PMP EXAM STUDY GUIDE

By Richard Man

CONTENTS

INTRODUCTION

This study guide includes an additional section on Agile and Hybrid approaches, which reflects the growing importance of these methodologies in project management. The section on Exam Tips and Tricks now includes mock exams and quizzes for additional practice, as well as guidance on developing a study plan and staying on track. The PMP Exam e-learning course section has also been expanded to include more comprehensive guidance on mastering the course content. This guide is tailored to the latest PMBOK Guide 2021, ECO 2021, and PMP exam questions and standards of ethics from 2021, ensuring that it is the most up-to-date and comprehensive PMP exam prep guide available.

This guide features repetitive presentation of ideas to highlight how the processes of project management are interconnected. An additional benefit is repetition aids in memory, providing stronger information retention.

The PMP Exam

- Understanding the PMP certification process
- Exam format and structure
- Exam eligibility criteria

Project Integration Management Summary

a. Develop a Project Charter: This process develops the project charter, which defines the project's purpose, scope, and objectives.

b. Develop the Project Management Plan: This process develops a project management plan, which defines the project's approach, scope, schedule, budget, and other key aspects.

c. Direct and Manage Project Work: This process executes the project management plan and monitors the project's progress.

d. Manage Project Knowledge: This process manages the project's knowledge and information to ensure that it is accessible and useful.

e. Monitor and Control Project Work: This process monitors the project's progress and performance and takes corrective actions if necessary.

f. Perform Integrated Change Control: This process manages changes to the project's scope, schedule, budget, and other aspects.

g. Close the Project or Phase: This process closes the project or phase and ensure that all deliverables are complete and accepted.

Project Scope Management Summary

a. Plan Scope Management: This process creates a scope management plan that outlines how the project's scope will be defined, validated, and controlled. It includes identifying key stakeholders, establishing scope boundaries, and determining the level of detail required for project requirements.

b. Collect Requirements: This process gathers and documents stakeholder needs and requirements to define the project scope. It includes techniques such as interviews, workshops, surveys, and focus groups to ensure all requirements are captured.

c. Define Scope: This process develops a detailed project scope statement that includes the project's deliverables, objectives, and constraints. This statement will serve as a baseline for the project and will be used to guide decision-making throughout the project's lifecycle.

d. Create a Work Breakdown Structure (WBS): This process breaks down the project scope into smaller, more manageable work packages. This enables the project team to better understand the project's requirements, estimate costs and timelines more accurately, and assign resources more effectively.

e. Validate the Scope: This process ensures the project deliverables meet the stakeholder's requirements. Deliverables are reviewed against the scope statement and formal acceptance is obtained for the intended deliverables.

f. Control the Scope: This process monitors and controls changes to the project scope to ensure the project remains on track. This includes documenting and reviewing scope changes, determining their impact on the project, and implementing approved changes through the project's change control process.

Project Schedule Management Summary

a. Plan Schedule Management: This process creates a comprehensive schedule management plan that outlines the project schedule development process, the tools and techniques to be used, and the roles and responsibilities of the project team.

b. Define Activities: This process breaks down the project deliverables into smaller, more manageable components and creates a list of activities that must be completed to produce each deliverable.

c. Sequence Activities: This process identifies the relationships between project activities and determines the most logical order in which they should be completed.

d. Estimate Activity Durations: This process estimates the amount of time required to complete each project activity based on historical data, expert judgment, and other relevant factors.

e. Develop Schedule: This process creates a detailed project schedule that includes start and end dates for each activity, dependencies, milestones, and other relevant information.

f. Control Schedule: This process monitors the project schedule on an ongoing basis to identify any deviations from the planned schedule in order to take corrective action to keep the project on track. This includes updating the project schedule, adjusting activity durations, and making other changes as necessary to ensure that the project is completed on time and within budget.

Project Cost Management Summary

a. Plan Cost Management: In this process the cost management plan is created, which outlines the project's overall approach to cost management. The plan includes the project's cost management policies, procedures, and guidelines, as well as the roles and responsibilities of the project team in managing costs.

b. Estimate Costs: This process estimates the costs of the resources required to complete each project activity. This includes the cost of labor, materials, equipment, and any other expenses that might be incurred during the project's execution. The accuracy of the cost estimates is crucial in determining the project budget and in managing costs throughout the project lifecycle.

c. Determine Budget: This process aggregates the estimated costs of all project activities to establish the project budget. This budget should include all direct and indirect costs associated with the project, including contingency reserves and management reserves.

d. Control Costs: This process monitors project costs and takes corrective action as necessary to ensure that the project remains within budget. This includes monitoring actual costs against the budgeted costs, identifying variances, analyzing the causes of variances, and implementing corrective actions to address any deviations from the budget.

Project Quality Management Summary

a. Plan Quality Management: This process involves identifying quality requirements and standards for the project and developing a comprehensive plan that outlines how these requirements will be met. The plan will include details on quality control and assurance activities, quality metrics, and the roles and responsibilities of team members involved in quality management.

b. Manage Quality: In this process the project team implements the quality management plan by executing quality control and assurance activities, ensuring that project deliverables meet the established quality standards. The team will continuously monitor the project's progress against the quality plan, document and report quality issues, and take corrective action as necessary.

c. Control Quality: This process involves monitoring and controlling the quality of the project deliverables throughout the project lifecycle, from planning to closure. The project team will use established quality control and assurance activities to measure the project's performance against the quality plan and make necessary adjustments to meet the established standards. The team will also document quality issues, identify their root causes, and implement corrective and preventive actions to prevent similar issues from arising in the future.

Project Resource Management Summary

a. Plan Resource Management: This process develops a comprehensive plan for how project resources are identified, acquired, managed, and used throughout the project lifecycle. The plan will include information on resource requirements, availability, allocation, and utilization.

b. Estimate Activity Resources: This process estimates the type and quantity of resources required for each project activity, including personnel, equipment, and materials. This estimation is crucial to ensuring that the project is appropriately staffed and resourced.

c. Acquire Resources: In this process, the project team acquires the necessary resources to execute the project plan, including personnel, equipment, and materials. The team will need to identify potential sources for these resources, negotiate contracts, and manage the procurement process.

d. Develop Team: This process builds and develops the project team, including developing team member skills and fostering a positive team environment. This ensures the team can work effectively and efficiently to achieve project objectives.

e. Manage Team: In this process, the project team manages the performance of the project team and takes steps to ensure that the team works effectively and efficiently. This includes providing feedback, addressing issues and conflicts, and taking corrective action when necessary.

f. Control Resources: This process monitors and controls project resources to ensure that they are being used effectively and efficiently. This includes tracking resource utilization, identifying and addressing issues, and making adjustments as necessary to keep the project on track.

Project Communications Management Summary

a. Plan Communications Management: This process develops a plan for how project information is communicated to stakeholders. It determines the communication needs of all stakeholders and creates a stakeholder communication matrix. It defines the communication methods and frequency of each stakeholder or group. It establishes guidelines for project documentation and how it is stored and distributed. It identifies potential communication risks and develops a contingency plan.

b. Manage Communications: In this process, the project team executes the communications management plan, including distributing project information to stakeholders. Communicate project progress and updates to stakeholders according to the communication plan. Manage stakeholder expectations and address any concerns or issues they may have. Ensure all project documentation is accurate and up-to-date. Facilitate communication between team members and stakeholders.

c. Monitor Communications: This process involves monitoring project communications to ensure that stakeholders receive the appropriate information in a timely manner. Evaluate the effectiveness of the communication plan and make adjustments as necessary. Measure stakeholder satisfaction with the communication process. Monitor project progress and adjust communication strategies as needed. Continuously improve the communication process through feedback and lessons learned.

Project Risk Management Summary

a. Plan Risk Management: This process is the foundation for effective risk management. The project team develops a plan that outlines how risks will be identified, analyzed, and managed. The plan includes roles and responsibilities, risk categories, and risk thresholds.

b. Identify Risks: This process involves identifying potential project risks and documenting them for further analysis. The project team can use a variety of techniques, such as brainstorming, checklists, and expert judgment, to identify risks.

c. Perform Qualitative Risk Analysis: This process analyzes the probability and impact of identified risks and prioritizing them for further analysis. The project team assesses the likelihood and impact of each risk and assigns a risk score to prioritize them for further analysis.

d. Perform Quantitative Risk Analysis: This process analyzes the probability and impact of identified risks using numerical techniques and models. The project team uses data and statistical analysis to quantify the impact of risks and to determine the probability of their occurrence.

e. Plan Risk Responses: This process develops a plan for how to respond to identified risks. The project team develops strategies for risk mitigation, risk avoidance, risk transfer, and risk acceptance. The plan also includes contingency plans for high-priority risks.

f. Control Risks: This process monitors project risks, assesses their status, and implements appropriate corrective actions. The team also revises the risk management plan as needed to address any changes in the project environment.

Project Stakeholder Management Summary

a. Identify Stakeholders: To identify all project stakeholders, the project team must conduct a thorough analysis of the stakeholders' interests, expectations, and potential impact on the project. This process identifies internal and external stakeholders, documenting their needs and expectations, and prioritizing them based on their level of influence and interest in the project.

b. Plan Stakeholder Engagement: Once the stakeholders have been identified, the project team must develop a plan for how to engage with them effectively. This plan should include strategies for managing stakeholder expectations, communication channels, and methods for gathering stakeholder feedback throughout the project. The team should also consider the stakeholders' preferred communication styles, cultural differences, and potential conflicts that may arise.

c. Manage Stakeholder Engagement: In this process, the project team must actively manage stakeholder relationships to ensure that their needs and expectations are being met throughout the project. This involves providing stakeholders with regular updates on the project's progress, addressing their concerns, and soliciting their feedback. The team should also be prepared to adapt the stakeholder engagement plan as necessary to maintain positive relationships.

d. Monitor Stakeholder Engagement: Throughout the project, the project team must monitor stakeholder relationships to ensure that their expectations are being met. This process gathers feedback from stakeholders regularly, measures their satisfaction levels, and takes corrective action as necessary to address any issues that arise. The team should also be prepared to adjust the stakeholder engagement plan based on feedback and changing circumstances.

Agile and Hybrid Approaches Summary

a. Agile Manifesto and Principles: This section introduces the Agile Manifesto and its underlying principles, which emphasize collaboration, flexibility, and customer satisfaction.

b. Agile frameworks and methodologies: This section provides an overview of popular Agile frameworks and methodologies, including Scrum, Kanban, and Lean.

c. Hybrid approaches and their benefits: This section explains the concept of hybrid project management and the benefits of combining Agile and traditional project management approaches.

d. Agile project management tools and techniques: This section covers the various tools and techniques used in agile project management, such as user stories, burndown charts, and retrospectives.

e. Agile project roles and responsibilities: This section describes the roles and responsibilities of the agile project team, including the product owner, scrum master, and development team.

f. Hybrid project management frameworks: This section discusses the various hybrid project management frameworks, such as PRINCE2 Agile and AgilePM, and how they can be used to combine agile and traditional project management approaches.

g. Benefits and challenges of using hybrid approaches: This section explores the benefits and challenges of using hybrid approaches, including improved flexibility, faster delivery, and increased stakeholder engagement, as well as potential conflicts between different project management methodologies.

Ethics and Professional Conduct Summary

a. Code of Ethics and Professional Conduct: This section covers the ethical principles and guidelines that project managers should follow in their professional conduct. It includes an overview of the PMI Code of Ethics and Professional Conduct, which outlines the expectations for professional conduct and ethical behavior.

b. Responsibilities of a project manager: This section covers the roles and responsibilities of a project manager, as defined by the PMBOK Guide 2021. It includes an overview of the project manager's duties, such as defining project objectives, managing project scope, and ensuring project quality. It also covers the project manager's responsibilities in terms of stakeholder management, communication, risk management, and project closure.

Project Management Exam Prep, Exam Tips and Tricks Summary

a. Time management techniques: This section covers proven time management techniques to help you optimize your study time and manage time effectively during the exam. We will provide you with strategies for creating a study schedule, allocating time during the exam, and managing your time efficiently.

b. Exam-taking strategies: This section will give you tips on how to approach and tackle exam questions. We will provide you with strategies for analyzing questions, eliminating wrong answers, and identifying the correct answer. These strategies are designed to help you maximize your score and minimize the chances of missing any crucial questions.

c. Key concepts and formulas to remember: This section covers essential concepts and formulas that are frequently tested on the PMP exam. We will provide you with a concise summary of the 10 knowledge areas, 49 processes, and formulas related to earned value management. By understanding these crucial project management concepts, you will be better prepared to pass the PMP exam.

d. Practice questions and answers: This section includes a comprehensive set of practice questions designed to simulate the PMP exam. We have included detailed explanations and references to the PMBOK Guide, ECO 2021, and other relevant resources. Our practice questions cover all knowledge areas and process groups, allowing you to test your understanding and identify areas where you need further study.

CATEGORIES OF QUESTIONS:

- Situational
- Knowledge-based Questions

- Formula-based Questions
- Interpersonal and Leadership Skills
- Ethics and Professional Responsibility
- Initiating
- Planning
- Executing
- Monitoring and Controlling
- Closing

INTRODUCTION TO THE PMP EXAM:

The Project Management Professional (PMP) certification is one of the most globally recognized certifications for project managers. It is awarded by the Project Management Institute (PMI) and demonstrates a project manager's expertise in leading and directing projects.

Understanding the PMP certification process:

To earn the PMP certification, candidates must meet specific educational and professional experience requirements, pass a rigorous exam, and adhere to a professional code of ethics. The PMP exam covers five process groups: initiating, planning, executing, monitoring and controlling, and closing, and ten knowledge areas: project integration, scope, schedule, cost, quality, resource, communications, risk, stakeholder, and agile/hybrid approaches.

Exam format and structure:

The PMP exam consists of 180 multiple-choice questions, which must be answered within four hours. Out of the 180 questions, 25 are pretest questions that do not contribute to the final score. The passing score for the exam is determined through a psychometric analysis and is not disclosed to the candidates.

Exam eligibility criteria:

To be eligible for the PMP certification, candidates must meet specific educational and professional experience requirements. Candidates must have a four-year degree, 36 months of non-overlapping project management experience, and 35 hours of project management education. Or a high school diploma or associate's degree with 60 months of non-overlapping project management experience, and 35 hours of project management education.

Note:

Preparing thoroughly for the PMP exam is crucial for candidates looking to pass this rigorous certification. The PMBOK Guide, practice exams, and other resources can be invaluable in helping candidates prepare for the exam. Additionally, it is important to note that there have been recent changes to the exam format and content, and candidates should be aware of these changes when studying.

It is also important for PMP certification holders to adhere to continuing education requirements to maintain their certification. This ensures that individuals with this certification stay up-to-date on the latest industry standards and best practices.

Furthermore, it is worth noting that there is a cost associated with taking the PMP exam, which can vary depending on PMI membership status and location. Nonetheless, the benefits of achieving this certification, such as increased career opportunities and earning potential, can far outweigh the cost of the exam.

PROJECT INTEGRATION MANAGEMENT

Project Integration Management is a key knowledge area in project management that deals with the coordination and integration of all the project management processes and activities.

Develop a Project Charter: In this process, we develop a document which clearly defines the project's purpose, scope, and objectives.

The Project Charter document formally authorizes the existence of a project and provides the project manager with the authority to apply organizational resources to project activities. The project charter is a high-level document that outlines the project's purpose, scope, objectives, stakeholders, and high-level requirements. It serves as the foundation for the project and provides the project manager with a clear understanding of what the project entails.

The following are the key inputs, tools and techniques, and outputs of the Develop a Project Charter process:

Inputs:

The Statement Of Work (SOW): A narrative description of products, services, or results to be delivered by the project.

The Business Case: The reason for the project, which includes the expected benefits, costs, and risks.

Agreements: Contracts, Memoranda Of Understanding (MOUs), Service Level Agreements (SLAs), etc.

Enterprise Environmental Factors: Internal and external factors that may affect the project, such as organizational culture and structure, government regulations, industry standards, etc.

Organizational Process Assets: Organizational policies, procedures, guidelines, and knowledge bases.

Tools and techniques:

Expert Judgment: Inputs from knowledgeable and experienced individuals or groups.

Facilitation Techniques: Techniques such as brainstorming, conflict resolution, and problem-solving that help in managing group dynamics and reaching a consensus.

They can be formal or informal discussions between stakeholders and project team members.

Outputs:

Project Charter: A document that formally authorizes the project, defines its high-level objectives and requirements, identifies stakeholders, and assigns the project manager with the authority to apply organizational resources to project activities.

Examples of project charters include the following:

Example 1: Development of a new product

Project title: Development of a new smartphone application

Purpose: To develop a new smartphone application that will enhance user experience and generate revenue for the organization

Scope: The project will involve the development of a user-friendly and visually appealing smartphone application that will provide users with access to a wide range of services and products.

Objectives: To complete the project within 12 months, to achieve a user base of 1 million within the first year of launch, and to generate $5 million in revenue within the first two years of launch.

Example 2: Construction of a new facility

Project title: Construction of a new manufacturing facility

Purpose: To construct a new manufacturing facility that will enable the organization to meet growing demand for its products and services.

Scope: The project will involve the construction of a new manufacturing facility with state-of-the-art equipment and facilities that will enable the organization to meet growing demand for its products and services.

Objectives: To complete the project within 24 months, to achieve LEED Gold certification for the facility, and to achieve a 20% reduction in operating costs compared to the existing facility.

The Develop a Project Charter process is a crucial step in project integration management, as it provides a high-level overview of the project's purpose, scope, objectives, and stakeholders. The project charter serves as the foundation for the project, and it is essential for ensuring that all project management processes and activities are aligned with the project's goals. Furthermore, to the inputs, tools and techniques, and outputs mentioned above, the Develop a Project Charter process may also involve conducting a feasibility study to determine whether the project is viable and conducting a stakeholder analysis to identify key stakeholders and their needs and expectations.

Developing a project charter is a crucial initial step in project management that defines the project's purpose, objectives, scope, and high-level requirements. It is a formal document that authorizes the project manager to use organizational resources to perform project activities. The project charter also serves as a communication and alignment tool, as it provides a common understanding of the project's goals and objectives for all stakeholders.

One of the crucial aspects of the project charter is that it assigns the project manager the authority to apply organizational resources to project activities. This means that the project manager can make decisions regarding project scope, budget, and schedule, and can allocate resources such as personnel, equipment, and funding. For instance, if the project manager identifies a crucial risk that might impact the project's success, he/she can allocate additional resources to mitigate the risk.

Before developing the project charter, it is essential to conduct a feasibility study to determine whether the project is viable and achievable. A feasibility study examines the technical, economic, operational, and schedule feasibility of the project. For example, if an organization wants to develop a new software application, the feasibility study will analyze whether the required technology, expertise, and infrastructure are available to complete the project successfully.

Another important activity involved in developing a project charter is conducting a stakeholder analysis. Stakeholder analysis is the process of identifying, analyzing, and managing stakeholders' interests and expectations related to the project. The project manager needs to understand the stakeholders' needs and expectations to manage their requirements effectively. For example, if the stakeholders have conflicting interests, the project manager needs to develop a strategy to manage those conflicts.

The project charter is typically created by the project sponsor or initiator, with input from the project manager and other key stakeholders. The project sponsor is the person or group who authorizes and funds the project and is accountable for its success. The project manager, on the other hand, is responsible for managing the project's day-to-day activities to achieve the project's objectives.

In the project charter development process, the project sponsor and project manager work collaboratively to define the project's purpose, objectives, scope, and requirements. The project manager provides input on the project's feasibility and stakeholder analysis and also assists in defining the project's constraints and assumptions. The project charter is then reviewed and approved by all stakeholders, including the project sponsor, project manager, and any other key stakeholders.

***

Develop A Project Management Plan

In this process, we will learn how to create a project management plan, which defines the project's approach, scope, schedule, budget, and other key aspects.

The Project Management Plan defines, documents, and maintains a project plan that acts as a guide for the entire project. The project management plan is a key deliverable and serves as a roadmap for the project team to follow throughout the project's lifecycle.

To develop a project management plan, the project manager needs to follow a structured approach that includes the following artifacts:

The Project Scope: It is important to determine a project's boundaries. The Project Scope statement outlines what will be included in the project and what will be excluded from it. It also identifies the project's objectives, its deliverables, and the success criteria for those deliverables.

The Project Schedule: This is a timeline for the project that outlines the key milestones and deadlines associated with the project. It documents the project's critical path, project dependencies, and any resource constraints.

The Project Budget: A Project Budget is created from the estimated project costs identified. The budget contains the costs associated with all the necessary resources, such as labor, materials, equipment, and overheads.

The Project Stakeholders: The project stakeholder identification outlines everyone who has an interest in the project and determines their level of involvement, expectations, and communication preferences.

The Project Risks: All identified risks, big and small, need a plan on how to manage the risks should they occur. The Project Risk plan outlines these risks and their mitigation actions.

The Project Quality Standards: This documents the quality standards that will be used to evaluate the project's deliverables and ensure that they are met.

The Project Communication Plan: Defines the communication needs of all the stakeholders, and develops a plan that outlines the methods, frequency, and content of the communications for the project stakeholders.

Here are a few examples to illustrate how these steps can be applied in practice:

Example 1: Developing a project management plan for a software development project

Step 1: Define the project scope: The project is to develop a new software application that will automate the company's sales processes. The project scope includes the development of the application, testing, documentation, and user training.

Step 2: Develop the project schedule: The project timeline is six months, and the critical path involves developing the application, testing, and user training. There is a dependency on the availability of a third-party software library, which may cause delays.

Step 3: Determine the project budget: The project budget is $500,000, which includes the costs of hiring developers, testers, and trainers, and purchasing software licenses, and equipment.

Step 4: Identify the project stakeholders: The stakeholders include the sales team, the IT department, management, and end-users. The sales team will provide the requirements, and the IT department will oversee the project's technical aspects.

Step 5: Assess the project risks: The risks include delays caused by the third-party software library, technical issues, and user adoption. The risk management plan includes contingency actions for each risk.

Step 6: Establish the project quality standards: The quality standards include adherence to coding standards, testing standards, and user interface design standards.

Step 7: Develop a project communication plan: The communication plan includes weekly progress reports, biweekly meetings with stakeholders, and monthly status updates for management.

Project management is a crucial process for organizations that want to successfully execute projects. It involves the planning, execution, monitoring, and control of a project from start to finish. One of the essential components of project management is the development of a project management plan. This plan serves as a roadmap for the project and outlines the project's scope, objectives, timelines, deliverables, and resources.

Developing a project management plan requires a systematic approach that considers various factors, such as the project's Environmental, Social, and Governance (ESG) impacts. Organizations must ensure that their projects align with their ESG values and comply with relevant regulations and standards.

To develop an effective project management plan, organizations can use a range of tools and techniques. These include expert judgment, data analysis, and stakeholder engagement.

Expert judgment involves consulting with subject matter experts in various fields to gain insights into the project's technical requirements, risks, and opportunities. Data analysis, on the other hand, involves using data to identify trends, patterns, and insights that can inform project planning. Finally, stakeholder engagement involves consulting with stakeholders to identify their needs, expectations, and concerns and incorporating them into the project management plan.

One crucial aspect of developing a project management plan is reviewing and updating it throughout the project's lifecycle. This ensures that the plan remains relevant and useful as the project progresses and that it accounts for any changes or challenges that may arise.

Another crucial component of project management is the role of the project management Office (PMO). A PMO is a centralized department or function that provides guidance and support for project management activities. It is responsible for developing and maintaining project management standards, processes, and templates, including the project management plan. A PMO can also provide training and support to project managers and team members, helping them to develop and implement effective project management practices.

***

Direct and Manage Project Work

In this process, we discuss how to execute the project management plan and monitor the project's progress.

The Direct and Manage Project Work process is crucial in project integration management. It involves executing the project management plan, implementing the approved changes, and producing the project deliverables. The project manager and the project team work together to complete the work defined in the project management plan, ensuring that it meets the project's objectives and requirements.

It involves coordinating people and resources, managing stakeholder expectations, and ensuring that the work is completed according to the project plan.

Some of the key activities that take place in this process include:

Implementing the project management plan: The project management plan is implemented by executing the tasks and activities that have been identified in the plan. This includes assigning tasks to team members, setting up communication channels, and establishing procedures for monitoring and controlling the project.

Managing project resources: This involves ensuring that the necessary resources are available to carry out the project work. This includes managing the project budget, allocating resources to specific tasks, and coordinating the work of external contractors and vendors.

Managing stakeholder expectations: Stakeholders must be kept informed of the project's progress and any issues or changes that may impact the project's success. Communication plans and status reports should be developed and shared with stakeholders on a regular basis.

Ensuring quality: Quality must be monitored and managed throughout the project to ensure that deliverables meet the required standards. This includes developing and implementing quality control procedures, performing inspections and audits, and addressing any issues that arise.

Examples of Direct and Manage Project Work in action might include:

A project manager is coordinating the efforts of a team of software developers working on a new mobile app. They are responsible for ensuring that the developers have the resources they need to complete the work, that stakeholders are kept informed of progress, and that quality standards are maintained throughout the project.

A construction project manager is overseeing the construction of a new building. They are responsible for managing the project budget, scheduling subcontractors, communicating with the client, and ensuring that the project is completed on time and to the required quality standards.

The Direct and Manage Project Work process is one of the most important processes in project management. It is a part of the project execution phase, which starts after the Develop The Project Management Plan process and continues until the project is completed or terminated. This process involves executing the project plan and managing the project team to achieve the project's objectives.

The first step in the Direct and Manage Project Work process is to implement the project plan. This includes assigning tasks to team members, allocating resources, and establishing communication channels. To facilitate this process, project managers use a variety of tools and techniques such as project management software, Gantt charts, and network diagrams. These tools help project managers to visualize the project's timeline, assign tasks, and track progress.

As the project work is being executed, it's important to monitor and control it. This involves tracking progress, identifying and addressing issues, and making adjustments to the project plan as needed. One tool commonly used in this process is performance reports. These reports provide an overview of the project's progress, including information about the schedule, budget, and quality. Performance reports can help project managers to identify any deviations from the project plan and take corrective action if necessary.

Another important aspect to consider is risk management. Project managers need to identify potential risks, assess their likelihood and impact, and develop strategies to mitigate or respond to them. One tool commonly used in this process is a risk register. A risk register is a document that lists all the potential risks to the project and provides information about their likelihood, impact, and mitigation strategies. By using a risk register, project managers can proactively identify and address risks before they become problems.

In addition to risk management, quality management is also an important part of the Direct and Manage Project Work process. Quality management involves ensuring that the project deliverables meet the stakeholders' requirements and are of high quality. One tool commonly used in this process is a quality control checklist. A quality control checklist is a document that lists all the quality requirements for the project and provides a way to track whether they have been met or not. By using a quality control checklist, project managers can ensure that the project deliverables meet the stakeholders' expectations.

Throughout the Direct and Manage Project Work process, project managers need to manage changes to the project plan. This includes receiving and reviewing change requests, evaluating their impact on the project, and approving or rejecting them. One tool commonly used in this process is a Change Control Board. A change control board is a group of stakeholders who are responsible for evaluating change requests and deciding whether to approve them for inclusion in the project. By using a change control board, project managers can ensure that changes to the project plan are evaluated objectively and consistently for impact on the project's published scope, schedule, budget, and risk.

***

Manage Project Knowledge

In this process, we will learn how to manage the project's knowledge and information to ensure that it is accessible and useful.

The Manage Project Knowledge process is a part of Project Integration Management and focuses on managing knowledge and information related to the project. The aim of this process is to ensure that project knowledge is easily accessible and useful for the project team members throughout the project lifecycle. This includes capturing, organizing, storing, retrieving, and sharing knowledge and information in a way that benefits the project.

Examples of how Manage Project Knowledge can be applied in a project:

Lessons Learned: Throughout the project, team members will gain knowledge and experience that can be used to improve future projects. The Manage Project Knowledge process involves capturing and documenting these lessons learned so that they can be shared with the wider organization.

Knowledge Repository: The project team may have access to a variety of knowledge sources, such as manuals, guidelines, and templates. The Manage Project Knowledge process involves organizing this information in a way that is easy to access and use. This could involve creating a centralized knowledge repository that team members can access throughout the project.

Information Sharing: Project team members may have different roles and responsibilities, but they all need access to relevant project information. The Manage Project Knowledge process involves sharing information and knowledge in a way that is appropriate for each team member. This could involve creating reports, dashboards, or other communication channels that provide relevant information to team members.

Collaboration: Collaboration is key to project success, and the Manage Project Knowledge process involves creating an environment where team members can collaborate effectively. This could involve using tools and technologies that facilitate collaboration, such as project management software, communication tools, or document-sharing platforms.

In summary, the Manage Project Knowledge process is about managing project knowledge and information to ensure that it is accessible and useful for the project team members. By implementing this process, project teams can improve collaboration, share knowledge and information effectively, and capture lessons learned for future projects.

Knowledge management is a crucial component of project management and can greatly benefit both the project team and the organization as a whole. At its core, knowledge management involves the creation, capture, sharing, and use of information and knowledge to improve project outcomes.

One example of how knowledge management has improved project outcomes in the past is through the use of lessons learned. By capturing and sharing the lessons learned from previous projects, teams can avoid making the same mistakes and build upon successful strategies. This not only improves the current project but also increases the overall efficiency and effectiveness of future projects.

To effectively manage project knowledge, various tools, and techniques can be used, such as knowledge management systems, expert systems, and artificial intelligence. Knowledge management systems can be used to store and share information and knowledge, while expert systems can provide automated decision-making support based on previous experiences. Artificial intelligence can also be used to analyze data and make predictions, further enhancing the knowledge management process.

Effective stakeholder engagement is another important aspect of knowledge management. By engaging stakeholders, project teams can identify their knowledge needs and preferences, ensuring that the knowledge management approach aligns with their needs and increasing their engagement and ownership in the project.

Continuous improvement is also crucial to successful knowledge management. The process should be regularly reviewed and updated, incorporating feedback from the project team and stakeholders. This ensures that the knowledge management approach remains relevant and effective throughout the project.

In terms of specific tools and techniques, collaboration tools and document-sharing platforms are common options for managing project knowledge. For example, platforms like Microsoft Teams or Google Drive can be used to share and collaborate on documents, while project management software like Asana or Trello can be used to track project progress and capture lessons learned.

***

Monitor and Control Project Work

In this process, we discuss how to monitor the project's progress and performance and take corrective actions if necessary.

The Monitor and Control Project Work process is a crucial process in project management, as it helps project managers to monitor project performance and identify any variances from the project plan. This process allows the project manager to take corrective actions if necessary to keep the project on track and ensure that it meets its objectives.

There are several activities involved in the Monitor and Control Project Work process, including:

Monitoring project performance: This involves measuring the progress of the project against the project plan, identifying any variances, and analyzing the reasons for the variances.

Analyzing project performance: This involves analyzing the data collected during project performance monitoring to identify trends and patterns that can improve project performance.

Taking corrective actions: This involves taking corrective actions to address any variances from the project plan and ensure that the project remains on track. Corrective actions can include adjusting the project plan, revising the project scope, or changing the project schedule.

Updating project documents: This involves updating project documents, such as the project plan, risk register, and stakeholder register, to reflect any changes made to the project because of corrective actions taken.

Reporting project status: This involves reporting the project status to stakeholders, including project sponsors, project team members, and other stakeholders who have an interest in the project.

For example, if a project is behind schedule, the project manager may use the Monitor and Control Project Work process to identify the reasons for the delay and take corrective actions to bring the project back on schedule. This may involve revising the project schedule, increasing the project team's resources, or reducing the project scope.

The Monitor and Control Project Work process is an essential part of project management, as it helps to ensure that the project is progressing according to plan and that any issues or deviations from the plan are identified and addressed promptly. This process involves tracking, reviewing, and regulating the progress and performance of the project, and taking corrective actions as needed to keep the project on track.

Inputs to the Monitor and Control Project Work process include project management plan updates, project document updates, and work performance data. Project management plan updates can include changes to the project schedule, cost estimates, resource allocation, risk management plans, and quality management plans. Project document updates can include changes to project charters, stakeholder registers, communication plans, and issue logs. Work performance data can include information on project scope, schedule, cost, quality, risk, and stakeholder engagement.

Outputs of the Monitor and Control Project Work process include change requests, project management plan updates, and project document updates. Change requests are formal proposals to modify the project plan and may arise from issues or risks identified during the monitoring and control process. Project management plan updates may include changes to the project scope, schedule, cost estimates, resource allocation, risk management plan, and quality management plan. Project document updates may include changes to project charters, stakeholder registers, communication plans, and issue logs.

Continuous monitoring and control of the project is crucial, as it allows project managers to identify potential issues and take corrective actions before they escalate and become significant variances. For example, if a project manager is continuously monitoring the project schedule, they may notice that a particular task is taking longer than expected and take corrective action, such as reallocating resources or adjusting the schedule to avoid delays.

There are several tools and techniques that can be used in the Monitor and Control Project Work process. One such tool is earned value management, which is a project performance measurement technique that integrates scope, cost, and schedule to help project managers assess project performance and identify potential variances. Another tool is trend analysis, which involves analyzing project data over time to identify patterns and trends, and to identify potential issues or opportunities. Root cause analysis is also a useful technique for identifying the underlying causes of project issues and developing effective corrective actions.

***

Perform Integrated Change Control

In this process, we will learn how to manage changes to the project's scope, schedule, budget, and other aspects.

Performing Integrated Change Control is a crucial process within the Project Integration Management knowledge area, as it provides a structured approach to managing changes throughout the project lifecycle. The process involves reviewing, evaluating, and approving or rejecting change requests to ensure that they align with the project's objectives, scope, schedule, and budget.

The Perform Integrated Change Control process has the following key inputs, tools and techniques, and outputs:

Inputs:

Project management plan: This document contains all the project plans and provides a baseline against which changes are evaluated.

Change requests: These are formally documented requests to modify a project component, such as the scope, schedule, or budget.

Work performance data: This is the raw data collected during project execution, such as status reports, progress measurements, and issue logs.

Organizational process assets: These are the policies, procedures, and guidelines that govern how changes are managed within the organization.

Tools and techniques:

Change control tools: These include change control boards, change control systems, and configuration management systems that help track and manage changes.

Expert judgment: This involves seeking the advice and opinions of subject matter experts to evaluate the impact of proposed changes.

Meetings: These are formal or informal discussions among stakeholders to review and discuss change requests.

Outputs:

Approved change requests: These are change requests that have been evaluated and approved for implementation.

Change log: This is a document that captures all the change requests and their status throughout the project lifecycle.

Project management plan updates: These are updates to the project management plan resulting from approved change requests.

Project document updates: These are updates to project documents, such as the requirements document or the risk register, resulting from approved change requests.

Examples to help illustrate the Perform Integrated Change Control process:

Example 1: A construction project is running behind schedule, and the project manager receives a change request to extend the project timeline by six months. The project manager evaluates the change request, consults with subject matter experts, and determines that the extension is necessary to complete the project successfully. The change request is approved, and the project management plan is updated to reflect the new timeline.

Example 2: A software development project is in the testing phase, and the quality assurance team identifies a crucial defect that could impact the project's success. The project manager receives a change request to allocate additional resources to fix the defect. The project manager evaluates the change request, consults with the development team, and determines if additional resources are necessary to resolve the issue. The change request is approved, and the project management plan and requirements document are updated to reflect the change.

Perform Integrated Change Control is a crucial process in project management that involves reviewing and approving or rejecting proposed changes to a project's scope, schedule, budget, or other components. This process is iterative, meaning it may require multiple rounds of reviews and evaluations before a change request is approved or rejected.

For example, if a team member proposes a change to the project scope, the change request will go through a series of reviews and evaluations to determine the feasibility, impact, and potential risks of implementing the change. The change request may be sent back to the team member for further clarification or refinement, or it may be approved and integrated into the project plan.

The process of Perform Integrated Change Control is closely linked to other Project Integration Management processes, such as Develop the Project Charter, Develop the Project Management Plan, Direct and Manage the Project Work, and Monitor and Control Project Work. These processes work together to ensure that changes to the project are properly evaluated, approved, and implemented while maintaining alignment with project objectives and stakeholder expectations.

For example, during the Develop Project Management Plan process, the project management team defines the procedures for managing changes to the project, including the development of a change management plan. A change management plan outlines the procedures and responsibilities for managing changes, such as who reviews and approving change requests and how changes will be communicated to stakeholders.

Effective stakeholder communication and engagement are essential components of the Perform Integrated Change Control process. By keeping stakeholders informed and engaged throughout the change control process, the project team can manage expectations and ensure alignment with project objectives. This can also help to build trust and support for the project among stakeholders.

For example, if a change request is approved that affects a stakeholder's area of the project, the project team should communicate the details of the change and how it will impact the stakeholder. By doing so, the project team can ensure that the stakeholder understands the implications of the change and can prepare accordingly.

***

Close Project or Phase:

In this process, we will learn how to close the project or phase and ensure that all deliverables are complete and accepted.

The Close Project or Phase process is the ending process in the Project Integration Management knowledge area. Its purpose is to formally close out a project or a project phase. This process is important because it ensures that all the project objectives have been met, all deliverables have been completed and accepted, and all necessary documentation has been properly archived.

The Close Project or Phase process comprises four principal activities:

Administrative Closure: This activity involves the formal termination of all project activities, including the release of resources, the closing of contracts, and archiving of project documents.

Contract Closure: This activity involves the closure of all contracts related to the project, including settlement of all outstanding payments, resolution of any disputes, and termination of all contractual obligations.

Final Product, Service, or Result Transition: This activity involves the transfer of the final product, service, or result to the appropriate stakeholders, along with any associated documentation, training materials, and support information.

Lessons Learned: This activity involves documenting and analyzing the project's successes and failures, identifying the root causes of any problems, and providing recommendations for future improvements.

Here are three examples of how the Close Project or Phase process might be applied in different project scenarios:

A software development project: Once the final product has been developed and thoroughly tested, the project team would use the Close Project or Phase process to formally transition the product to the customer or end user. This could involve providing training and support materials, as well as archiving all project documentation and closing any contracts with vendors or contractors.

A construction project: Once a building has been constructed and inspected, the Close Project or Phase process would transition the building to the owner or property manager. This would involve providing any necessary documentation, such as building plans and specifications, as well as closing out any contracts with subcontractors or suppliers.

A marketing campaign: Once a marketing campaign has been executed and analyzed, the Close Project or Phase process would be used to formally close out the project and document any lessons learned. This could involve archiving campaign materials, closing out contracts with advertising agencies or media outlets, and providing recommendations for future campaigns.

Benefits of the project or phase closure process:

- Identify lessons learned that can be applied to future projects
- Free up resources for other projects
- Evaluate the success of the project and recognize team members for their contribution
- Ensure that all legal and contractual requirements are met
- Provide a solid foundation for the initiation of a new project or phase

PROJECT SCOPE MANAGEMENT:

Project Scope Management is the process of defining, documenting, and controlling the scope of a project. The goal of this process is to ensure that the project's objectives and deliverables are clearly defined and meet stakeholder needs and requirements.

Plan Scope Management

This process involves creating a scope management plan that outlines how the project's scope will be defined, validated, and controlled. It includes identifying key stakeholders, establishing scope boundaries, and determining the level of detail required for project requirements.

This process is a crucial part of project scope management, as it involves creating a comprehensive plan that will guide the project's scope definition, validation, and control. The plan should outline how the project team will identify, document, and manage the project's scope, including how changes to scope will be handled.

Here are some key elements that might be included in a Plan Scope Management document:

Scope Statement: This should define the project's objectives, deliverables, and boundaries. It should clearly describe what the project will and will not include, and what the success criteria will be.

Stakeholder Analysis: This should identify all stakeholders who will be impacted by the project's scope, and define their roles and responsibilities.

Scope Management Plan: This should outline the process for defining, validating, and controlling the project's scope, including how scope changes will be handled.

Requirements Management Plan: This should describe how the project team will manage requirements throughout the project lifecycle, including how they will be documented, validated, and verified.

Configuration Management Plan: This should describe how the project team will manage changes to project documents and deliverables, including version control, approval processes, and audit trails.

Change Management Plan: This should describe the process for requesting, reviewing, and approving changes to the project's scope, including how changes will be communicated and documented.

Some examples of how these elements might be applied in practice include:

A construction project might use a Plan Scope Management document to define the scope of work, identify key stakeholders (such as the client, the architect, and the contractors), and outline the process for managing changes to the project's scope.

An IT project might use a Plan Scope Management document to define the project's objectives, requirements, and boundaries, and to outline the process for validating and verifying requirements, managing changes to scope, and communicating with stakeholders.

A marketing campaign might use a Plan Scope Management document to define the scope of work, identify key stakeholders (such as the client, the creative team, and the media buyers), and outline the process for managing changes to the campaign's scope, including approving new creative concepts or media placements.

Scope management is a crucial aspect of project management that entails defining, validating, and controlling the project scope to ensure successful project delivery. The scope refers to the work that must be done to complete the project, including the products, services, and outcomes that the project is expected to deliver. By managing the scope effectively, the project team can ensure that the project is completed within the set time, cost, and quality constraints.

Scope management starts with the Plan Scope Management process, which involves developing a scope management plan that outlines the procedures for managing changes to the project scope. This plan should include the project scope statement, the work breakdown structure (WBS), and the scope baseline. The scope baseline is a document that defines the project scope, schedule, and budget and is used as a reference point for managing changes to the project scope.

The WBS is a tool that is used to break down the project scope into smaller, more manageable components. This hierarchical structure defines the deliverables, work packages, and activities that are required to complete the project. By breaking down the project scope into smaller components, it is easier to manage and control the project.

Expert judgment and historical data are also useful tools and techniques for managing the project scope. Expert judgment involves consulting with subject matter experts or experienced project managers to estimate project requirements and identify potential risks to the project scope. Historical data refers to data from past projects that can be used to estimate project requirements and identify potential risks to the project scope.

Scope creep is an uncontrolled expansion of the project scope beyond its original objectives. This can happen when changes are made to the project scope without proper management or when stakeholders request additional features or functions that were not part of the original scope. Scope creep can lead to delays, increased costs, and reduced project quality.

To manage scope creep, it is important to have a change control process in place. This process should define the procedures for evaluating change requests, determining the impact of the changes on the project scope, and obtaining approval from the project stakeholders before implementing the changes. By following a change control process, the project team can control scope creep and ensure that the project is delivered within the set time, cost, and quality constraints.

Collect Requirements

This process involves gathering and documenting stakeholder needs and requirements to define the project scope. It includes techniques such as interviews, workshops, surveys, and focus groups to ensure all requirements are captured.

Collecting requirements is an important process in project scope management. It involves identifying, gathering, and documenting all of the requirements and needs of stakeholders, which helps define the scope of the project. The process requires the project team to engage with stakeholders and use various techniques to capture all requirements, including interviews, workshops, surveys, and focus groups.

To ensure that all requirements are captured, it is essential to involve all stakeholders in the process. The project team must identify all stakeholders and determine their expectations and requirements. The team can then use various techniques to collect requirements. For example, interviews can be conducted with individual stakeholders to understand their specific needs and preferences. Workshops can be held to gather requirements from multiple stakeholders simultaneously. Surveys can be distributed to stakeholders to collect their feedback on the project requirements.

Focus groups can also be used to gather requirements, especially when there are conflicting opinions among stakeholders. In a focus group, stakeholders can discuss their requirements and preferences, and the team can use the information to develop a consensus among the stakeholders.

It is essential to document all requirements in a clear and concise manner, which helps ensure that all stakeholders have a shared understanding of the project scope. The project team should use a consistent format to document requirements, which can include a requirement statement, the source of the requirement, and its priority level.

For example, a requirement statement can be: "The project should be completed within six months." The source of the requirement could be the customer, and the priority level could be high. By documenting all requirements in this way, the project team can track them throughout the project and ensure that they are met.

Requirements validation and verification are two essential processes in project management that ensure the requirements are aligned with the stakeholders' needs and the project objectives. Without these processes, the project team may end up delivering a solution that does not meet the stakeholders' needs or does not align with the project objectives, resulting in project failure.

Validation is the process of ensuring that the requirements are aligned with the stakeholders' needs and the project objectives. It involves verifying that the requirements address the project's purpose and goals, as well as the needs and expectations of the stakeholders. Validation techniques include prototyping, testing, and walkthroughs. For example, prototyping involves creating a working model of the solution that allows stakeholders to see how the solution will meet their needs. Testing involves executing the requirements to ensure that they function as intended. Walkthroughs involve reviewing the requirements with stakeholders to ensure that they understand them and that they align with their needs and expectations.

Verification is the process of ensuring that the requirements are complete, consistent, and accurate. It involves checking that the requirements meet the project's standards and specifications, are unambiguous, and do not conflict with other requirements. Verification techniques include reviews, inspections, and testing. For example, reviews involve reviewing the requirements to ensure that they meet the project's standards and specifications. Inspections involve a formal review process that involves a team of experts who review the requirements to identify errors and defects. Testing involves executing the requirements to ensure that they function as intended and that they meet the project's standards and specifications.

Both validation and verification are crucial to the success of the project. They ensure that the requirements are accurate, complete, and aligned with the stakeholders' needs and the project objectives. Involving stakeholders in the validation and verification processes is crucial to ensure that their needs are being met. By involving stakeholders, the project team can ensure that the solution meets their expectations and is aligned with the project's purpose and goals.

Define Scope

This process involves developing a detailed project scope statement that includes the project's deliverables, objectives, and constraints. This statement will serve as a baseline for the project and will be used to guide decision-making throughout the project's lifecycle.

In project management, the process of defining scope is a crucial step that lays the foundation for the entire project. This process involves developing a detailed project scope statement that clearly outlines the project's deliverables, objectives, and constraints. The scope statement serves as a reference point for all project stakeholders, including the project team, sponsors, and customers, and provides a clear understanding of what the project will deliver.

The scope statement should include a detailed description of the project's product or service, along with any constraints or assumptions that may impact the project's success. These constraints may include factors such as budget, time constraints, resource availability, or regulatory requirements. It's important to identify these constraints early on in the project to ensure that they are properly managed throughout the project's lifecycle.

To create a comprehensive scope statement, project managers may use a variety of tools and techniques, such as brainstorming sessions, mind maps, or decision trees. The goal is to ensure that all stakeholders have a clear understanding of the project's scope and that there are no misunderstandings or surprises later on.

Here's an example of a project scope statement:

Project Title:

Website Redesign Project

Objective:

The objective of this project is to redesign our company website to improve user experience and increase conversions.

Deliverables:

- A new website design that is visually appealing and easy to navigate
- A responsive website that is optimized for mobile devices
- Improved website speed and performance
- Integration with our customer relationship management (CRM) system
- Updated content and images

Constraints:

- The project must be completed within a budget of $50,000
- The project must be completed within a timeframe of 3 months
- The website must comply with all relevant regulatory requirements and accessibility guidelines

By clearly defining the project scope, stakeholders can better understand the project's goals, expectations, and limitations. This helps to ensure that the project is completed on time, within budget, and to the satisfaction of all stakeholders.

Project scope management is an essential aspect of project management, and it involves defining, planning, monitoring, controlling, and verifying the project's scope. Effective scope management ensures that the project team delivers the required products or services within the specified budget, timeline, and quality standards.

Stakeholder analysis is an important step in project planning, and it helps project managers to identify potential sources of scope creep or conflicts early on. Stakeholders are individuals, groups, or organizations that have an interest in the project's outcome or can influence the project's success.

To identify and analyze stakeholders in the context of scope management, project managers can use techniques such as stakeholder mapping, stakeholder identification, and stakeholder analysis. Stakeholder mapping involves categorizing stakeholders based on their level of interest and power, while stakeholder identification involves creating a list of potential stakeholders. Stakeholder analysis involves assessing the stakeholders' needs, expectations, and influence on the project's scope.

For example, in a construction project, stakeholders may include the project sponsor, project team, contractors, suppliers, regulatory agencies, and local communities. The project sponsor may have a high level of interest and power in the project's outcome, while the local communities may have a high level of interest but low power.

Scope verification is the process of ensuring that the project's scope has been achieved. The scope statement serves as a reference point for all project stakeholders, and it outlines the project's objectives, deliverables, and acceptance criteria. To verify the project's scope, project managers can use techniques such as inspections, reviews, and walkthroughs.

For example, in a software development project, scope verification may involve testing the software to ensure that it meets the specified requirements and acceptance criteria. The project team can conduct inspections and reviews to verify that the software meets the quality standards and user expectations.

Change management is an important aspect of project scope management, and it involves managing scope changes that arise during the project. Change management includes processes for identifying, evaluating, and approving scope changes and ensuring that the project team implements the changes effectively.

To manage scope changes, project managers can use techniques such as change control boards, change requests, and change logs. Change control boards are groups of stakeholders that evaluate and approve scope changes, while change requests are documents that describe the proposed changes and their impact on the project's scope, schedule, and budget. Change logs track the status of scope changes and ensure that the project team implements the changes according to the approved plan.

For example, in a marketing campaign project, scope changes may arise due to changes in market conditions, customer preferences, or budget constraints. The project team can use change control boards to evaluate and approve scope changes and change logs to track the status of changes.

Quality management is an essential aspect of project scope management, and it involves ensuring that the project's deliverables meet the required quality standards. Quality management includes processes for planning, executing, and monitoring quality activities throughout the project's lifecycle.

To manage quality, project managers can use techniques such as quality planning, quality control, and quality assurance. Quality planning involves identifying the quality standards and requirements for the project's deliverables, while quality control involves monitoring and controlling the quality of the project's products or services. Quality assurance involves ensuring that the project team follows the established quality standards and processes.

For example, in a manufacturing project, quality management may involve defining the quality standards for the products, conducting inspections and tests to ensure that the products meet the standards, and implementing corrective actions to address quality issues.

Create the Work Breakdown Structure (WBS)

This process involves breaking down the project scope into smaller, more manageable work packages. This enables the project team to better understand the project's requirements, estimate costs and timelines more accurately, and assign resources more effectively.

The "Create WBS" process is a key step in project scope management. It involves breaking down the project scope into smaller, more manageable work packages that can be easily understood and executed by the project team. A work breakdown structure (WBS) is a hierarchical decomposition of the project scope into smaller components that can be more easily managed and controlled.

The WBS is an essential tool for project planning and control. It enables the project team to identify all the deliverables required to complete the project, and to organize them into a logical sequence. This helps to ensure that all project requirements are met and that the project is completed on time, within budget, and to the required quality standards.

Creating a WBS involves the following steps:

Identify the major deliverables: The project team must identify the major deliverables required to complete the project. These are usually listed in the project charter or scope statement.

Break down the deliverables: Each major deliverable is then broken down into smaller components. This process continues until the components are small enough to be easily understood and managed.

Assign codes: Each component is assigned a unique code to identify it within the WBS. This makes it easier to track progress and identify any issues that arise.

Validate the WBS: The WBS should be reviewed and validated by the project team to ensure that all deliverables have been included and that the hierarchy is logical and manageable.

Update the WBS: The WBS should be updated throughout the project as new deliverables are identified or existing ones are modified.

For example, let's say a construction company is tasked with building a new office building. The major deliverables for the project might include foundation work, framing, roofing, electrical work, plumbing, HVAC, and finishing work. Each of these major deliverables can be broken down into smaller components, such as excavation, pouring concrete, installing steel beams, running electrical wiring, installing plumbing fixtures, and so on. Each of these components would be assigned a unique code within the WBS.

By breaking down the project scope into smaller, more manageable work packages, the project team can better understand the project requirements, estimate costs and timelines more accurately, and assign resources more effectively. This leads to a more efficient and effective project management process, which ultimately results in a successful project outcome.

The Work Breakdown Structure (WBS) is a crucial tool in project management as it helps to organize project tasks into manageable and well-defined deliverables. Nonetheless, the importance of WBS goes beyond project planning and control, as it also plays a crucial role in project communication.

By breaking down the project into smaller, more manageable tasks, the WBS provides a common understanding of project deliverables. This helps to align the expectations of the project team, sponsors, and customers. For example, if the project involves building a house, the WBS can break down the project into deliverables such as the foundation, walls, roofing, plumbing, and electrical systems. Each of these deliverables can then be further broken down into smaller tasks, such as pouring the foundation, framing the walls, and installing the electrical wiring.

The WBS is also closely linked with other project management processes, such as cost estimating, schedule development, and resource planning. For example, cost estimates can be developed by analyzing the cost of each deliverable in the WBS. The WBS can also be used to develop the project schedule by estimating the time required for each deliverable. Resource planning can be facilitated by identifying the resources required for each deliverable in the WBS.

Project management software can be used to create and maintain the WBS. For example, Microsoft Project provides a WBS view that can be used to create a hierarchical WBS. The software can help automate the process of assigning codes and tracking progress, which saves time and reduces errors.

Nonetheless, there are also challenges and risks associated with creating a WBS. One common risk is scope creep, where additional tasks are added to the WBS without proper approval or justification. This can result in the project exceeding its budget or timeline. Another risk is inadequate stakeholder engagement, where key stakeholders are not involved in the development of the WBS, resulting in a lack of buy-in or misalignment of expectations.

To mitigate these risks, it is important to involve all key stakeholders in the development of the WBS, including the project team, sponsors, and customers. It is also important to ensure that the WBS is based on a thorough understanding of project requirements and to regularly review and update the WBS throughout the project lifecycle.

There are various types of WBS templates, including hierarchical, matrix-based, or tree-based templates. Hierarchical WBS templates are the most commonly used, where deliverables are organized in a top-down fashion, with each level representing a more detailed breakdown of the previous level. Matrix-based templates are useful when the project involves multiple disciplines or teams, with each deliverable organized by discipline or team. Tree-based templates are useful when the project involves multiple parallel deliverables, with each deliverable organized into a separate branch.

Validate Scope

This process involves ensuring that the project deliverables meet the stakeholder's requirements. It includes reviewing deliverables against the scope statement and obtaining formal acceptance of the completed deliverables.

Project scope validation is a crucial process that ensures the project deliverables meet the stakeholder's expectations and requirements. This process involves reviewing the completed deliverables against the scope statement to ensure that they are complete, correct, and satisfactory.

The purpose of scope validation is to ensure that the project is progressing in the right direction, and the stakeholders are satisfied with the project's progress. The validated scope is a crucial input to the control scope process, which helps ensure that the project stays on track.

Examples of how the scope validation process works:

A software development company has completed the development of a new software product. The company will validate the scope of the project by testing the software against the requirements specified in the scope statement. Once the software has been tested and meets the requirements, it can be delivered to the stakeholders.

A construction company has built a new office building for a client. The company will validate the scope of the project by conducting a final walkthrough with the client. During the walkthrough, the company will ensure that the building meets all of the client's requirements and specifications. Once the client approves the building, it can be handed over to them.

An event management company has organized a conference for a client. The company will validate the scope of the project by reviewing the conference against the scope statement. The company will ensure that all the sessions, speakers, and logistics of the conference meet the client's requirements. Once the client approves the conference, it can be considered complete.

Obtaining formal acceptance from stakeholders is a crucial step in the project validation process. This ensures that the stakeholders have approved the project deliverables and that the project is moving in the right direction. Formal acceptance is typically obtained through a formal sign-off process, where stakeholders review the deliverables and indicate their acceptance of them.

For example, imagine a software development project where the project team has developed a new mobile app. The app is complete, and the project team has tested it thoroughly to ensure that it meets the requirements set out in the project scope statement. Nonetheless, before the app can be released to the public, the project sponsor must review and approve the final product. The sponsor's formal acceptance signifies that the app meets the requirements and is ready for release.

Scope changes can impact the project validation process. When changes to the scope statement occur, the validation process may need to be repeated to ensure that the updated deliverables meet the new requirements. This can have a significant impact on the project timeline and budget, so it's essential to manage scope changes carefully.

For example, suppose a project is being developed to build a new office building. The project scope statement outlines the specifications of the building, including the size, layout, and materials to be used. Suppose the stakeholders decide they want to add a new wing to the building after construction has already begun. In that case, the validation process will need to be repeated to ensure that the new wing meets the same requirements as the original building.

Quality control plays a crucial role in the scope validation process. While the text mentions that completed deliverables are reviewed for completeness and correctness, it is essential to emphasize the importance of quality control measures in ensuring that the deliverables meet the necessary standards of quality.

For example, imagine a construction project where the project team is building a new bridge. Once the bridge is complete, the project team will perform a quality control check to ensure that the bridge meets the necessary safety standards. This includes testing the structural integrity of the bridge, ensuring that it can withstand the weight of traffic, and checking that all safety features, such as guardrails and lighting, are working correctly.

Control Scope

This process involves monitoring and controlling changes to the project scope to ensure that the project remains on track. This includes documenting and reviewing scope changes, determining their impact on the project, and implementing approved changes through the project's change control process.

Project Scope Management is a crucial aspect of project management. The Control Scope process is the fifth and final process in the Project Scope Management knowledge area. It is concerned with monitoring and controlling changes to the project scope to ensure that the project remains on track.

The Control Scope process is an essential process because it allows project managers to manage scope creep, which is one of the most significant challenges in project management. Scope creep occurs when there are uncontrolled changes to the project scope, leading to increased project costs, delays, and reduced quality. As such, controlling scope is crucial to ensure that the project objectives are achieved on time, within budget, and to the expected quality.

The Control Scope process involves the following steps:

Documenting scope changes: This step involves documenting all scope changes that have occurred since the last scope change control process. It includes recording the nature of the change, the reason for the change, and the impact of the change on the project's schedule, cost, and quality.

Reviewing scope changes: This step involves reviewing all scope changes to determine their impact on the project. It includes assessing whether the changes are necessary and whether they align with the project's objectives. The project manager must evaluate whether the changes will affect the project's cost, schedule, and quality.

Determining the impact of scope changes: This step involves determining the impact of the scope changes on the project's cost, schedule, and quality. The project manager must assess whether the changes will cause the project to exceed its budget or schedule and whether they will affect the quality of the project deliverables.

Implementing approved changes: This step involves implementing the approved scope changes through the project's change control process. The project manager must ensure that the changes are implemented correctly and that they do not adversely affect the project's objectives.

Here is an example to illustrate the Control Scope process:

Suppose a project manager is overseeing the construction of a new office building. During the course of the project, the client requests that an additional floor be added to the building. The project manager must follow the Control Scope process to evaluate the impact of this change on the project.

The project manager documents the scope change by recording the nature of the change, the reason for the change, and the impact of the change on the project's schedule, cost, and quality. They then review the scope change and assess whether it aligns with the project's objectives. The project manager determines that the change is necessary and will not adversely affect the project's objectives.

Next, the project manager evaluates the impact of the scope change on the project's cost, schedule, and quality. They determine that the additional floor will increase the project's cost and extend the project's schedule by two weeks. Nonetheless, the quality of the project deliverables will not be affected.

Finally, the project manager implements the approved scope change through the project's change control process. They ensure that the additional floor is constructed according to the client's specifications and that it does not adversely affect the project's objectives.

Project Scope Management is a crucial part of project management, as it ensures that the project's objectives are achieved while meeting stakeholder requirements. It consists of six processes, one of which is Control Scope. Control Scope is the process of monitoring the status of the project scope and managing changes to the scope baseline. In this process, several key elements should be considered to ensure successful scope management.

One essential element of the Control Scope process is the change control board. This board is responsible for evaluating and approving scope changes, ensuring that changes are made only after proper evaluation and analysis. The board should be composed of representatives from all relevant stakeholders, including team members, sponsors, and customers. For example, in a construction project, the change control board may include the project manager, the architect, the contractor, and the client.

Another crucial element is the communication plan. It is vital to communicate scope changes to all relevant stakeholders to ensure that everyone is aware of the changes and can adjust their plans or expectations accordingly. The communication plan should identify the frequency, format, and recipients of project status reports, including scope changes. For example, in a software development project, the project manager may send a weekly email update to the team, highlighting any scope changes made during the week.

Monitoring the scope is also a crucial element of the Control Scope process. It is essential to ensure that the project remains aligned with the project objectives throughout the project's lifecycle. This can be achieved through regular monitoring and review of the scope statement, scope baseline, and work breakdown structure. For example, in a marketing campaign project, the project manager may review the project scope at each project milestone to ensure that it aligns with the marketing objectives.

The Control Scope process uses several tools and techniques to manage scope changes effectively. One of these tools is variance analysis, which compares the actual project performance to the baseline. For example, in a construction project, variance analysis may be used to compare the actual cost of materials to the budgeted cost of materials. Another tool is trend analysis, which analyzes project performance over time to identify any trends. For example, in a manufacturing project, trend analysis may be used to identify any patterns in product defects. Earned value management is another technique that compares the actual project performance to the planned value of the project. For example, in a software development project, earned value management may be used to compare the actual progress of the project to the planned schedule.

PROJECT SCHEDULE MANAGEMENT

Project Schedule Management is a crucial area of project management that focuses on developing and maintaining a project schedule. The Project Schedule Management process involves several steps, including Plan Schedule Management, Define Activities, Sequence Activities, Estimate Activity Durations, Develop Schedule, and Control Schedule.

Plan Schedule Management

This process involves creating a comprehensive schedule management plan that outlines the project schedule development process, the tools and techniques that will be used, and the roles and responsibilities of the project team.

This process involves creating a comprehensive schedule management plan that outlines the project schedule development process, the tools and techniques that will be used, and the roles and responsibilities of the project team. The plan also defines how the project schedule will be monitored and controlled throughout the project's life cycle.

Here are some of the key components of a Schedule Management Plan:

Schedule Development Approach: This defines the approach that will be used to develop the project schedule. This could include a traditional waterfall approach, an iterative approach, or an agile approach.

Roles and Responsibilities: This section outlines the roles and responsibilities of the project team members involved in schedule management, such as the project manager, scheduler, and project team members.

Schedule Control: This section defines how the project schedule will be monitored and controlled throughout the project's life cycle. This could include regular status reports, change control procedures, and contingency planning.

Schedule Baseline: This is a snapshot of the project schedule at a specific point in time. It is used as a reference point to measure progress and to compare actual results against planned results.

Tools and Techniques: This section outlines the tools and techniques that will be used to develop and maintain the project schedule. This could include software tools, such as Microsoft Project or Primavera, as well as manual techniques, such as Gantt charts or network diagrams.

As a project manager, developing a schedule management plan is a crucial task in ensuring the success of a project. It is essential to consider external factors such as project constraints, stakeholder requirements, and the project's overall business goals while developing the schedule management plan. These factors can significantly impact the project schedule and should be taken into account during the planning process.

For example, if the project has a strict deadline due to contractual obligations, the project manager should consider this constraint while developing the schedule management plan. Similarly, if the project requires specific resources that are in high demand or have limited availability, the project manager should consider this factor while developing the schedule management plan.

Communication and collaboration among team members are also crucial during the schedule development process. The project manager should involve team members in the planning process and seek their input on the feasibility of the schedule. This collaboration can help identify potential challenges and ensure that the schedule is realistic and achievable.

For example, the project manager can involve team members in a brainstorming session to identify potential risks and challenges that may impact the project schedule. This session can help identify critical paths, dependencies, and potential conflicts that need to be addressed in the schedule management plan.

Revising and updating the schedule management plan as the project progresses is equally important. The project manager should continuously monitor the project's progress against the schedule and update the plan as necessary to reflect any changes in scope, timelines, or resources.

For example, if the project scope changes, the project manager should update the schedule management plan to reflect the new requirements and adjust the schedule accordingly. Similarly, if unforeseen delays occur, the project manager should update the plan to reflect the new timelines.

Define Activities

This process involves breaking down the project deliverables into smaller, more manageable components and creating a list of specific activities that must be completed to produce each deliverable.

The Define Activities process is a key step in developing a project schedule, and involves breaking down the project deliverables into smaller, more manageable components. This process essentially involves identifying all the tasks or activities that are required to produce each of the project deliverables.

Here are some key steps involved in the Define Activities process:

Review the project scope and requirements: It's important to have a clear understanding of the project scope and requirements before you begin identifying specific activities. This will help ensure that you don't miss any crucial tasks or activities.

Break down the deliverables: Once you have a clear understanding of the project scope and requirements, you can start breaking down the project deliverables into smaller components. For example, if one of the project deliverables is a new website, you might break it down into tasks such as designing the website layout, coding the website, and testing the website functionality.

Identify dependencies: As you're identifying specific activities, it's important to consider any dependencies between tasks. For example, you might not be able to start coding the website until the website layout has been designed.

Assign resources: Once you have a list of specific activities, you can start assigning resources to each task. This might involve identifying specific team members or departments that will be responsible for each task.

Create a schedule: Finally, you can use the list of activities and assigned resources to create a project schedule. This schedule should include timelines for each task, as well as dependencies between tasks.

Here's an example of how the Define Activities process might work in practice:

Let's say you're managing a project to develop a new software product. One of the project deliverables is a user manual. Here are some steps you might take to define the activities required to produce the user manual:

Review the project scope and requirements: You review the project scope and requirements and confirm that a user manual is required.

Break down the deliverable: You break down the user manual deliverable into smaller components, such as writing the introduction, writing the chapter on installation, and writing the chapter on troubleshooting.

Identify dependencies: You realize that the chapter on installation can't be written until the software has been developed and installed.

Assign resources: You assign the technical writing team to write the user manual.

Create a schedule: Using the list of activities and assigned resources, you create a schedule that includes timelines for each task, and dependencies between tasks.

Identifying activities accurately is crucial in project management as it helps ensure the successful completion of a project within the specified time, budget, and quality. Inaccurate or incomplete identification of project activities can lead to delays, cost overruns, and failure to meet the project objectives. Therefore, it is essential to involve relevant stakeholders in the Define Activities process to ensure that all crucial activities are identified, dependencies are considered, and resources are assigned appropriately.

Stakeholders can provide valuable insights into the project's requirements and expectations, making it easier to identify all necessary activities. Subject matter experts, team members, and customers can contribute to the identification of activities based on their knowledge and experience. For example, subject matter experts can provide technical knowledge and expertise, while team members can provide insights into the day-to-day activities required to complete the project.

The Define Activities process involves several tools and techniques that can help improve the accuracy of activity identification. Decomposition is one such tool that involves breaking down the project deliverables into smaller, manageable components. This helps to identify all the necessary activities required to complete the project. For example, in a construction project, the decomposition of the building into its constituent components such as foundation, walls, roof, and finishes can help identify all the required activities.

Expert judgment is another technique used in the Define Activities process, where experienced professionals provide their opinions and insights into activity identification. For example, a project manager can seek the opinion of a construction expert to identify all the necessary activities required to complete a building project.

Rolling wave planning is a technique that involves planning the project in stages, with detailed planning for the near-term activities and high-level planning for the longer-term activities. This approach allows for flexibility in the project schedule, as the project progresses and new information becomes available. Templates are also useful tools that can help streamline the activity identification process by providing a structured approach to identifying all necessary activities.

It is important to update the activity list regularly to ensure that the project schedule reflects the latest project status. As the project progresses, new information becomes available that can impact the activity list, such as changes in the project scope, resource availability, or external factors. Therefore, regular updates to the activity list can help ensure that the project schedule remains accurate and up-to-date.

Sequence Activities

This process involves identifying the relationships between project activities and determining the most logical order in which they should be completed.

The "Sequence Activities" process is a crucial step in the project schedule management process. It involves identifying all the project activities, and their dependencies, and determining the most logical order in which they should be executed to ensure the project is completed on time and within budget.

To sequence activities effectively, you need to have a clear understanding of the project scope, objectives, and requirements. You also need to identify all the project activities and their respective durations, dependencies, and constraints.

Some common techniques used in sequencing activities include:

Precedence Diagramming Method (PDM): This technique involves creating a network diagram that shows the relationship between the project activities. The network diagram can be used to identify the critical path, which is the longest path in the network, and determines the project's duration.

Dependency Determination: This technique involves identifying the dependencies between the project activities. There are four types of dependencies: finish-to-start (FS), start-to-start (SS), finish-to-finish (FF), and start-to-finish (SF).

Leads and Lags: This technique involves adding or subtracting time to the project activities to account for time overlaps or delays between activities. Leads and lags are typically added to the activity's predecessor, allowing for some flexibility in the project schedule.

Let's consider an example to illustrate this process.

Suppose you are managing a construction project to build a new office building. The project involves several activities, including site preparation, foundation pouring, framing, roofing, electrical, plumbing, and finishing. Here's an example of how you would sequence the activities:

Site preparation: This activity needs to be completed before foundation pouring can begin.

Foundation pouring: This activity needs to be completed before framing can begin.

Framing: This activity needs to be completed before roofing can begin.

Roofing: This activity needs to be completed before electrical and plumbing can begin.

Electrical and plumbing: These activities can be performed concurrently since they do not have any dependencies between them.

Finishing: This activity can be performed once all the previous activities are completed.

By sequencing the activities in this manner, you can ensure that the project is completed on time and within budget. It also helps you identify the critical path, which is the sequence of activities that determines the project's duration. By focusing on the Critical path, you can prioritize your resources and ensure that the project stays on track.

Sequencing activities is a crucial process in project management that involves arranging tasks in a logical order to achieve the project objectives efficiently. This process is crucial because it ensures the project is completed on time and within budget. Without proper sequencing, a project may experience delays and cost overruns, resulting in an unsuccessful project outcome.

One of the key benefits of sequencing activities is the identification of potential schedule risks. By arranging the project tasks in the right sequence, project managers can identify activities that are crucial to the project's success and prioritize them accordingly. For example, suppose a construction project requires the installation of a roof before the interior work can begin. In that case, sequencing activities can ensure that this task is scheduled appropriately to prevent delays in completing the project.

There are different types of dependencies between project activities, such as finish-to-start (FS), start-to-start (SS), finish-to-finish (FF), and start-to-finish (SF). Finish-to-start dependencies are the most common type of dependency used in project management. This type of dependency means that the next task cannot start until the previous one has finished. For example, if a project involves building a house, the foundation must be completed before starting the construction of the walls.

Start-to-finish dependencies are less frequently used in project management. In this type of dependency, the next task can only finish after the previous one has started. This dependency type is useful in cases where a specific activity must be ongoing for a set period, and the next task cannot begin until that period ends. For instance, in a software development project, the testing phase may require ongoing execution until a specific number of test cases are passed before the next phase can begin.

Project management software tools play a crucial role in sequencing activities. Many project management software tools include features that automate the creation of network diagrams and Critical path analysis. These features allow project managers to create a visual representation of the project schedule and identify the Critical path, which is the sequence of activities that must be completed on time to achieve the project's objectives. Project management software tools can save project managers significant time and effort in creating and managing project schedules, which is particularly helpful for complex projects with multiple dependencies.

Estimate Activity Durations

This process involves estimating the amount of time required to complete each project activity, based on historical data, expert judgment, and other relevant factors.

In project management, estimating activity durations is a crucial process that involves predicting how long each task or activity will take to complete. Accurate estimation of activity durations is essential for developing a realistic project schedule and ensuring that the project is completed on time.

The estimate activity duration process involves using various techniques to determine the duration of each activity, including historical data, expert judgment, and other relevant factors. Some of the factors that may be considered include the complexity of the activity, the skills and experience of the team members assigned to the activity, the availability of resources, and any external constraints or dependencies.

To estimate activity durations, project managers can use several techniques, including analogous estimating, parametric estimating, and three-point estimating. Analogous estimating involves using historical data from similar projects to predict activity durations, while parametric estimating uses statistical data to calculate activity durations based on specific variables. Three-point estimating involves using three estimates - optimistic, pessimistic, and most likely to develop a range of potential activity durations.

For example, let's say a project involves developing a new website for a client. The project manager can estimate the activity durations for each task by looking at historical data from similar projects, consulting with team members with relevant experience, and considering any constraints or dependencies that may affect the timeline. For instance, if the project requires integrating a third-party tool, the project manager may need to consider the time required for testing and troubleshooting, which could impact the overall duration of the activity.

Accurate estimation is a crucial aspect of project management as it is essential for developing a realistic project schedule. Project managers must have a thorough understanding of the activities involved in the project and the time required to complete each task. Inaccurate estimation can lead to delays, cost overruns, and other project problems.

For example, if a project manager underestimates the time required to complete a task, it can lead to unrealistic project timelines, which may cause the team to rush through the project and produce a low-quality deliverable. On the other hand, if a project manager overestimates the time required, it can lead to unnecessary delays, which can increase costs and decrease customer satisfaction.

Estimating activity durations is also related to risk management. By identifying potential risks that could impact the timeline of project activity, project managers can develop contingency plans to mitigate those risks and ensure that the project stays on track. For example, if a project involves a crucial activity that requires specialized equipment, the project manager should identify potential equipment failures and develop a contingency plan to address such failures. This could involve identifying backup equipment, developing a maintenance schedule, or exploring other options to minimize the impact of equipment failure.

Communication and collaboration among team members during the estimation process are crucial. By involving team members with relevant experience and skills, project managers can obtain more accurate estimates and ensure that everyone is on the same page regarding the timeline for each activity. Team members who have previously worked on similar projects can provide valuable insights into the time required for each task and any potential risks associated with each activity.

For example, if a project involves developing a new software application, the project manager could involve the development team in the estimation process. The development team can provide insights into the time required for each development phase, any potential issues that could arise during development, and any other considerations that could impact the project timeline.

The use of tools and software for estimating activity durations can also be beneficial. There are various tools available that can help project managers with this process, such as project management software, online calculators, and other applications. These tools can provide project managers with a more structured approach to estimating activity durations and can help ensure that all factors are considered in the estimation process.

For example, project management software can allow project managers to break down activities into smaller, more manageable tasks, assign resources to each task, and estimate the time required to complete each task. The software can also allow project managers to track progress, identify potential delays, and adjust the project schedule accordingly.

Develop Schedule

This process involves creating a detailed project schedule that includes start and end dates for each activity, dependencies, milestones, and other relevant information.

The Develop Schedule process is a crucial step in project management that involves creating a detailed project schedule that outlines the start and end dates for each activity, dependencies, milestones, and other relevant information.

The primary objective of this process is to produce an accurate and comprehensive project schedule that can be used to manage project resources, monitor project progress, and ensure that the project is completed within the specified timeline.

Here are some key steps involved in the Develop Schedule process:

Define Activities: The first step is to identify and define all the project activities that are required to complete the project. This includes breaking down the project scope into smaller, manageable components and identifying the specific tasks that need to be completed to achieve project objectives.

Sequence Activities: The next step is to establish the sequence in which the project activities will be executed. This involves identifying dependencies between activities and determining the order in which they should be completed.

Estimate Activity Resources: Once the activities are defined and sequenced, the next step is to estimate the resources required to complete each activity. This includes identifying the people, equipment, and materials needed for each task.

Estimate Activity Durations: Based on the resources required for each activity, the next step is to estimate the duration of each activity. This involves determining the amount of time needed to complete each task, taking into account any constraints or limitations that may impact the timeline.

Develop Schedule: With all the necessary information gathered, the project schedule can now be developed. This involves creating a comprehensive timeline that outlines the start and end dates for each activity, as well as any milestones or deliverables that must be achieved at specific points in the project.

It's worth noting that developing a project schedule is an iterative process that requires ongoing monitoring and adjustment as the project progresses. As new information becomes available or unexpected challenges arise, the schedule may need to be revised to ensure that the project remains on track.

To give you an example, let's say that a project involves building a new office building. The Develop Schedule process would involve breaking down the project into smaller components, such as site preparation, foundation work, framing, electrical and plumbing work, and finishing.

The activities would be sequenced based on dependencies, such as the need to complete foundation work before framing can begin. Resource and duration estimates would then be developed for each activity, taking into account the availability of workers, equipment, and materials.

Using this information, a detailed project schedule would be created that outlines the start and end dates for each activity, as well as any milestones or deliverables that must be achieved along the way. The project schedule would be monitored and adjusted as necessary to ensure that the project remains on track and is completed within the specified timeline.

Developing a project schedule is an important aspect of project management. It involves identifying the activities that need to be completed, estimating the time required to complete each activity, and determining the order in which the activities should be completed. In order to create an effective project schedule, it is important to consider several factors, including identifying the types of dependencies between activities, identifying limitations of resources, and using tools and techniques to develop the schedule.

Identifying Types of Dependencies: One of the first steps in developing a project schedule is identifying the types of dependencies that exist between activities. There are three main types of dependencies: mandatory, discretionary, and external. Mandatory dependencies are those that are inherent to the project and must be completed in a specific order. For example, building the foundation of a house must be completed before the walls can be erected. Discretionary dependencies are those that are not inherent to the project and can be completed in any order. For example, painting a room can be done before or after installing the carpet. External dependencies are those that are outside the control of the project team, such as waiting for a permit to be approved or for a supplier to deliver materials.

Identifying Limitations of Resources: Another important factor to consider when developing a project schedule is identifying the limitations of resources. Resources can be limited in terms of availability or capacity. For example, if there are only two carpenters available to work on a project, the project schedule will need to be adjusted to reflect this limitation. Similarly, if a piece of equipment can only process a certain number of units per hour, this will need to be taken into account when developing the schedule.

Using Tools and Techniques: There are several tools and techniques that can be used to develop a project schedule. One commonly used tool is the network diagram, which shows the relationships between activities and the Critical path. The Critical path is the sequence of activities that must be completed on time in order for the project to be completed on schedule. Another technique is the use of the Critical path method (CPM), which is a mathematical algorithm used to calculate the Critical path and determine the shortest possible project duration. The analysis of line of balance (LOB) is another tool that can be used to determine resource availability and allocation and to optimize resource utilization.

Control Schedule

This process involves monitoring the project schedule on an ongoing basis to identify any deviations from the planned schedule and taking corrective action to keep the project on track. This includes updating the project schedule, adjusting activity durations, and making other changes as necessary to ensure that the project is completed on time and within budget.

Control Schedule is an important process in project management that ensures that the project is completed within the planned time frame and budget. The process involves monitoring the project schedule regularly, comparing it with the planned schedule, and identifying any variances. Once the variances are identified, corrective actions are taken to bring the project back on track.

Here are some key steps involved in the Control Schedule process:

Monitor the Project Schedule: This step involves regularly reviewing the project schedule and comparing it with the planned schedule. This helps identify any deviations or variances from the planned schedule.

Analyze the Schedule Variance: Once the deviations are identified, the next step is to analyze the causes of the variances. This helps determine whether the variances are acceptable or require corrective action.

Take Corrective Action: If the variances are not acceptable, corrective actions need to be taken to bring the project back on track. This can include adjusting activity durations, re-sequencing activities, or changing resource assignments.

Update the Project Schedule: Once corrective actions are taken, the project schedule needs to be updated to reflect the changes. This helps ensure that the project team has the latest information on the project schedule.

Communicate Schedule Changes: It's important to communicate any schedule changes to the project team, stakeholders, and other relevant parties. This helps ensure that everyone is aware of the changes and can adjust their plans accordingly.

Here is an example of how the Control Schedule process works in practice:

Suppose you are managing a construction project that involves building a new office building. Your project schedule shows that the project should be completed in 12 months. Nonetheless, after six months, you realize that the project is running behind schedule due to delays in obtaining permits and approvals from the local authorities.

In this case, you would need to take corrective action to bring the project back on track. This could include re-sequencing activities, hiring additional resources, or renegotiating timelines with suppliers. Once the corrective actions are taken, you would update the project schedule and communicate the changes to the project team and other stakeholders.

Overall, the Control Schedule process is essential for ensuring that a project is completed within the planned time frame and budget. By monitoring the project schedule regularly and taking corrective actions, when necessary, project managers can keep the project on track and ensure its success.

Project management involves a range of processes and techniques that are aimed at ensuring successful project delivery. One of the key aspects of project management is the control of the project schedule. This involves implementing a range of processes and techniques to ensure that the project schedule is managed effectively and any changes are controlled and monitored.

Change Control is an important process that should be in place to manage any changes made to the project schedule. This process involves ensuring that any changes made to the schedule are reviewed and approved before they are implemented. For example, if there is a delay in the delivery of a key component, the change control process should be initiated to ensure that the impact on the project schedule is assessed and any necessary changes are made.

The Schedule Baseline is the approved version of the project schedule against which actual progress is measured. This is an important aspect of the control schedule process, as it provides a reference point for measuring progress and identifying any deviations. For example, if the project is behind schedule, the schedule baseline can be used to identify where the project has deviated from the planned schedule.

Earned Value Management (EVM) is a technique used to measure project performance against the project baseline. This involves assessing the planned value, earned value, and actual cost of the project to determine whether the project is on track. For example, if the planned value of a project is $100,000 and the actual cost is $80,000, the project is said to be performing well.

Schedule Performance Index (SPI) and Schedule Variance (SV) are two key performance indicators used to measure the project's schedule performance. SPI measures the project's progress against the schedule baseline, while SV measures the difference between the planned and actual progress. For example, if the SPI is 1.2, it means that the project is progressing at a rate that is 20% faster than planned. If the SV is -10%, it means that the project is 10% behind schedule.

Risk Management is an important aspect of project management and should be integrated with the Control Schedule process. This involves identifying and managing any risks that could impact the project schedule. For example, if there is a risk that a key team member may leave the project, a risk management plan should be developed to mitigate the impact of this risk on the project schedule.

PROJECT COST MANAGEMENT

Is the process of planning, estimating, budgeting, and controlling the costs involved in a project. It involves creating a Cost Management Plan that outlines the processes for estimating, budgeting, and controlling costs throughout the project lifecycle. This plan should include the methodologies, tools, and techniques to be used in cost management.

Plan Cost Management:

In this process, the cost management plan is created, which outlines the project's overall approach to cost management. The plan includes the project's cost management policies, procedures, and guidelines, as well as the roles and responsibilities of the project team in managing costs.

Plan Cost Management is the first process in the Project Cost Management knowledge area. Its purpose is to establish the policies, procedures, and documentation for planning, managing, expending, and controlling project costs effectively.

The output of this process is the Cost Management Plan, which is a component of the overall project management plan. It outlines how the project team will manage and control costs throughout the project lifecycle. The plan should be tailored to meet the specific needs of the project and the organization.

The Cost Management Plan should include the following information:

Cost Management Policies: The policies should describe how the project team will manage and control costs. They should include information on cost estimation, budgeting, cost control, and reporting.

Cost Estimation Procedures: The procedures should describe how the project team will estimate costs for the project. They should include information on the methods and techniques used to estimate costs, such as bottom-up or top-down estimating.

Cost Baseline: The cost baseline is the approved time-phased budget for the project. It is used as a basis for comparison to actual costs and is an important element of project cost control.

Funding Requirements: The funding requirements describe how the project will be funded and how the project team will obtain the necessary resources to complete the project.

Reporting Formats: The reporting formats describe how the project team will report project costs to stakeholders. They should include information on the frequency and level of detail of the reports.

Roles and Responsibilities: The roles and responsibilities of the project team should be clearly defined in the Cost Management Plan. This includes who is responsible for cost estimation, budgeting, cost control, and reporting.

Change Control Procedures: The change control procedures describe how the project team will manage changes to the project scope, schedule, or budget.

Some examples of tools and techniques that can be used in the Plan Cost Management process include expert judgment, analytical techniques, and meetings.

Expert judgment is often used to help develop the Cost Management Plan. Experts in cost estimation and project cost control can provide valuable insights into the development of the plan.

Analytical techniques, such as cost-benefit analysis and earned value management, can be used to help determine the best approach to managing project costs.

Meetings are also important in the Plan Cost Management process. The project team should meet to discuss the Cost Management Plan and ensure that it is aligned with the overall project objectives.

One of the key concepts to understand in cost management is the difference between cost management and cost control. Cost management is the process of planning, estimating, and budgeting for costs, while cost control is the process of monitoring and controlling project costs to ensure they remain within the approved budget. Cost management is proactive and focuses on preventing cost overruns, while cost control is reactive and focuses on identifying and addressing cost overruns once they have occurred. For example, during the planning phase, a project manager may estimate the cost of a particular activity to be $10,000. During the execution phase, the actual cost of the activity may be $12,000. Cost control would involve identifying why the actual cost was higher than estimated and taking corrective action to bring it back in line with the approved budget.

It is important to note that the Cost Management Plan should be updated throughout the project lifecycle to ensure that it remains relevant and effective. As the project progresses, there may be changes to the scope, schedule, or resources that impact project costs. Therefore, the Cost Management Plan should be reviewed and updated regularly to reflect these changes. For example, if a project team member leaves the project and a replacement needs to be hired, the Cost Management Plan should be updated to reflect the new resource costs.

Another crucial aspect of Cost Management is the consideration of risk management. Risk management is the process of identifying, analyzing, and responding to project risks to minimize their impact on project objectives. Risks can have a significant impact on project costs, and therefore, it is crucial to include risk management in the Plan Cost Management process. The Cost Management Plan should include a risk management plan that outlines how risks will be identified, assessed, and managed to minimize their impact on project costs. For example, if there is a risk of a supplier not delivering materials on time, the risk management plan should include strategies for mitigating this risk, such as identifying alternate suppliers or ordering materials in advance to avoid delays.

Estimate Costs

This process involves estimating the costs of the resources required to complete each project activity. This includes the cost of labor, materials, equipment, and any other expenses that may be incurred during the project's execution. The accuracy of the cost estimates is crucial in determining the project budget and in managing costs throughout the project lifecycle.

In project management, estimating costs is a crucial process in determining the overall budget for a project. This involves identifying and estimating the costs associated with all the resources required to complete each project activity. The accuracy of cost estimates is essential in managing costs throughout the project lifecycle, as it helps to avoid cost overruns and ensure that the project is completed within the allocated budget.

To estimate costs, project managers typically use a variety of techniques, including analogous estimating, parametric estimating, and bottom-up estimating. Analogous estimating involves using historical data from similar projects to estimate costs for the current project. Parametric estimating uses statistical data to calculate costs based on specific project parameters, such as the size or complexity of the project. Bottom-up estimating involves estimating the costs of individual project components and then aggregating them to arrive at an overall project cost estimate.

Examples of how cost estimates can be used in project management:

A construction project manager estimates the cost of materials, equipment, and labor required to build a new bridge. The cost estimate helps to determine the overall project budget and identify any potential cost overruns that need to be managed.

A software development project manager estimates the cost of resources required to develop a new application, including the cost of software licenses, hardware, and personnel. The cost estimate helps to determine the project budget and ensure that the project is completed within the allocated resources.

A marketing project manager estimates the cost of advertising and promotional materials for a new product launch. The cost estimate helps to determine the marketing budget and ensure that the project is completed within the allocated funds.

Project cost management is a crucial aspect of project management that involves estimating, budgeting, and controlling project costs. Accurate cost estimation is essential for successful project execution, and it starts with a clear understanding of the project scope. The more defined the project scope, the more accurate the cost estimates will be. Project managers must ensure that they have a clear understanding of the project scope before estimating costs.

For instance, consider a construction project. A well-defined scope will help project managers estimate the number of resources needed, the duration of the project, and the corresponding costs. Nonetheless, if the project scope is unclear, it will be challenging to estimate costs accurately. Project managers may end up underestimating or overestimating the project costs, which could impact the project's overall success.

As part of the Plan Cost Management process, project managers should develop a cost management plan that defines how costs will be estimated, budgeted, and controlled throughout the project. The cost management plan is an essential document for ensuring that cost management activities are consistent with project objectives, and stakeholders are informed about cost-related decisions.

For example, a cost management plan for a software development project might define the methodologies and tools used for cost estimation and tracking, the reporting formats, and the stakeholders responsible for reviewing and approving cost-related decisions.

Project managers should also consider the use of contingency reserves as part of their cost management plan. Contingency reserves are typically included in cost estimates to account for unforeseen risks or uncertainties that may impact project costs. For instance, a construction project may have a contingency reserve for unexpected delays caused by weather conditions. These reserves are a vital tool for managing project risks and avoiding cost overruns.

Moreover, the use of specialized software tools for cost estimating and management is becoming increasingly popular among project managers. These tools can streamline the cost estimating process, automate calculations, and generate reports. For instance, a project manager can use cost estimation software to calculate the cost of resources needed for a particular project. This approach can help project managers make more accurate cost estimates and save time in the estimation process.

Determine Budget

> This process involves aggregating the estimated costs of all project activities to establish the project budget. This budget should include all direct and indirect costs associated with the project, including contingency reserves and management reserves.

The "Determine Budget" process is the process of aggregating the estimated costs of all project activities to establish the project budget. This process is a part of the Project Cost Management knowledge area in the PMBOK Guide. The purpose of this process is to determine the total cost required to complete the project and to establish a cost baseline against which project performance can be measured and controlled.

To determine the budget, the project manager needs to collect and compile cost estimates for all the project activities. These cost estimates should include all direct and indirect costs associated with the project, such as labor, materials, equipment, facilities, and any other expenses related to the project.

In addition to the estimated costs, the project manager should also include contingency reserves and management reserves in the project budget. Contingency reserves are funds set aside to cover unforeseen risks and uncertainties that may arise during the project. Management reserves are funds set aside to cover changes in scope or other unexpected events that may impact the project.

Once all the cost estimates are compiled, the project manager should aggregate them to establish the project budget. This budget should be approved by the project sponsor or other appropriate stakeholders before it is finalized.

Here's an example to illustrate the "Determine Budget" process:

Let's say that you are a project manager in charge of building a new office building. To determine the budget, you need to collect cost estimates for all the activities involved in the project, such as excavation, foundation, framing, electrical, plumbing, and finishing work.

You estimate that the total cost of all the activities will be $10 million. Nonetheless, to account for any unforeseen risks or uncertainties, you decide to include a 10% contingency reserve, bringing the total budget to $11 million. In addition, you also set aside a 5% management reserve, bringing the total budget to $11.55 million.

You present the project budget to the project sponsor and other stakeholders for approval. Once it is approved, the budget becomes the cost baseline against which project performance is measured and controlled.

Effective cost management is a crucial aspect of project management. Managing costs ensures that projects are delivered within the approved budget and that resources are used efficiently. The "Determine Budget" process is an essential part of the cost management plan and is closely related to other cost management processes in the project life cycle.

Cost Estimation Techniques: There are several techniques for estimating project costs, including the analog estimation, parametric estimation, and three-point estimation. Analog estimation is a technique that uses historical data from similar projects to estimate costs. Parametric estimation uses statistical modeling to estimate costs based on variables such as project size, complexity, and duration. The three-point estimation technique takes into account three different scenarios: best-case, worst-case, and most likely, to determine a range of potential costs.

Direct and Indirect Costs: Direct costs are expenses that are directly tied to the project, such as labor costs and materials. Indirect costs are expenses that are not directly related to the project, such as rent or utilities. For example, in a construction project, direct costs might include materials, labor, and equipment, while indirect costs might include permits and fees, insurance, and administrative expenses.

Establishing and Managing the Cost Baseline: The cost baseline is the approved budget for the project, and it is established during the "Determine Budget" process. The cost baseline provides a reference point against which project performance can be measured. It is crucial to manage the cost baseline throughout the project to ensure that the project remains on track and within the approved budget. This includes monitoring project expenses, identifying cost variances, and taking corrective action as needed.

Controlling Costs: Effective cost control involves monitoring project expenses and making adjustments to keep the project on track. This includes analyzing cost variances, identifying the root causes of deviations from the budget, and implementing corrective actions. The "Control Costs" process is an essential part of cost management and involves monitoring the project's actual expenditures against the budget and making adjustments as needed.

Example: Suppose a company is building a new office building. The direct costs for the project include the cost of materials, labor, and equipment. The company estimates that the total direct costs for the project will be $5 million. Nonetheless, there are also indirect costs associated with the project, such as permits and fees, insurance, and administrative expenses. These indirect costs are estimated to be $1 million, bringing the total estimated cost of the project to $6 million.

Halfway through the project, the cost of materials increased significantly, resulting in a cost variance of $500,000, compared to the established cost baseline of $6 million.". The project manager identifies the root cause of the variance and implements corrective action, such as finding alternative materials or negotiating better prices with suppliers, to bring the project back on track.

Control Costs

This process involves monitoring project costs and taking corrective action as necessary to ensure that the project remains within budget. This includes monitoring actual costs against the budgeted costs, identifying variances, analyzing the causes of variances, and implementing corrective actions to address any deviations from the budget.

Control Costs is a crucial process in project cost management, as it involves monitoring project costs and taking corrective action to ensure that the project remains within budget. Here's a breakdown of the process and its key steps:

Monitor Actual Costs: The first step in the process is to track the actual costs of the project. This involves regularly comparing the actual costs incurred against the budgeted costs to determine if the project is on track financially.

Identify Variances: Identify any variances between actual and budgeted costs. A variance is the difference between the actual cost and the budgeted cost, and it can be either positive or negative.

Analyze Causes of Variances: Once variances have been identified, it's important to analyze the causes of these deviations from the budget. There are several potential reasons for variances, such as inaccurate cost estimates, unexpected changes in project scope, or unanticipated costs.

Implement Corrective Actions: After analyzing the causes of variances, it's time to take corrective action to address any deviations from the budget. This may involve adjusting the project scope, renegotiating contracts with vendors, or finding ways to reduce costs.

To give you an example, let's say you're managing a construction project to build a new office building. During the Control Costs process, you notice that the actual costs of materials and labor are higher than expected, and you've exceeded your budget. After analyzing the causes of the variances, you determine that the construction crew has been working overtime, which is driving up labor costs.

To address this issue, you might take corrective action by adjusting the work schedule to reduce overtime hours or negotiating a lower hourly rate with the construction crew. By taking these actions, you can bring your project costs back in line with your budget.

Project cost management is an essential aspect of project management, and it involves planning, estimating, budgeting, and controlling costs throughout a project's lifecycle. In this context, the term "budget" refers to the approved cost baseline for the project, which serves as a reference point for monitoring project costs.

The Cost Management Plan is a crucial component of project cost management, and it outlines how project costs will be estimated, budgeted, and controlled throughout the project's lifecycle. This plan includes a description of the processes, tools, and techniques that will be used to manage project costs, as well as the roles and responsibilities of the project team members involved in cost management.

One essential aspect of project cost management is defining performance metrics to measure progress and identify variances. Performance metrics could include cost variance, schedule variance, and earned value analysis. For example, cost variance compares the actual cost of work performed to the planned cost of work, furthermore, while schedule variance compares the actual duration of work performed to the planned duration of work.

Project management software can be very helpful in tracking actual costs and identifying variances. Commonly used software in project cost management includes Microsoft Project, Primavera, and Smartsheet. These tools can help project managers track project costs, create budgets, and generate reports on cost performance.

Change control is another crucial aspect of project cost management. The Control Costs process is closely linked to the Change Control process, and any changes to the project scope or budget must be approved through the Change Control process before they can be implemented. This ensures that any changes to the project do not impact project costs without proper approval and evaluation.

PROJECT QUALITY MANAGEMENT:

Project Quality Management is an important area in project management that ensures that the project delivers products or services that meet or exceed stakeholder expectations.

Plan Quality Management

This process involves identifying quality requirements and standards for the project and developing a comprehensive plan that outlines how these requirements will be met. The plan will include details on quality control and assurance activities, quality metrics, and the roles and responsibilities of team members involved in quality management.

"Plan Quality Management" is the process of defining how the project's quality requirements will be met and ensuring that the project's deliverables meet the necessary quality standards. This process is the first step and is crucial to ensuring that project objectives are met.

Here are some key steps involved in the "Plan Quality Management" process:

Identify Quality Requirements: The first step is to identify the quality requirements for the project. This involves determining the quality standards that must be met and the criteria that will be used to measure quality.

Determine Quality Metrics: The next step is to define the metrics that will be used to measure quality. Quality metrics will be used to assess whether the project's deliverables meet the quality standards set out in the quality requirements.

Develop Quality Management Plan: Based on the quality requirements and metrics, a comprehensive quality management plan should be developed. This plan should include details on quality control and assurance activities, as well as the roles and responsibilities of team members involved in quality management.

Define Quality Control Activities: Quality control activities are designed to ensure that project deliverables meet the defined quality standards. These activities should be identified and outlined in the quality management plan.

Define Quality Assurance Activities: Quality assurance activities are designed to ensure that the project's overall quality management approach is effective. These activities should be identified and outlined in the quality management plan.

Gain Acceptance: The quality management plan should be reviewed and approved by stakeholders, including the project sponsor and other key stakeholders, to ensure that everyone understands and agrees with the approach.

Examples of quality requirements could include things like "all software code must be reviewed by at least two people before being released" or "all documentation must be reviewed by a subject matter expert before being finalized." Quality metrics might include things like "number of defects per 1,000 lines of code" or "customer satisfaction ratings on a scale of 1 to 5."

Plan Quality Management is the process of defining quality requirements and determining how they will be achieved throughout the project lifecycle. This process is crucial for project success as it ensures that project deliverables meet stakeholder expectations and requirements. In this text, we will explain the importance of stakeholder analysis, the need to update the quality management plan regularly, the use of quality tools and techniques, and the linkage to other project management processes.

Stakeholder analysis is essential in the Plan Quality Management process as it helps to identify and involve stakeholders in the quality planning process. Stakeholders can provide valuable input that ensures that quality requirements are properly defined and prioritized. For instance, a project manager of a construction project could involve the client, engineers, and architects in the quality planning process to understand their requirements, expectations, and concerns. This input can help to define quality objectives, criteria, and standards that meet their needs.

The quality management plan is a living document that should be regularly updated throughout the project lifecycle to reflect changes in quality requirements, metrics, and control/assurance activities. For example, a software development project might start with a basic set of quality requirements, but as the project progresses, the requirements might change based on the needs of stakeholders. The quality management plan should be updated accordingly to ensure that the project team is aware of the changes and can adjust their work accordingly.

Quality tools and techniques are crucial in the Plan Quality Management process as they provide a structured approach to identify, analyze, and manage quality requirements. Some examples of quality tools and techniques include brainstorming, benchmarking, and statistical process control. Brainstorming involves generating ideas and solutions to a problem through a group discussion. Benchmarking is a process of comparing the project's performance to that of other projects or industry standards. Statistical process control involves monitoring and controlling processes to ensure that they are within acceptable quality limits.

The Plan Quality Management process should be linked to other project management processes such as risk management and change management. This linkage ensures that quality requirements are considered in these areas as well. For example, during the risk management process, the project team should consider the potential impact of risks on quality requirements. Similarly, during the change management process, the project team should evaluate the impact of changes on quality requirements and update the quality management plan accordingly.

Manage Quality

In this process, the project team implements the quality management plan by executing quality control and assurance activities, ensuring that project deliverables meet the established quality standards. The team will continuously monitor the project's progress against the quality plan, document and report quality issues, and take corrective action as necessary.

The "Manage Quality" process is a part of Project Quality Management that focuses on implementing the quality management plan to ensure that project deliverables meet the established quality standards. It involves executing quality control and assurance activities, continuously monitoring project progress against the quality plan, documenting and reporting quality issues, and taking corrective action as necessary.

Examples of activities that might take place during the "Manage Quality" process:

Performing inspections and tests: Inspections and tests are performed to ensure that the project deliverables meet the required quality standards. For example, if a construction project is underway, inspections may be conducted on the foundation to ensure that it is stable and meets the required strength and durability standards.

Reviewing work results: The project team reviews work results to ensure that they meet quality standards. For example, if a software development project is underway, the team might review the code to ensure that it is well-documented, efficient, and meets the required functionality and security standards.

Conducting quality audits: Quality audits are conducted to identify any deficiencies in the quality management plan and project execution. For example, a quality audit may be conducted on a manufacturing project to ensure that the equipment used meets the required safety and quality standards.

Analyzing quality data: Quality data is analyzed to identify trends and patterns that may indicate potential quality issues. For example, if a manufacturing project is underway, data on defect rates might be analyzed to identify areas for improvement.

Taking corrective action: If quality issues are identified, corrective action is taken to address them. For example, if a construction project is underway, corrective action may be taken to reinforce the foundation if it does not meet the required strength and durability standards.

Quality planning is a crucial component of the project management process. It involves defining the quality standards, processes, and tools to be used for ensuring quality deliverables. Quality planning helps to identify potential quality issues upfront, which can save time and resources in the long run. For example, let's say that a project involves building a new website for a client. The quality planning process would involve identifying the quality standards for the website, such as load times, functionality, and design elements. It would also involve determining the processes and tools to be used for testing and validating the website before delivery to the client.

Executing quality control and assurance activities is another essential part of managing quality in a project. It is essential to understand the difference between quality control and quality assurance.

Quality control is about inspecting deliverables to ensure that they meet the required quality standards. For example, in our website project, quality control would involve testing the website for bugs, broken links, and other issues that could affect its performance. On the other hand, quality assurance focuses on ensuring that the processes used to create the deliverables are effective and efficient. In our website project, quality assurance would involve evaluating the tools and processes used to develop and test the website.

Documentation is also crucial to the Manage Quality process. Keeping accurate records of quality issues and their resolution is essential for future reference. Documentation helps to keep track of quality issues and their resolution and provides a record for future reference. In our website project, documentation would involve keeping a log of all bugs and issues found during the testing process, as well as their resolution. This documentation can be used for future reference and to ensure that similar issues are not repeated in future projects.

Stakeholder involvement is also crucial to ensuring the success of the quality management process. Stakeholders can provide valuable input on quality requirements and help to identify potential quality issues. Effective communication with stakeholders is crucial to ensuring that quality expectations are met. In our website project, stakeholders would include the client, the development team, and any other parties involved in the project. Effective communication with these stakeholders would involve regular meetings to discuss quality issues and ensure that everyone is on the same page.

Control Quality

This process involves monitoring and controlling the quality of the project deliverables throughout the project lifecycle, from planning to closure. The project team will use established quality control and assurance activities to measure the project's performance against the quality plan and make necessary adjustments to meet the established standards. The team will also document quality issues, identify their root causes, and implement corrective and preventive actions to prevent similar issues from arising in the future.

Control Quality is a crucial process in Project Quality Management that ensures the project deliverables meet the established quality standards. This process involves monitoring and controlling the project's quality throughout its lifecycle, starting from planning to closure.

During Control Quality, the team will measure performance against the quality plan. The quality control activities involve inspecting the project deliverables to ensure they meet the specified requirements, while the quality assurance activities involve reviewing the overall quality management approach and recommending changes to improve quality.

The project team will document quality issues that arise during the Control Quality process and identify their root causes. They will then implement corrective and preventive actions to prevent similar issues from arising in the future. Corrective actions address quality issues that have already occurred, while preventive actions focus on avoiding quality issues before they occur.

Examples of the Control Quality process in action:

In a software development project, the project team performs regular testing to ensure the software meets the specified requirements. They use tools such as automated testing software and code review to identify any quality issues and make necessary adjustments.

In a construction project, the project team performs regular inspections of the work to ensure it meets the specified standards. They may also use tools such as materials testing to ensure the quality of the materials used in the project.

In a manufacturing project, the project team performs regular quality checks on the production line to ensure that the products meet the specified requirements. They may also use statistical process control to monitor the production process and make necessary adjustments to maintain quality.

Quality management is essential, and Control Quality ensures required standards are met. In this process, several key elements need to be considered to ensure that the project's quality is maintained, and stakeholders' requirements are met.

Additionally, one of these key elements is the concept of quality audits. Quality audits are independent evaluations of the project's quality management system. These audits help identify any gaps or areas for improvement in the project's quality management approach. For example, during a quality audit, the project team may discover that some of the project's quality control measures are not being implemented correctly, which could lead to quality issues down the line.

Another important element of Control Quality is the use of quality metrics. Quality metrics are used to measure and monitor the project's quality performance. Quality metrics can be used to track progress, identify trends, and determine if the project is meeting its quality objectives. For example, if the project team is using a metric to track the number of defects found in the project deliverables, they can quickly identify if the number of defects is increasing and take corrective action to prevent the issue from escalating.

Stakeholder engagement is also a crucial aspect of Control Quality. Stakeholder engagement helps ensure that the project's quality requirements are clearly defined, understood, and met. The project team should engage with stakeholders to gather their feedback on the project's quality and make necessary adjustments to ensure that their requirements are met. For example, if a stakeholder indicates that the quality of the deliverables is not meeting their expectations, the project team can use this feedback to make necessary improvements.

PROJECT RESOURCE MANAGEMENT

Project Resource Management is a key area in project management that involves effectively identifying, acquiring, managing, and utilizing resources throughout the project lifecycle.

Plan Resource Management

This process involves developing a comprehensive plan for how project resources will be identified, acquired, managed, and used throughout the project lifecycle. The plan will include information on resource requirements, availability, allocation, and utilization.

In this process, the project manager identifies and documents the resource requirements for the project, including both human and non-human resources, such as equipment, materials, and facilities. The project manager then develops a plan for how these resources will be acquired, allocated, and used throughout the project lifecycle.

For example, suppose a company is planning to develop a new software product. The project manager will need to identify the human resources required for the project, such as software developers, quality assurance engineers, and project managers. Additionally, they will need to identify the non-human resources required, such as computers, software licenses, and testing equipment.

Once the resource requirements have been identified, the project manager will develop a plan for how these resources will be acquired, allocated, and used throughout the project lifecycle. This may involve hiring additional staff, purchasing equipment, or negotiating with vendors for necessary resources.

The plan will also include information on how resources will be managed throughout the project, such as how conflicts over resource allocation will be resolved and how changes to the resource plan will be handled. By having a comprehensive plan for resource management, the project manager can ensure that the project has the necessary resources to meet its objectives and that these resources are used effectively throughout the project lifecycle.

As a project manager, it is important to develop a comprehensive resource management plan that takes into account various factors that can impact the availability and utilization of resources. This includes lead times for equipment procurement, availability of key personnel, budget constraints, and potential risks to resource availability or utilization. In addition, ethical considerations must be taken into account when allocating resources and resolving conflicts over resource allocation.

Determining Resource Availability, the resource management plan should include information on how the project manager will determine the availability of resources. This can include lead times for equipment procurement or the availability of key personnel. For example, if the project requires specialized equipment that has a long lead time for procurement, the project manager should take this into account and ensure that the procurement process is started well in advance of when the equipment is needed. Similarly, if key personnel are required for the project, the project manager should assess their availability and ensure that they are allocated to the project in a timely manner.

Resource Constraints The resource management plan should also mention any resource constraints that may impact the project. This can include a limited budget or a tight deadline. For example, if the project has a tight deadline, the project manager may need to allocate additional resources to the project to ensure that it is completed on time. Alternatively, if the budget is limited, the project manager may need to find ways to optimize the use of available resources to ensure that the project is completed within the budget constraints.

Risk Management The resource management plan should also address potential risks to resource availability or utilization. For example, if a key team member becomes unavailable due to illness or other reasons, the plan should include contingencies for how the project will proceed. This can include identifying backup resources or reallocating resources from other projects to ensure that the project remains on track. In addition, the plan should include a risk management strategy that identifies potential risks to resource availability and outlines how these risks will be mitigated.

Ethical Considerations Given that the standards of ethics are an integral part of project management, it is important to include information on how the resource management plan will take ethical considerations into account. This can include ensuring that resources are allocated fairly and that conflicts over resource allocation are resolved in an ethical manner. For example, if there are competing demands for resources from different projects or stakeholders, the project manager should ensure that resources are allocated based on the project's priority and overall benefit to the organization. In addition, the project manager should ensure that all team members are treated fairly, and that there is no discrimination based on race, gender, or other factors.

Estimate Activity Resources

This process involves estimating the type and quantity of resources required for each project activity, including personnel, equipment, and materials. This estimation is crucial to ensuring that the project is properly staffed and resourced.

The Estimate Activity Resources process is a part of the Project Resource Management knowledge area and is focused on identifying and estimating the resources required for each project activity. This process is important as it helps to ensure that the project is adequately staffed and resourced to achieve the project objectives.

During this process, the project team must determine the types and quantities of resources that are required for each activity. This may include personnel, equipment, materials, and other resources. The project team must also consider any constraints or limitations that may impact the availability or use of these resources.

For example, if a project activity requires the use of a specific piece of equipment, the project team must estimate the availability of that equipment and whether it can be used for the duration of the activity. Similarly, if a project activity requires a certain number of personnel, the project team must estimate the availability of those personnel and their skills and expertise.

The output of the Estimate Activity Resources process is a resource management plan that details the types and quantities of resources required for each activity, as well as any constraints or limitations that may impact their use. This plan is used to guide the acquisition and allocation of resources throughout the project.

Resource estimation is a crucial process in project management that involves determining the type and quantity of resources required for each project activity to achieve project objectives. Accurate estimation of resources is essential to ensure that the project is properly staffed and resourced to meet project goals. Failure to do so can lead to project delays, budget overruns, and other issues that can negatively impact project success.

The Estimate Activity Resources process involves several tools and techniques to estimate resources accurately.

Expert judgment involves consulting with individuals who have expertise in a specific area to help estimate resource requirements. For example, a construction project manager may consult with an architect or engineer to estimate the amount of steel required for a building's foundation.

Analogous estimating which involves using historical data from similar projects to estimate resource requirements. For instance, a software development project manager may use data from a previous project to estimate the number of software developers required for a new project.

Parametric estimating is another technique used in resource estimation, which involves using statistical data and mathematical models to estimate resource requirements. This method is often used when there is a significant amount of historical data available. For example, a transportation project manager may use statistical data on the time and cost required for a similar road construction project to estimate the resources required for a new project.

Bottom-up estimating is a technique that involves estimating the resources required for each project activity individually and then aggregating them to obtain a total estimate. This method is often used when there is insufficient historical data or when there is a need for a detailed breakdown of resource requirements. For example, a marketing project manager may estimate the number of graphic designers, copywriters, and video editors required for each advertising campaign activity before aggregating them to determine the total resources required for the project.

When estimating resources, the project team must also consider constraints or limitations that may impact the availability or use of resources. For instance, the team may need to consider factors such as resource availability, resource utilization rates, and resource allocation conflicts when estimating the types and quantities of resources required for each activity. For example, a manufacturing project manager may need to consider the availability of raw materials, the capacity of production equipment, and the number of employees available to determine the resources required for a new production line.

Acquire Resources

In this process, the project team acquires the necessary resources to execute the project plan, including personnel, equipment, and materials. The team will need to identify potential sources for these resources, negotiate contracts, and manage the procurement process.

In project management, resource management is a crucial aspect of the overall project planning and execution process. Acquiring resources is a process that involves obtaining all the necessary resources required to execute the project plan. This includes personnel, equipment, and materials. The following is a more detailed explanation of the Acquire Resources process:

Resource Identification: The first step in the process of acquiring resources is to identify the specific resources that will be needed to complete the project. This includes identifying the necessary personnel, equipment, and materials required.

Example: In a construction project, resource identification would involve identifying the types of machinery, tools, and equipment needed to carry out the project.

Resource Availability Assessment: After identifying the resources needed, the project team will need to assess the availability of those resources. This involves determining if the resources are currently available or if they need to be sourced from external suppliers.

Example: In the construction project, the project team would assess if the machinery and equipment needed are available in-house or if they need to be rented or sourced from external suppliers.

Contract Negotiation: Once the resources are identified and assessed, the project team will need to negotiate contracts with suppliers. This involves agreeing on the terms and conditions of the contract, including pricing, delivery schedules, and any warranties or guarantees.

Example: In the construction project, the project team would negotiate a contract with the supplier for the rental or purchase of the necessary machinery and equipment.

Procurement Management: The final step in the Acquire Resources process is managing the procurement process. This includes coordinating with suppliers to ensure the timely delivery of resources, monitoring the quality of the resources received, and ensuring that all contractual obligations are met.

Example: In the construction project, the project team would manage the procurement process by ensuring that the machinery and equipment are delivered on time and that they meet the required quality standards.

Project resources are crucial to the success of any project, and as a project manager, it is your responsibility to ensure that the right resources are acquired, used effectively, and allocated appropriately. The following text will provide a comprehensive overview of how to determine the quantity and quality of resources required, estimate resource costs, assess resource risks, prioritize resource allocation, optimize resource utilization, and manage conflicts and changes in resource requirements throughout the project's lifecycle.

Determining the Quantity and Quality of Resources Required:

The first step in resource management is to determine the quantity and quality of resources required for the project. This involves identifying the specific tasks that need to be completed and the resources required to complete them. For example, if the project involves building a bridge, the resources required may include materials, equipment, labor, and expertise in engineering and construction.

To determine the quality of resources required, the project manager should consider the required skill level, experience, and certifications necessary to complete the project tasks. For instance, a project that involves software development may require developers with expertise in specific programming languages.

Estimating Resource Costs

Once the resources required have been identified, the project manager must estimate the costs associated with acquiring them. This includes the cost of purchasing or leasing equipment, the cost of hiring personnel, and any other expenses associated with the resources required. For example, if the project involves purchasing materials, the project manager must estimate the cost of acquiring those materials, including shipping and handling costs.

Assessing Resource Risks:

Resource risks refer to any potential risks associated with acquiring or utilizing resources. For instance, a potential risk may be that the equipment required for the project is not available on time or is not working properly. To mitigate these risks, the project manager should have contingency plans in place and be prepared to adjust the project schedule as necessary.

Ensuring Effective Resource Utilization

Effective resource utilization is crucial to ensuring that the project is completed on time and within budget. This involves ensuring that the acquired resources are used efficiently throughout the project's lifecycle. For instance, if the project involves hiring personnel, the project manager should ensure that those personnel are assigned tasks that match their skill set and expertise.

Prioritizing Resource Allocation

Prioritizing resource allocation involves determining which resources should be acquired and used based on the project objectives and constraints. For example, if the project involves building a bridge, the project manager may prioritize acquiring the equipment necessary for the foundation before acquiring other resources.

Optimizing Resource Utilization

Optimizing resource utilization involves using techniques such as resource leveling and resource smoothing to ensure that resources are used effectively throughout the project's lifecycle. For instance, if the project involves hiring personnel, the project manager may use resource leveling techniques to ensure that the workload is distributed evenly among team members.

Managing Conflicts and Changes in Resource Requirements

Conflicts and changes in resource requirements are inevitable in any project. To manage conflicts, the project manager should have conflict resolution strategies in place, such as negotiation or mediation. To manage changes in resource requirements, the project manager should be prepared to adjust the project plan as necessary and communicate those changes effectively to all stakeholders.

Develop Team

This process involves building and developing the project team, including developing team member skills and fostering a positive team environment. This is essential to ensuring that the team is able to work effectively and efficiently to achieve project objectives.

The Develop Team process is a crucial part of project resource management. Its primary objective is to develop a team that is cohesive, collaborative, and competent in delivering the project objectives. The process involves a series of activities aimed at building a high-performing team, which can work together to deliver the project successfully.

Some of the key activities involved in the Develop Team process include:

Defining Team Roles and Responsibilities: The project manager needs to define the roles and responsibilities of each team member to ensure that everyone understands their duties and the expectations for the project.

Building Trust and Collaboration: The project manager needs to build trust and encourage collaboration among team members. This can be achieved by establishing an open communication environment, fostering mutual respect, and encouraging teamwork.

Providing Training and Development: The project manager needs to ensure that team members have the necessary skills and knowledge to perform their roles effectively. This may involve providing training, coaching, mentoring, or other forms of development support.

Resolving Conflicts: The project manager needs to be proactive in identifying and resolving conflicts among team members. This can be achieved by encouraging open communication, providing a safe environment for expressing opinions, and addressing conflicts promptly and effectively.

Recognizing and Rewarding Performance: The project manager needs to recognize and reward high-performing team members to maintain motivation and promote continued success.

Examples of the Develop Team process in action might include:

The project manager sets up a team-building exercise to help team members get to know each other better and build trust.

The project manager identifies a team member who lacks certain skills and arranges for them to receive training to develop those skills.

The project manager mediates a conflict between two team members who have different ideas about how to approach a particular task.

The project manager acknowledges the hard work and dedication of a team member who has consistently delivered high-quality work on time.

Developing a high-performing team is crucial for project success. A team that not only has the necessary skills but also works well together can deliver results efficiently, proactively identify and resolve issues, and adapt to changes in the project environment. In this text, we will explore the importance of developing a high-performing team and how project managers can achieve this.

Communication and Feedback: Clear communication channels and open dialogue are crucial to building a cohesive team. Project managers should establish these channels and encourage team members to communicate effectively. Regular feedback can help team members understand their strengths and weaknesses, improve their performance, and build trust within the team. For example, a project manager could organize weekly team meetings where team members can share progress, concerns, and feedback.

Diversity and Inclusion: Promoting diversity and inclusion in project teams is essential in today's global and diverse work environment. The project manager should ensure that all team members feel valued and respected, regardless of their background, culture, or identity. This can be achieved by creating an inclusive environment, providing equal opportunities, and addressing any biases or discrimination. For instance, a project manager could encourage team members to share their cultural traditions and organize team-building activities that celebrate diversity.

Continual Improvement: Developing a team is an ongoing process that requires continual improvement. The project manager should regularly assess the team's performance, identify areas for improvement, and provide opportunities for learning and development. For example, a project manager could organize training sessions to enhance team members' skills or assign a mentor to team members who need additional support.

Empowerment and Accountability: Empowering team members and holding them accountable are crucial for developing a high-performing team. The project manager should provide team members with the necessary resources and authority to complete their tasks effectively. At the same time, team members should be held accountable for their actions and results. For instance, a project manager could delegate tasks to team members based on their skills and experience, and hold them accountable for meeting deadlines and achieving goals.

Leadership and Vision: Effective leadership and a clear vision are essential for developing a high-performing team. The project manager should lead by example, inspire team members, and provide them with a clear vision of the project's goals and objectives. This can help align team members' efforts and motivate them to work towards a common goal. For example, a project manager could set ambitious but achievable goals for the team and inspire them to go above and beyond to achieve them.

Manage Team

In this process, the project team manages the performance of the project team and takes steps to ensure that the team is working effectively and efficiently. This includes providing feedback, addressing issues and conflicts, and taking corrective action when necessary.

In the Manage Team process, the project manager and the project team work together to ensure that the team is working effectively and efficiently. This involves a range of activities such as providing feedback, addressing issues and conflicts, and taking corrective action when necessary. The main goal of this process is to ensure that the project team is performing at its best and that everyone is working towards the same goals.

One important aspect of managing the team is providing feedback. This can involve giving feedback on individual performance, team performance, and overall project performance. Feedback should be constructive and aimed at helping team members improve their skills and work more effectively. It is important to provide feedback regularly and in a timely manner so that team members have the opportunity to make improvements.

Another important aspect of managing the team is addressing issues and conflicts. Project teams are made up of individuals with different personalities, skills, and backgrounds, and conflicts can arise from time to time. It is important for the project manager to identify these issues and conflicts early and to take steps to resolve them quickly. This can involve facilitating discussions between team members, providing mediation, and taking other actions to promote communication and understanding.

Finally, managing the team also involves taking corrective action when necessary. This can involve addressing performance issues, making changes to the team structure or roles, or taking other steps to ensure that the team is working effectively. The project manager should work closely with the project team to identify areas where improvements can be made and to implement appropriate corrective actions.

Project Resource Management is a crucial aspect of project management that involves identifying, acquiring, and managing resources such as personnel, equipment, and material needed to complete a project successfully. One of the most crucial components of this process is managing the project team, which involves supervising team members, coordinating their activities, and monitoring their progress. In this text, we will explore the Manage Team process in detail, emphasizing the importance of effective communication and discussing the role of the project manager.

First and foremost, timely feedback is an essential aspect of managing a project team. Providing feedback helps team members identify areas where they need to improve and can help improve their performance. For instance, if a team member is struggling to complete a task, providing feedback can help them understand what they are doing wrong and how they can improve. An example of this is when a project manager notices that a team member is not completing tasks on time. The project manager can provide feedback to the team member, explaining how the delay is affecting the project's progress and offering suggestions for improvement.

Secondly, effective communication is crucial in managing a project team. Good communication helps to build trust, foster teamwork, and ensure that everyone is on the same page. It is essential to establish communication protocols and ensure that all team members understand them. An example of effective communication is when a project manager holds regular team meetings to update everyone on the project's progress, assign tasks, and address any concerns or questions team members may have.

In addition, the project manager plays a crucial role in managing the project team. The project manager is responsible for providing feedback, addressing conflicts, and taking corrective action when necessary. It is essential for the project manager to have excellent leadership skills, communication skills, and the ability to build strong relationships with team members. For instance, when conflicts arise, the project manager should be able to resolve them effectively by identifying the root cause of the conflict, facilitating open communication, and finding a mutually acceptable solution.

Furthermore, the project manager should ensure that team members are motivated and engaged. This can be achieved by creating a positive work environment, recognizing team members' contributions, and providing opportunities for career development. An example of this is when a project manager provides training opportunities for team members to help them acquire new skills that can benefit the project and their careers.

Finally, the project manager should monitor team performance regularly. This involves tracking progress, identifying potential issues, and taking corrective action when necessary. For instance, if a team member is consistently falling behind schedule, the project manager should intervene by providing additional support or resources to help the team member catch up.

Control Resources

This process involves monitoring and controlling project resources to ensure that they are being used effectively and efficiently. This includes tracking resource utilization, identifying and addressing issues, and making adjustments as necessary to keep the project on track.

Control Resources is a crucial process in project resource management that involves monitoring and controlling project resources to ensure that they are being used effectively and efficiently. The process ensures that the project is being completed within the allocated resources, and any issues with resource utilization are identified and addressed promptly.

During the Control Resources process, project managers monitor the usage of project resources such as materials, equipment, and personnel to ensure they are being used as planned. They track the actual usage of resources against the planned usage to identify any variances and take corrective actions if necessary. This process helps to ensure that the project is delivered within the defined scope, schedule, and budget.

For instance, suppose a project requires the use of certain specialized equipment. In that case, the project manager would monitor the usage of that equipment to ensure it is being used efficiently and effectively. If there are any issues with equipment utilization, the project manager would take corrective actions, such as providing additional training to the operators or finding alternative solutions to reduce equipment downtime.

The Control Resources process is an essential component of project management, as it ensures that project resources are used effectively and efficiently to achieve project goals. This process is a part of the Monitoring and Controlling process group and focuses on monitoring and controlling project resources to ensure that they are used in the most efficient and effective way possible.

Inputs

The inputs to the Control Resources process include the project management plan, project documents, work performance data, and organizational process assets. The project management plan provides the overall framework for resource management, while project documents such as the resource breakdown structure (RBS), the resource calendar, and the risk register provide additional information on resource allocation and utilization. Work performance data is used to evaluate the effectiveness of resource utilization, while organizational process assets, such as policies and procedures, provide guidance on ethical and regulatory compliance.

Tools and Techniques

The Control Resources process uses a variety of tools and techniques to monitor and control project resources. These include data analysis, project management information systems (PMIS), and meetings. Data analysis involves reviewing work performance data to identify trends and issues related to resource utilization, while PMIS provides a centralized platform for resource tracking and reporting. Meetings such as status review meetings, performance review meetings, and resource allocation meetings provide opportunities for project stakeholders to review resource utilization and make necessary adjustments.

Outputs

The primary outputs of the Control Resources process are work performance information, change requests, and updates to project documents. Work performance information provides an overview of resource utilization and highlights any issues or concerns that require action. Change requests may be generated if resource utilization is not in line with project requirements, while updates to project documents such as the RBS, the resource calendar, and the risk register reflect any changes to resource allocation and utilization.

Resource optimization is an essential aspect of the Control Resources process, as it ensures that project resources are used in the most efficient and effective way possible to maximize their value and minimize waste. Resource optimization involves identifying the crucial resources required for the project and allocating them in a manner that ensures that they are used optimally. This helps to ensure that the project is completed on time, within budget, and to the desired quality standards.

Resource utilization issues may arise during a project that can impact project performance. For example, if a crucial resource becomes unavailable, the project team may need to find alternative resources to fill the gap or reschedule activities until the resource becomes available. Similarly, if a team member is not performing as expected, the project manager may need to provide additional training or support or consider replacing the team member if necessary. These issues can be addressed by reviewing the resource utilization data and adjusting resource allocation and utilization as required.

Stakeholder engagement is crucial in resource management, as stakeholders can have a significant impact on resource availability and utilization. Project managers must take into account the needs and expectations of stakeholders when managing resources and communicate with them regularly to ensure that their requirements are being met.

Ethical behavior is essential in resource management, as project managers must ensure that resources are used ethically and in compliance with organizational policies and regulations. Ethical behavior includes treating resources and team members fairly and transparently, avoiding conflicts of interest, and ensuring that resources are not used for personal gain.

PROJECT COMMUNICATIONS MANAGEMENT

Project Communications Management is the knowledge area that deals with the processes required to ensure timely and appropriate planning, collection, creation, distribution, storage, retrieval, management, control, monitoring, and ultimate disposition of project information. This information includes project status, progress, risks, issues, and other relevant information necessary for effective project management. Project Communications Management is all about getting the right information to the right people at the right time.

Plan Communications Management

This process involves developing a plan for how project information will be communicated to stakeholders. Determine the communication needs of all stakeholders and create a stakeholder communication matrix. Define the communication methods and frequency for each stakeholder or group. Establish guidelines for project documentation and how it will be stored and distributed. Identify potential communication risks and develop a contingency plan.

The first process in Project Communications Management is Plan Communications Management. This process involves developing a comprehensive plan for how project information will be communicated to stakeholders. The goal of this process is to ensure that all stakeholders receive the right information at the right time, in the right format, and through the right channels.

To develop the plan, the project manager must first determine the communication needs of all stakeholders. This includes identifying who the stakeholders are, what information they need, when they need it, and how they prefer to receive it. This information can be captured in a stakeholder communication matrix, which outlines the communication requirements of each stakeholder or group.

Next, the project manager must define the communication methods and frequency for each stakeholder or group. This could include emails, meetings, status reports, newsletters, or other methods. The frequency of communication will depend on the needs of each stakeholder and the level of detail required.

Another important aspect of Plan Communications Management is establishing guidelines for project documentation. This includes defining the types of documents that will be created, who will create them, and how they will be stored and distributed. This ensures that all project documentation is consistent, accurate, and easily accessible to all stakeholders.

Identifying potential communication risks and developing a contingency plan is also crucial in this process. Risks could include miscommunication, misunderstandings, or failure to receive crucial information. The contingency plan should outline what steps will be taken in the event that a communication breakdown occurs.

Overall, the Plan Communications Management process is crucial for ensuring that all stakeholders receive the right information at the right time. By developing a comprehensive plan, the project manager can avoid miscommunication and ensure that the project stays on track.

Here are a few examples of how the Plan Communications Management process could be applied in a real project scenario:

Example 1: A software development project is underway, and the project manager needs to ensure that all stakeholders are informed about the project status. The project manager first identifies all stakeholders, including the development team, senior management, and end-users. The project manager then develops a stakeholder communication matrix, which outlines the information needs of each stakeholder. The project manager decides to hold weekly status meetings with the development team, monthly status meetings with senior management, and bi-weekly status reports for end-users. The project manager also establishes guidelines for project documentation, including coding standards, design documents, and test plans. Finally, the project manager identifies potential communication risks, such as misinterpretation of requirements, and develops a contingency plan that includes additional testing and documentation.

Example 2: A construction project is underway, and the project manager needs to ensure that all stakeholders are informed about safety protocols. The project manager first identifies all stakeholders, including construction workers, safety inspectors, and project sponsors. The project manager then develops a stakeholder communication matrix, which outlines the safety requirements of each stakeholder. The project manager decides to hold daily safety meetings with construction workers, weekly safety inspections with safety inspectors, and monthly safety reports for project sponsors. The project manager also establishes guidelines for project documentation, including safety plans, accident reports, and incident logs. Finally, the project manager identifies potential communication risks, such as failure to report safety incidents, and develops a contingency plan that includes additional safety training and reporting requirements.

Plan Communications Management is the process of developing an appropriate approach for project communication that meets the needs and expectations of all stakeholders. The communication plan is created during this process, and it outlines the communication requirements, stakeholders' communication needs, the communication methods, and the timing of the communication.

One crucial aspect to consider during the Plan Communications Management process is identifying the stakeholders early in the project. It ensures that their communication needs are understood and included in the communication plan. Stakeholders are individuals or groups who have an interest in the project, and they can impact or be impacted by the project's outcome.

For instance, suppose a project aims to develop a new software system for a company. In that case, stakeholders can be the company's management team, the software development team, the end-users, the quality assurance team, the marketing team, and any external vendors or partners involved. By identifying these stakeholders early in the project, the communication plan can be tailored to meet their specific communication needs.

Cultural differences are also an essential consideration when developing a communication plan. Communication can be challenging when dealing with stakeholders from different cultures, languages, and backgrounds. Therefore, it is necessary to understand these differences and develop a communication plan that addresses them.

For example, if a project team is working on a global project with stakeholders from different countries, the communication plan must consider language and cultural differences. The team can use translation services or hire local representatives to ensure that the communication is effective for all stakeholders.

A feedback loop is another crucial aspect of the communication plan. The communication plan must include mechanisms to gather feedback from stakeholders to ensure that their needs are being met. The feedback can be collected through surveys, meetings, or any other communication channel deemed appropriate.

For instance, after launching a new product, the project team can gather feedback from end users on the product's functionality, features, and user-friendliness. The feedback can be used to improve the product or update the communication plan to address any issues or concerns.

Lastly, assessing the effectiveness of the communication plan periodically is essential to ensure that it remains relevant and effective throughout the project. The project team must review and update the communication plan regularly to ensure that it meets the project's evolving needs.

For example, if a project has a significant change in scope or timeline, the communication plan must be updated to reflect the changes and address any new communication needs that arise. Periodic reviews of the communication plan can help ensure that it remains relevant and effective throughout the project.

Manage Communications

In this process, the project team executes the communications management plan, including distributing project information to stakeholders. Communicate project progress and updates to stakeholders according to the communication plan. Manage stakeholder expectations and address any concerns or issues they may have. Ensure all project documentation is accurate and up-to-date. Facilitate communication between team members and stakeholders.

In this process, the project team is responsible for distributing project information to stakeholders, communicating project progress and updates to stakeholders, managing stakeholder expectations, addressing concerns or issues that stakeholders may have, ensuring project documentation is accurate and up-to-date, and facilitating communication between team members and stakeholders. The key activities involved in this process are as follows:

Execute the Communications Management Plan: In this activity, the project team puts the communications management plan into action by following the communication protocols and procedures outlined in the plan.

Example: If the communication plan specifies that weekly status reports should be sent to stakeholders, the project team should ensure that the reports are created, reviewed, and distributed on time.

Distribute Project Information: In this activity, the project team shares project information with stakeholders, such as status reports, meeting minutes, and other project documents, as specified in the communications management plan.

Example: If the project manager needs to provide an update on the project status to the senior management team, the project manager should use the communication plan to determine the best format and frequency of updates, such as a weekly email or a monthly presentation.

Manage Stakeholder Expectations: In this activity, the project team manages stakeholder expectations by ensuring that stakeholders have a clear understanding of the project's goals, objectives, and progress.

Example: If the project manager realizes that the project will be delayed due to unforeseen circumstances, the project manager should use the communication plan to communicate the delay to stakeholders and discuss options for addressing the delay.

Address Stakeholder Concerns or Issues: In this activity, the project team addresses concerns or issues that stakeholders may have by providing them with accurate and timely information.

Example: If a stakeholder expresses concern about the project's budget, the project manager should use the communication plan to provide the stakeholder with an update on the budget and explain how any issues will be addressed.

Ensure Project Documentation is Accurate and Up-to-Date: In this activity, the project team ensures that all project documentation is accurate and up-to-date, as specified in the communications management plan.

Example: If the project manager needs to provide a progress report to stakeholders, the project manager should use the communication plan to ensure that the report is accurate, complete, and up-to-date.

Facilitate Communication Between Team Members and Stakeholders: In this activity, the project team facilitates communication between team members and stakeholders to ensure that everyone has the information they need to complete their work.

Example: If a stakeholder needs to communicate with a team member about a specific task, the project manager should use the communication plan to facilitate the conversation and ensure that the necessary information is exchanged.

Project management involves various processes that aim to achieve project objectives within the defined constraints of time, scope, cost, quality, resources, and risks. Effective communication is crucial to the success of any project as it ensures that project stakeholders are informed, engaged, and aligned towards the project objectives. The Manage Communications process is a key process in project management that helps to plan, create, distribute, monitor, and control project communications to meet the information needs of project stakeholders.

The Manage Communications process is part of the Project Communications Management knowledge area, which is one of the ten knowledge areas in the PMBOK Guide 2021. The importance of effective communication in project management cannot be overstated. According to a study by the Project Management Institute (PMI), ineffective communication is the primary cause of project failure in one-third of all projects. Effective communication can help to build trust, reduce conflict, enhance collaboration, manage expectations, and promote project success.

The Manage Communications process is related to other project management processes, such as project integration, stakeholder engagement, and risk management. Communication plays a crucial role in project integration as it ensures that all project components are properly coordinated and integrated to achieve project objectives. For example, the Manage Communications process can help to ensure that the project scope, schedule, and budget are aligned and communicated to all project stakeholders. Effective communication can also help to identify and mitigate project risks by ensuring that risks are properly identified, assessed, and communicated to all relevant stakeholders.

Stakeholder engagement is another important process that is closely related to the Manage Communications process. The Manage Communications process can help to ensure that all project stakeholders are identified, analyzed, and engaged throughout the project lifecycle. For example, the Manage Communications process can help to identify the communication needs of different stakeholders and develop appropriate communication strategies and plans to meet those needs. Effective communication can also help to ensure that stakeholders are engaged and motivated to contribute to project success.

The Manage Communications process involves various activities that can be customized to fit different project needs. These activities include planning communications, managing information, reporting performance, managing stakeholders, and distributing information. For example, in a construction project, the Manage Communications process can involve developing a communication plan that outlines how project progress will be reported to different stakeholders, such as the project owner, the construction team, and the local community. The communication plan can also specify the communication channels and frequency of communication. The Manage Communications process can also involve monitoring project performance and reporting progress to stakeholders through regular progress meetings, status reports, and project dashboards.

Monitor Communications

This process involves monitoring project communications to ensure that stakeholders receive the appropriate information in a timely manner. Evaluate the effectiveness of the communication plan and make adjustments as necessary. Measure stakeholder satisfaction with the communication process. Monitor project progress and adjust communication strategies as needed. Continuously improve the communication process through feedback and lessons learned.

Project Communications Management is a crucial area that ensures effective communication between the project team and with stakeholders. The process of Monitoring Communications is essential to ensure that the project communication plan is meeting the needs of stakeholders, and any required adjustments are made promptly.

To monitor project communications, the project manager should analyze the effectiveness of the communication plan by examining the feedback received from stakeholders. This feedback can be in the form of surveys, meetings, and other communication channels. The feedback can help to identify any communication gaps and areas that need improvement.

After analyzing the feedback, the project manager should make necessary adjustments to the communication plan. These adjustments may include changes to the communication channels, the frequency of communication, or the format of the information shared. The project manager should also ensure that stakeholders are receiving the right information at the right time.

Stakeholder satisfaction with the communication process is an essential aspect of Monitoring Communications. Project managers can measure stakeholder satisfaction by conducting surveys, interviews, and focus groups. The feedback received can help to identify areas where stakeholders are not satisfied with the communication process, and necessary changes can be made to address their concerns.

Monitoring project progress is another important aspect of Monitoring Communications. The project manager should analyze the project's progress to ensure that it is consistent with the communication plan. Any deviations from the plan should be identified and addressed promptly. The project manager should also adjust communication strategies as needed to ensure that stakeholders are kept informed of any changes in the project's progress.

Finally, continuous improvement of the communication process is crucial. The project manager should use feedback and lessons learned to improve the communication plan continually. The lessons learned can be documented and shared with the team and stakeholders to ensure that everyone benefits from the improvements.

Project Communications Management is a crucial element in successful project management. It involves developing, executing, and controlling communications to meet the project's requirements and the stakeholders' expectations. The communications plan outlines the project's communication approach and ensures that the project team and stakeholders receive the right information at the right time.

Roles and Responsibilities: One of the crucial components of the communications plan is identifying the roles and responsibilities of the project team and stakeholders. Each team member and stakeholder should have a clear understanding of their communication responsibilities to ensure effective communication throughout the project. For example, the project manager may be responsible for developing the communication plan, while the project team is responsible for providing timely and accurate information to stakeholders.

Communication Technology: In today's digital age, technology plays a significant role in project communications management. Project managers can use various communication technologies, such as email, videoconferencing, and instant messaging to enhance communication and ensure that stakeholders receive the right information at the right time. For example, a project manager can use a project management tool, such as Asana or Trello, to assign tasks and monitor progress in real-time. Using technology also allows the project manager to overcome geographic barriers and communicate with stakeholders worldwide.

Cultural Sensitivity: Cultural sensitivity is essential to project communications management, especially when working with stakeholders from different backgrounds. The project manager should ensure that communication is culturally sensitive and respectful to avoid any misunderstandings or conflicts. For example, the project manager can adapt their communication style to suit the stakeholders' cultural expectations. They may also need to consider translation services or interpreters to ensure that communication is clear and effective.

Contingency Planning: Contingency planning is crucial in project communications management. Unforeseen events, such as natural disasters, technical issues, or stakeholder conflicts, can disrupt communication and derail the project. The project manager should develop contingency plans to address these risks and mitigate the impact on the project. For example, the project manager can have a backup communication plan in case of a power outage or internet connectivity issues. They can also develop alternative communication channels in case of a stakeholder conflict.

PROJECT RISK MANAGEMENT

Is an essential part of any successful project. The project team must develop a comprehensive plan to identify, analyze, and manage risks throughout the project lifecycle.

Plan Risk Management

This process is the foundation for effective risk management. The project team develops a plan that outlines how risks will be identified, analyzed, and managed. The plan includes roles and responsibilities, risk categories, and risk thresholds.

Plan Risk Management is a crucial process in project risk management, as it provides a foundation for the entire risk management process. It is the first step that the project team takes to develop a risk management plan that outlines how they will identify, analyze, and manage risks throughout the project.

During this process, the project team develops a risk management plan that includes a set of guidelines, policies, and procedures for risk management. The plan also outlines the roles and responsibilities of each team member involved in risk management, including the project manager, project sponsor, and stakeholders.

Moreover, the plan identifies potential risk categories, such as technical risks, schedule risks, cost risks, and external risks, and establishes risk thresholds that determine the level of risk that the project team is willing to accept. This information helps the team to focus their efforts and resources on high-priority risks that could impact the project's success.

For instance, let's say a project involves building a new office building. The project team would identify potential risks, such as construction delays, budget overruns, or changes in local building codes. They would then analyze each risk's potential impact on the project's timeline, budget, and scope.

Based on their analysis, the team would establish risk thresholds that determine the level of risk that the project team is willing to accept. For instance, the project team might decide that they are willing to accept a 10% budget overrun risk, but anything above that would require immediate action.

Risk management is a crucial component of project management. To effectively manage risks, the first step is to create a plan for how risks will be identified, assessed, and managed throughout the project. This is where the Plan Risk Management process comes in.

The Plan Risk Management process is important because it sets the tone for the entire risk management process. This process ensures that risks are identified and managed in a consistent and effective manner. Without a solid plan for risk management, the project team may miss crucial risks, fail to allocate resources properly, and ultimately fail to deliver the project on time and within budget.

The output of the Plan Risk Management process includes several key deliverables. The first is the risk management plan, which outlines the approach to risk management that will be taken throughout the project. This plan includes details such as the roles and responsibilities of the project team members, the process for identifying and assessing risks, and the methods that will be used to manage risks.

Another output of the Plan Risk Management process is the risk register. This is a document that contains a list of all the identified risks and their potential impact on the project. The risk register also includes information about the likelihood of each risk occurring and the potential consequences if it does occur.

Finally, the Plan Risk Management process produces a risk assessment matrix. This matrix is used to prioritize risks based on their likelihood and impact on the project. A matrix is a useful tool for identifying which risks need to be addressed first and which risks can be addressed later.

It is important to note that risk management is an iterative process. While risks are identified, analyzed, and managed throughout the project, the risk management plan and risk register should be updated regularly. New risks may emerge, and the impact of existing risks may change. Therefore, the project team must continuously monitor and adjust the risk management plan and the risk register as needed.

For example, let's say a construction project is in progress, and the project team has identified the risk of bad weather. The risk management plan outlines the process for assessing and managing this risk. Nonetheless, halfway through the project, a hurricane is forecasted in the area, which could have a significant impact on the project. In this case, the project team would need to update the risk register and risk management plan to address this new and potentially more severe risk.

Identify Risks

This process involves identifying potential project risks and documenting them for further analysis. The project team can use a variety of techniques, such as brainstorming, checklists, and expert judgment, to identify risks.

The Identify Risks process is a crucial step in project risk management as it helps the project team to identify potential risks that could impact the project's objectives. It involves systematically identifying, documenting, and prioritizing potential risks, which can then be analyzed and responded to accordingly.

The following are some of the techniques that can be used to identify risks:

Brainstorming: This technique involves gathering a group of stakeholders or subject matter experts to generate a list of potential risks. This can be done through a facilitated workshop or an online collaboration tool. During the brainstorming session, participants can freely share their ideas and concerns about the project, which can help uncover potential risks.

Checklists: Checklists are a useful tool for identifying risks, as they provide a comprehensive list of potential risks that have been identified in similar projects. Project teams can use existing checklists or develop their own customized checklists based on their specific project requirements.

Expert Judgment: The project team can seek the input of subject matter experts or experienced project managers to identify potential risks. Experts can provide insights into the potential risks based on their past experience, industry knowledge, and best practices.

Once potential risks have been identified, they should be documented in a risk register or risk log. The risk register should include a description of each risk, its potential impact on the project, the likelihood of occurrence, and the risk owner. The project team can then analyze each risk and develop a risk response plan to mitigate or eliminate the risk.

For example, let's consider a construction project to build a new office building. During the Identify Risks process, the project team might use brainstorming to identify potential risks, such as delays in obtaining building permits, adverse weather conditions, labor shortages, or changes in building codes. They could also use checklists to ensure that they have considered all relevant risks, such as risks related to site selection, materials, and equipment.

As a project manager, one of your primary responsibilities is to identify, assess, and manage project risks. Risk management is an essential process that involves identifying potential risks, evaluating the likelihood and impact of each risk, developing strategies to mitigate or avoid risks, and monitoring and controlling risks throughout the project life cycle.

One important aspect of risk management is prioritizing risks. Prioritizing risks involves determining which risks are the most crucial and require immediate attention. One approach to prioritizing risks is to use a risk matrix. A risk matrix is a tool that evaluates the likelihood and potential impact of each risk and assigns it a score.

For example, suppose you are managing a software development project, and one of the identified risks is a delay in delivering crucial components from a vendor. You would assess the likelihood of this risk occurring, such as the probability of the vendor encountering production issues or supply chain disruptions. You would also assess the potential impact of this risk, such as the impact on project timelines, cost, and quality. Based on this assessment, you would assign a score to this risk, which would then guide the development of a risk response plan.

Another aspect of risk management is regular risk reviews throughout the project life cycle. Risks can change over time, and new risks may emerge as the project progresses, so it's essential to regularly review and update the risk register to ensure that the project team is adequately prepared to respond to any potential risks.

For example, suppose you are managing a construction project, and one of the identified risks is a shortage of construction materials due to supply chain disruptions. As the project progresses, you may find that this risk has become more severe due to increased demand for construction materials or unexpected delays in delivery. By regularly reviewing and updating the risk register, you can ensure that the project team is aware of the changing risk landscape and can adjust their risk response strategies accordingly.

In addition to prioritizing risks and conducting regular risk reviews, effective risk management also involves developing a robust risk response plan. A risk response plan is a document that outlines how the project team will respond to identified risks.

For example, suppose you are managing a marketing campaign, and one of the identified risks is a negative social media backlash. Your risk response plan might include strategies for monitoring social media channels, developing a crisis communication plan, and engaging with stakeholders to address any concerns or issues.

Finally, it's essential to understand that risk management is an iterative process. As new risks emerge or existing risks change, you may need to adjust your risk response strategies. By continually monitoring and controlling risks throughout the project life cycle, you can ensure that your project stays on track and delivers the expected outcomes.

Perform Qualitative Risk Analysis

This process involves analyzing the probability and impact of identified risks and prioritizing them for further analysis. The project team assesses the likelihood and impact of each risk and assigns a risk score to prioritize them for further analysis.

Performing Qualitative Risk Analysis is an important process in Project Risk Management, and it helps the project team to identify and prioritize risks that need further attention. In this process, the team assesses the probability and impact of each identified risk and assigns a risk score to prioritize them for further analysis. The following are the steps involved in this process:

Identify Risks: The project team identifies potential risks that may impact the project objectives.

Assess Probability: The probability of each identified risk is assessed by the project team, based on historical data, expert judgment, and other relevant information. The probability can be expressed as high, medium, or low.

Assess Impact: The impact of each identified risk is assessed by the project team, based on the potential consequences of the risk event. The impact can be expressed as high, medium, or low.

Assign Risk Scores: The project team assigns a risk score to each identified risk, based on the probability and impact assessments. The risk score can be calculated by multiplying the probability and impact scores. For example, if the probability of a risk is medium and the impact is high, the risk score would be 6 (2 x 3).

Prioritize Risks: The project team prioritizes the risks based on the risk scores and identifies the high-priority risks that need further analysis and response planning.

For example, let's consider a software development project. The project team identifies the risk of delay in receiving hardware components required for software testing. The team assesses the probability of this risk as high, based on previous experience and supplier reliability. The impact of this risk is assessed as medium, as it may cause a delay in the project schedule. Based on these assessments, the team assigns a risk score of 6 (2 x 3) to this risk. The team then prioritizes this risk as a high priority and plans to further analyze and develop a response plan to mitigate this risk.

Performing Qualitative Risk Analysis is a crucial process in Project Risk Management, and it helps the project team proactively identify and prioritize risks that may impact project objectives. It provides a framework for further analysis and response planning, which can help to mitigate the impact of risks on the project.

Project risk management is an essential process that identifies, evaluates, and mitigates potential risks that may affect a project's success. To effectively manage project risks, it is important to understand the different types of risks, the risk matrix, and the importance of expert judgment.

Risk Categories: Project risks can be classified into various categories, including technical, financial, legal, and environmental. Technical risks arise from the use of complex technologies or systems that may fail or malfunction. Financial risks are related to the cost of the project and the availability of funds. Legal risks are associated with contractual obligations and regulatory compliance, while environmental risks pertain to natural disasters, climate change, or other ecological factors.

Risk Matrix: A risk matrix is a useful tool for identifying and assessing project risks. It is a table that helps to identify the level of risk based on probability and impact scores. Probability refers to the likelihood of a risk occurring, while impact refers to the consequences if the risk does occur. To calculate a risk score, the probability and impact scores are multiplied together. For example, if the probability of a risk occurring is 50% and the impact is severe, then the risk score is 5 (50% x 10). The risk matrix can help project managers prioritize risks and allocate resources accordingly.

Expert Judgment: Expert judgment is an essential component of the risk management process. It involves using the knowledge and experience of subject matter experts to evaluate risks that have not been encountered before. Expert judgment can help project teams assess risks more accurately and develop effective risk response strategies. For example, an experienced construction engineer can provide insight into technical risks associated with a complex building design. Similarly, a financial analyst can help evaluate financial risks related to cost estimates and funding availability.

Perform Quantitative Risk Analysis

This process involves analyzing the probability and impact of identified risks using numerical techniques and models. The project team uses data and statistical analysis to quantify the impact of risks and to determine the probability of their occurrence.

Performing quantitative risk analysis is a crucial step in project risk management that involves using data and statistical analysis to determine the probability and impact of identified risks. It helps the project team to understand the overall risk exposure and to prioritize the risks based on their potential impact on the project objectives.

To perform quantitative risk analysis, the project team needs to follow a structured approach that includes the following steps:

Define the probability and impact scales: The project team needs to define the scales for both probability and impact of the identified risks. These scales are used to assign a numerical value to the likelihood and consequence of each risk.

Collect data: The project team needs to collect data related to the identified risks. This can include historical data, expert opinions, industry benchmarks, and other relevant information.

Analyze the data: The project team needs to analyze the data using statistical techniques and models. This can include Monte Carlo simulation, decision tree analysis, and sensitivity analysis.

Determine the risk exposure: Based on the analysis, the project team can determine the overall risk exposure of the project. This includes identifying the risks that have the highest probability and impact and estimating the expected monetary value (EMV) of the risks.

Prioritize the risks: The project team can use the results of the analysis to prioritize the risks based on their potential impact on the project objectives. This helps the team to focus on the risks that require the most attention and to develop appropriate risk response strategies.

For example, suppose a construction project is facing the risk of delays due to adverse weather conditions. The project team can perform quantitative risk analysis by collecting data on historical weather patterns in the project location, and using statistical models to estimate the probability and impact of adverse weather conditions on the project schedule. Based on the analysis, the team can determine the expected delay and cost implications of the risk, and develop appropriate risk response strategies, such as rescheduling activities or adding contingencies to the schedule.

Quantitative risk analysis is an important aspect of project management, which helps to identify and analyze risks using numerical methods. This process involves several steps, which are as follows:

Risk identification: Before performing quantitative risk analysis, it is essential to identify all potential risks that may affect the project. This can be done using various techniques, such as brainstorming, checklists, and expert judgment. For example, a project manager of a construction project can identify potential risks such as natural disasters, equipment failure, or labor shortage by conducting a brainstorming session with the project team.

Risk register: The identified risks should be documented in a risk register, which includes information such as the risk description, probability, impact, and risk owner. The risk register is used as a reference document throughout the project to manage and monitor the risks. For instance, the risk register for a software development project can include information about the probability of software bugs, the impact on project timelines, and the person responsible for managing the risk.

Risk data quality assessment: The project team should assess the quality of the data used in the quantitative risk analysis. This involves evaluating the accuracy, completeness, and reliability of the data sources to ensure that the analysis results are valid. For example, if the data used to estimate the impact of a risk on the project is incomplete or inaccurate, the results of the risk analysis may not be reliable.

Quantitative risk analysis: This step involves analyzing the identified risks using numerical methods. The project team should estimate the probability and impact of each risk using techniques such as Monte Carlo simulation or decision tree analysis. For instance, a project manager of a marketing campaign can use Monte Carlo simulation to estimate the probability of achieving the campaign's goal, based on factors such as budget, target audience, and marketing channels.

Communication and stakeholder engagement: The project team should communicate the results of the quantitative risk analysis to the relevant stakeholders, including the project sponsor, project team members, and other stakeholders. This helps to ensure that everyone is aware of the project risks and the risk response strategies. For example, the project manager can present the results of the risk analysis to the project sponsor and stakeholders during a project status meeting.

Risk response planning: Based on the results of the quantitative risk analysis, the project team should develop risk response strategies for each identified risk. The risk response strategies can be classified as avoid, mitigate, transfer, or accept. For example, if the risk analysis for a construction project identifies the risk of equipment failure, the project team can develop a risk response strategy of mitigating the risk by conducting regular equipment maintenance.

Plan Risk Responses

This process involves developing a plan for how to respond to identified risks. The project team develops strategies for risk mitigation, risk avoidance, risk transfer, and risk acceptance. The plan also includes contingency plans for high-priority risks.

Plan Risk Responses is a crucial process in Project Risk Management. It involves developing a plan to address the risks that have been identified in the earlier stages of the risk management process. The main objective of this process is to reduce the probability and impact of negative risks, as well as to increase the probability and impact of positive risks.

Here are some steps involved in the Plan Risk Responses process:

Risk Mitigation Strategies: These are proactive strategies to reduce the probability and impact of risks. For instance, if there is a risk that the project will be delayed due to unforeseen circumstances, the project team can mitigate this risk by developing a contingency plan that includes additional resources, revised schedules, and more.

Risk Avoidance Strategies: These are strategies to eliminate the risk altogether. For example, if there is a risk that a certain material will not be available on time, the project team can choose a different material that is readily available.

Risk Transfer Strategies: These are strategies to transfer the risk to another party. For example, if there is a risk that a supplier may not deliver on time, the project team can transfer this risk to another supplier who is more reliable.

Risk Acceptance Strategies: These are strategies to accept the risk and deal with it if and when it occurs. For instance, if there is a risk that a certain task may take longer than expected, the project team can accept this risk and develop a contingency plan to deal with it if it occurs.

Contingency Plans: These are plans developed to deal with high-priority risks. These plans include detailed steps to be taken if the identified risk occurs.

Plan Risk Responses is a process in Project Risk Management that involves developing and implementing strategies to manage potential risks. This process is crucial for the success of any project because it enables project managers to identify and address potential problems before they occur. In this text, we will explore the Plan Risk Responses process and provide additional clarification and examples to align with the latest updates on the PMP certification exam.

Identifying Risk Owners and Stakeholders

It is crucial to involve risk owners and stakeholders in the Plan Risk Responses process. Risk owners are individuals or teams responsible for managing specific risks, and stakeholders have a vested interest in the project's success. Including them in the process helps ensure that their perspectives and insights are considered in developing the risk response plan. For example, a construction project manager should involve architects, engineers, contractors, and project sponsors as risk owners and stakeholders.

Defining Trigger Conditions

Trigger conditions are specific events or conditions that indicate when a risk response plan should be implemented. It is essential to define these conditions in the risk response plan to ensure that the plan is implemented at the appropriate time. For instance, if a construction project manager identifies a risk of delayed material delivery, the trigger condition could be a specific date or the project reaching a certain milestone.

Specifying Risk Response Owners and Actions

The risk response plan should clearly specify the owners of each risk response and the actions that should be taken in response to each identified risk. This can help ensure that there is clear accountability and responsibility for executing the plan. For example, if the identified risk is the possibility of a flood, the owner could be the safety officer, and the action could be to evacuate the site and move to a higher ground.

Establishing a System for Tracking and Monitoring

It is important to establish a system for tracking and monitoring the effectiveness of the risk response plan. This can help identify whether the plan is working as intended or whether adjustments are needed. For instance, if the identified risk is the potential for budget overrun, the project manager should track actual expenses against the budget and assess whether the implemented actions are effective.

Adhering to Ethical Standards

In the Plan Risk Responses process, project managers should adhere to ethical standards in identifying and responding to risks. They should ensure that all stakeholders are treated fairly and that the risk response plan does not cause harm to any individual or group. For example, if the identified risk is the possibility of a conflict of interest, the project manager should consult the project's ethics officer and follow the organization's code of conduct.

Control Risks

This process involves monitoring project risks and taking appropriate corrective action to mitigate their impact. The project team tracks identified risks, assesses their status, and implements appropriate corrective actions. The team also revises the risk management plan as needed to address any changes in the project environment.

Control Risks is a crucial process in project risk management that involves monitoring and controlling project risks to reduce their impact on project objectives. This process focuses on implementing appropriate corrective actions to reduce the likelihood and/or impact of identified risks and to ensure that risks are effectively managed throughout the project lifecycle.

To fully understand this process, let's break it down into its key components:

Monitoring Project Risks: In this step, the project team continuously monitors the identified risks to ensure that they are still valid and relevant. This involves collecting data on the status of each risk, including any changes in probability or impact, and assessing the current level of risk exposure.

Assessing Risk Status: Once the risks have been monitored, the team assesses their status to determine if they have changed in any way. This includes evaluating any changes in probability or impact, as well as any new risks that have emerged since the last assessment.

Implementing Corrective Actions: If the risk status assessment reveals that the risk exposure has increased, the team implements corrective actions to reduce the likelihood or impact of the risk. This may include developing new risk response strategies or modifying existing ones, as well as taking other actions to mitigate the risk.

Revising the Risk Management Plan: Finally, the project team revises the risk management plan as needed to address any changes in the project environment. This includes updating the risk register, modifying risk response strategies, and communicating any changes to relevant stakeholders.

To illustrate the Control Risks process, let's consider an example. Suppose a construction project is facing a risk of material shortages due to supply chain disruptions. The project team has identified this risk and has developed a risk response strategy to mitigate it, including identifying alternative suppliers and pre-ordering materials to ensure availability.

During the monitoring phase, the team tracks the status of the risk and observes that there has been a further disruption in the supply chain that could increase the risk exposure. In the risk status assessment phase, the team evaluates the current level of risk exposure and determines that it has indeed increased.

The team then implements corrective actions by revisiting the risk response strategy and identifying additional measures to further reduce the likelihood and/or impact of the risk, such as exploring alternative material sources or delaying non-crucial activities to conserve materials. Finally, the team revises the risk management plan to reflect the changes made and communicates these changes to stakeholders to ensure everyone is aware of the updated risk response strategy.

Project risk management is a crucial component of project management that ensures that potential risks are identified, assessed, and addressed in a timely manner. Within the overall risk management process, the Control Risks process plays a crucial role in monitoring and controlling identified risks throughout the project lifecycle.

The Control Risks process involves several key activities, including risk reassessment, risk response strategy adjustment, and risk response implementation. These activities help project managers continually monitor and adjust their risk response strategies to ensure that the project remains on track and that potential risks are minimized.

One important point to note is that the Control Risks process is just one part of the overall Risk Management process in project management. The larger risk management framework includes other processes, such as risk identification, risk assessment, and risk response planning. By understanding how the Control Risks process fits into the larger framework, project managers can better appreciate the importance of monitoring and controlling risks throughout the project lifecycle.

Regular communication with stakeholders is another crucial aspect of the Control Risks process. This helps to ensure that everyone is aware of any changes in risk exposure and the corresponding risk response strategies. For example, if a new risk is identified or an existing risk changes, it is important to communicate this information to stakeholders so that they can make informed decisions about the project. By keeping stakeholders informed, project managers can help to mitigate potential risks and ensure successful project outcomes.

Finally, it is essential to understand that the Control Risks process is an iterative one, meaning that it should be repeated throughout the project lifecycle as new risks emerge or existing risks change. This emphasizes the importance of continuous monitoring and adjustment of risk response strategies. For example, suppose a project manager identifies a new risk during the execution phase of a project. In that case, they will need to reassess the risk, develop an appropriate response strategy, and implement that strategy in a timely manner to ensure that the project remains on track.

PROJECT STAKEHOLDER MANAGEMENT

Project Stakeholder Management is a crucial aspect of project management that involves identifying, analyzing, and managing stakeholders' needs and expectations. It is the process of engaging and communicating with stakeholders to ensure that their needs are met and their expectations are aligned with project objectives. The main goal of project stakeholder management is to foster positive relationships with stakeholders and ensure their active participation in the project.

Identify Stakeholders

To identify all project stakeholders, the project team must conduct a thorough analysis of the stakeholders' interests, expectations, and potential impact on the project. This process involves identifying internal and external stakeholders, documenting their needs and expectations, and prioritizing them based on their level of influence and interest in the project.

Identifying stakeholders is an essential step in project management, as it helps project teams to better understand who may be affected by the project and what their needs and expectations are. This process involves several steps:

Identify internal stakeholders: These are individuals or groups within the organization that are directly impacted by the project. Examples may include project team members, executives, and employees who will be affected by changes to business processes or technology.

Identify external stakeholders: These are individuals or groups outside of the organization that may be affected by the project. Examples may include customers, suppliers, regulatory agencies, and the community.

Document stakeholder needs and expectations: Once stakeholders have been identified, it is important to document their needs and expectations. This may involve conducting interviews, surveys, or focus groups to gather information about what each stakeholder group expects from the project.

Prioritize stakeholders: Once stakeholder needs and expectations have been documented, they can be prioritized based on their level of influence and interest in the project. This helps project teams to better understand which stakeholders may require more attention and resources throughout the project lifecycle.

For example, let's say a company is planning to implement a new customer relationship management (CRM) system. Internal stakeholders may include employees in the sales and marketing departments who will be using the system, as well as executives who are funding the project. External stakeholders may include customers who will be using the system to interact with the company.

To identify these stakeholders, the project team may conduct interviews with employees and executives, as well as surveys with customers. They may also review regulatory requirements and engage with community groups that may be affected by the project. Once stakeholders have been identified, their needs and expectations can be documented and prioritized, which will help the project team to better manage their expectations and ensure that the project is a success.

Identifying project stakeholders is a crucial process in project management that requires careful consideration and planning. The success of a project heavily depends on the support and collaboration of its stakeholders, making it essential to identify, engage and manage them effectively. In this text, we will explore the importance of identifying stakeholders and explain the steps to achieve this, while incorporating examples to help illustrate the process.

Why identifying stakeholders is crucial in project management?

Identifying stakeholders is crucial in project management because stakeholders significantly impact a project's success. Stakeholders are individuals, groups, or organizations that have an interest or influence in the project and can affect or be affected by its outcome. These can include project sponsors, project team members, customers, users, suppliers, regulators, and the community. Failure to identify and manage stakeholders' expectations can lead to conflicts, delays, and project failures.

For instance, imagine a company that wants to introduce a new product to the market. They have conducted extensive research on the product and developed a launch plan that the marketing team has signed off on. Nonetheless, they did not consider the impact of the new product on the community. After the launch, the community begins to raise concerns about the product's impact on the environment, leading to negative press and, ultimately, loss of revenue for the company. In this example, the company failed to identify the community as a stakeholder and did not manage its expectations, leading to project failure.

Steps to identify stakeholders

Identify Internal Stakeholders: Internal stakeholders are individuals or groups that work within the organization that is responsible for the project. These can include executives, managers, employees, and team members.

Identify External Stakeholders: External stakeholders are individuals or groups outside of the organization that can affect or be affected by the project. These can include customers, suppliers, regulators, and the community.

Analyze Stakeholder Needs and Expectations: Once the stakeholders have been identified, it is essential to document their needs and expectations. This can be done by conducting interviews, surveys, focus groups, or analyzing existing data. This step helps to identify the requirements and goals of each stakeholder and prioritize them based on their level of influence and interest in the project.

Prioritize Stakeholders: After identifying the needs and expectations of each stakeholder, it is essential to prioritize them based on their level of influence and interest in the project. This helps to ensure that the project team focuses on the most crucial stakeholders and addresses their concerns effectively.

Develop a Stakeholder Management Plan: Once the stakeholders have been identified, and their needs and expectations have been prioritized, it is essential to develop a stakeholder management plan. This plan should outline how the project team will engage and manage stakeholders throughout the project's lifecycle to ensure that their needs and expectations are being met.

Examples of stakeholder identification

For instance, imagine a construction company that wants to build a new office building. The internal stakeholders of this project can include the project sponsor, project manager, and team members responsible for the project's design and construction. The external stakeholders can include the city's government, environmental agencies, the local community, suppliers, and tenants.

The project team can identify the stakeholders by conducting interviews, focus groups, or analyzing existing data. For example, they can conduct interviews with the city's government officials to understand the regulations and permits required to build the new office building. They can also conduct focus groups with the local community to understand their concerns and expectations regarding the project.

Once the stakeholders have been identified, the project team can prioritize them based on their level of influence and interest in the project. For instance, the city's government officials may have a high level of influence on the project, while the local community may have a high level of interest in the project.

Stakeholder analysis is a crucial process in project management that involves identifying and assessing stakeholders' power, interests, and influence to determine their impact on the project. By doing so, project teams can develop strategies to manage stakeholders effectively and prioritize their needs and expectations.

The importance of stakeholder analysis lies in the fact that it can significantly impact the success of a project. Understanding the needs and expectations of stakeholders can help project teams create more effective plans, avoid unnecessary delays, and prevent misunderstandings. Additionally, stakeholder analysis can help project teams avoid potential risks associated with stakeholder management, such as conflicts and resistance to change.

For example, let's say a company is planning to launch a new product. Stakeholder analysis would involve identifying and assessing all the stakeholders involved in the project, such as customers, employees, shareholders, regulators, suppliers, and competitors. For each stakeholder, the project team would need to determine their level of power, interest, and influence.

Power refers to the ability of a stakeholder to influence the project's outcome. For example, a regulator may have significant power over the project if they can approve or reject the product's launch. Interest refers to how invested a stakeholder is in the project's outcome. For example, customers may have a high level of interest in the product's features and benefits. Influence refers to how much a stakeholder can affect the project's success. For example, a competitor may have a significant influence on the project if they launch a similar product at the same time.

Based on the stakeholder analysis, project teams can develop strategies to manage stakeholder expectations effectively. For example, if customers have a high level of interest in the product's features and benefits, the project team can prioritize product development efforts to meet those needs. Additionally, if a regulator has significant power over the project, the team can work to ensure that all regulatory requirements are met to avoid any delays or rejections.

Nonetheless, stakeholder management can also pose potential risks. For example, stakeholders may have conflicting interests or priorities, which can result in disagreements and conflicts. Additionally, stakeholders may resist change, especially if they feel that their needs or expectations are not being met. To mitigate these risks, project teams should communicate regularly with stakeholders and address any concerns or issues as soon as they arise.

Plan Stakeholder Engagement

Once the stakeholders have been identified, the project team must develop a plan for how to engage with them effectively. This plan should include strategies for managing stakeholder expectations, communication channels, and methods for gathering stakeholder feedback throughout the project. The team should also consider the stakeholders' preferred communication styles, cultural differences, and potential conflicts that may arise.

Plan Stakeholder Engagement is an essential part of project stakeholder management, as it outlines the strategies and actions that the project team will take to engage with stakeholders effectively. This involves identifying stakeholders, understanding their needs, and developing a plan that addresses those needs and expectations.

The following are some of the key elements that should be included in the Plan for Stakeholder Engagement:

Identifying stakeholders: The project team must identify all stakeholders who will be affected by the project or have an interest in it. This includes internal and external stakeholders, such as team members, sponsors, customers, suppliers, and regulators.

Analyzing stakeholder needs and expectations: Once stakeholders have been identified, the project team should analyze their needs and expectations. This involves understanding the stakeholders' goals, priorities, and concerns, as well as any potential conflicts that may arise.

Developing engagement strategies: Based on the stakeholder analysis, the project team should develop engagement strategies that address the needs and expectations of each stakeholder. This may involve developing communication plans, conducting stakeholder meetings, or providing training to stakeholders.

Defining communication channels: The team should define the communication channels that will be used to engage with stakeholders. This includes determining the frequency, format, and type of communication that will be used.

Addressing cultural differences: The team should consider any cultural differences that may impact stakeholder engagement. This may involve developing communication plans that are tailored to the cultural preferences of each stakeholder group.

Managing conflicts: The team should identify potential conflicts that may arise and develop strategies for managing them. This may involve developing conflict resolution plans, conducting stakeholder mediation sessions, or escalating conflicts at higher levels of management.

Overall, the Plan for Stakeholder Engagement is a crucial document that helps project teams engage with stakeholders effectively. By considering stakeholder needs and expectations, developing engagement strategies, defining communication channels, and managing conflicts, project teams can ensure that stakeholders are satisfied with the project outcomes and are supportive throughout the project lifecycle.

Example: For example, let's say a project is being undertaken to build a new hospital. The stakeholders in this project could include the hospital administration, doctors, nurses, patients, insurance companies, and regulatory bodies. The project team would first identify these stakeholders and then analyze their needs and expectations.

The hospital administration may be interested in ensuring that the project is completed on time and within budget, while the doctors and nurses may be concerned about patient safety and the quality of care. Patients may be concerned about the convenience of the hospital location, and insurance companies may be interested in the cost of services.

Based on this analysis, the project team would develop engagement strategies that address the needs and expectations of each stakeholder. They may develop communication plans that include regular stakeholder meetings, project updates, and newsletters. They may also provide training to stakeholders to ensure that they are aware of project goals and can contribute effectively. Additionally, the team may develop conflict resolution plans to address any potential conflicts that may arise during the project.

As a project manager, one of your key responsibilities is to engage with stakeholders in a meaningful and effective way throughout the project lifecycle. Effective stakeholder engagement is crucial to project success, as it helps to ensure that project objectives are met and stakeholder needs and expectations are addressed.

To achieve effective stakeholder engagement, it is important to develop a Plan for Stakeholder Engagement as part of the project management plan. This plan outlines how stakeholders will be identified, engaged, and communicated with throughout the project lifecycle. The Plan Stakeholder Engagement is developed during the project initiation phase and is updated throughout the project lifecycle as needed.

Stakeholder identification is the first step in developing the Plan for Stakeholder Engagement. This involves identifying all stakeholders who may be affected by the project, including internal and external stakeholders. Examples of internal stakeholders include project team members, sponsors, and shareholders, while external stakeholders may include customers, suppliers, and regulatory agencies.

Once stakeholders have been identified, the next step is to assess their level of interest, power, and influence in the project. This is where stakeholder mapping comes in. Stakeholder mapping is a technique used to identify stakeholders' level of interest, power, and influence in the project. This can help project teams prioritize stakeholder engagement efforts and tailor communication strategies accordingly.

For example, a stakeholder with high power and high interest may require more frequent and detailed communication compared to a stakeholder with low power and low interest. On the other hand, a stakeholder with high power but low interest may require periodic updates rather than frequent communication.

Stakeholder engagement strategies and communication plans are then developed based on the stakeholder analysis. These strategies should be tailored to the specific needs and expectations of each stakeholder group.

Effective stakeholder engagement requires ongoing communication and feedback. Project managers should maintain open lines of communication with stakeholders throughout the project lifecycle to ensure that their needs and expectations are being met. This can involve regular meetings, status updates, and progress reports.

In addition, project managers should be proactive in addressing stakeholder concerns and issues. For example, if a stakeholder expresses concern about a particular aspect of the project, the project manager should work to address these concerns in a timely and effective manner.

Finally, it is important to monitor and evaluate stakeholder engagement efforts throughout the project lifecycle. This involves measuring stakeholder satisfaction and identifying areas for improvement. The Plan Stakeholder Engagement should be updated as needed based on feedback from stakeholders.

Manage Stakeholder Engagement

In this process, the project team must actively manage stakeholder relationships to ensure that their needs and expectations are being met throughout the project. This involves providing stakeholders with regular updates on the project's progress, addressing their concerns, and soliciting their feedback. The team should also be prepared to adapt the stakeholder engagement plan as necessary to maintain positive relationships.

In the Manage Stakeholder Engagement process, the project team is responsible for proactively managing stakeholder relationships to ensure their needs and expectations are met throughout the project lifecycle. The team must engage with stakeholders regularly, provide updates on project progress, address their concerns, and gather feedback to maintain positive relationships.

Here are some key steps to effectively manage stakeholder engagement:

Identify stakeholders: The first step is to identify all stakeholders, both internal and external, who have an interest or impact on the project. This includes customers, team members, sponsors, regulators, suppliers, and more.

Analyze stakeholders: Once stakeholders are identified, it is important to analyze their needs, expectations, and levels of influence. This helps in prioritizing stakeholder engagement efforts and tailoring communication and engagement strategies accordingly.

Develop stakeholder engagement plan: Based on the stakeholder analysis, a stakeholder engagement plan should be developed. The plan outlines the communication and engagement strategies, frequency and mode of communication, and roles and responsibilities of the project team.

Implement stakeholder engagement plan: The stakeholder engagement plan should be implemented by the project team. This involves regular communication, addressing stakeholder concerns, and gathering feedback to improve stakeholder satisfaction.

Monitor stakeholder engagement: The stakeholder engagement plan should be monitored regularly to ensure it is effective and delivering the desired outcomes. If necessary, the plan should be revised and updated based on feedback from stakeholders.

Example: Let's say you are managing a project to implement a new software system in a company. Your stakeholders include the project sponsor, IT department, end-users, and customers. In order to effectively manage stakeholder engagement, you would:

Identify all stakeholders and their needs and expectations.

Analyze stakeholder needs and expectations and prioritize engagement efforts.

Develop a stakeholder engagement plan that includes regular updates, feedback mechanisms, and engagement strategies tailored to each stakeholder group.

Implement the stakeholder engagement plan by regularly communicating project progress, addressing concerns, and gathering feedback to improve stakeholder satisfaction.

Monitor stakeholder engagement regularly and revise the plan as necessary based on feedback from stakeholders.

Stakeholder engagement is a crucial aspect of project management. It involves identifying stakeholders, understanding their needs and expectations, and involving them in project decision-making processes. Effective stakeholder engagement can lead to better project outcomes, increased stakeholder satisfaction, improved communication, and reduced risk of stakeholder resistance.

Communication channels are an essential aspect of stakeholder engagement. The project team should use various communication channels to engage stakeholders effectively. For instance, the team may choose to use email, phone calls, meetings, or any other communication method that is most suitable for each stakeholder group. By using appropriate communication channels, the project team can ensure that stakeholders are informed and involved in the project.

Feedback analysis is another crucial aspect of stakeholder engagement. The project team should not only gather feedback from stakeholders but also analyze the feedback and take action based on it. For instance, feedback analysis can help identify areas for improvement, assess stakeholder satisfaction levels, and inform decision-making. By analyzing feedback, the project team can understand stakeholder expectations and address any issues that may arise.

Stakeholder management techniques are also essential in managing stakeholder engagement. Techniques such as negotiation, persuasion, and conflict resolution can help the project team manage stakeholder expectations and resolve conflicts that may arise during the project. For instance, negotiation can be used to reach a mutually beneficial agreement with stakeholders, persuasion can be used to influence stakeholders' decisions, and conflict resolution can be used to resolve conflicts that may arise between stakeholders.

Ethical considerations are crucial in stakeholder engagement. The project team should adhere to ethical standards and avoid any conflicts of interest while engaging with stakeholders. For instance, confidentiality should be maintained while sharing sensitive information with stakeholders, transparency should be ensured while communicating project information, and fairness should be maintained while involving stakeholders in decision-making processes.

To sum up, managing stakeholder engagement is crucial to project success. Effective stakeholder engagement can lead to better project outcomes, increased stakeholder satisfaction, improved communication, and reduced risk of stakeholder resistance. The project team should use appropriate communication channels, analyze feedback, use stakeholder management techniques, and adhere to ethical standards while engaging with stakeholders. By doing so, the project team can ensure that stakeholders are informed and involved in the project, leading to successful project outcomes.

Monitor Stakeholder Engagement

Throughout the project, the project team must monitor stakeholder relationships to ensure that their expectations are being met. This process involves gathering feedback from stakeholders regularly, measuring their satisfaction levels, and taking corrective action as necessary to address any issues that arise. The team should also be prepared to adjust the stakeholder engagement plan based on feedback and changing circumstances.

In project management, stakeholder engagement is crucial for project success, as stakeholders can influence the project outcome positively or negatively. The process of monitoring stakeholder engagement is important because it helps project teams to stay attuned to the needs and concerns of stakeholders throughout the project lifecycle.

To monitor stakeholder engagement effectively, the project team must first identify the stakeholders and understand their expectations. This can be done through stakeholder analysis and communication planning, which are typically done at the beginning of the project.

Once the stakeholders are identified, the project team can then gather feedback from them regularly. This feedback can be collected through surveys, interviews, focus groups, or other methods, depending on the stakeholders' preferences and the project's scope. The project team should also measure stakeholder satisfaction levels to gauge the effectiveness of the stakeholder engagement plan.

If issues arise, the project team must take corrective action promptly to address them. This may involve revising the stakeholder engagement plan, adjusting project deliverables, or addressing stakeholder concerns directly. It is crucial to keep stakeholders informed of any changes or decisions made, as this helps to maintain their trust and engagement in the project.

Here's an example to illustrate the importance of monitoring stakeholder engagement:

Let's say a project team is developing a new software application for a client. One of the key stakeholders is the client's IT department, who will be responsible for maintaining and supporting the application after it is deployed.

During the project, the project team regularly meets with the IT department to gather feedback and discuss any issues that arise. Through these interactions, the project team learns that the IT department is concerned about the application's compatibility with their existing systems.

To address this concern, the project team works with the IT department to test the application's compatibility and makes necessary adjustments. This proactive approach helps to ensure that the application meets the IT department's needs and is easier to support after deployment.

Stakeholder engagement is a crucial aspect of project management, and it can have a significant impact on the success or failure of a project. Effective stakeholder management involves understanding who the stakeholders are, their needs and expectations, and how to engage with them throughout the project lifecycle. In this text, we will discuss the importance of stakeholder management, stakeholder analysis, communication planning, proactive stakeholder engagement, and the role of the project manager in stakeholder engagement.

Importance of Stakeholder Management

Stakeholder management is essential because stakeholders can significantly impact a project's success. Stakeholders are individuals or groups that have an interest or are affected by the project. They can include project sponsors, customers, suppliers, team members, and other individuals or groups. Stakeholder management involves identifying and analyzing stakeholders, developing strategies to engage and communicate with them, and managing their expectations throughout the project.

Effective stakeholder management requires a comprehensive stakeholder management plan that outlines the goals, objectives, and strategies for managing stakeholders. The plan should be developed early in the project and reviewed regularly to ensure that it remains relevant and effective. The plan should also be flexible enough to accommodate changes in the project's objectives or stakeholders.

Examples of Stakeholder Analysis and Communication Planning

Stakeholder analysis involves identifying and analyzing stakeholders to determine their interests, needs, and expectations. The analysis can be conducted through various methods, including surveys, interviews, and focus groups. A stakeholder analysis matrix can be used to document the results of the analysis, which can be used to develop a stakeholder management plan.

Communication planning involves developing a plan to communicate with stakeholders throughout the project. The plan should identify the stakeholders, their communication needs and preferences, and the communication channels to be used. The plan should also include a communication schedule that outlines when and how communication will occur. The plan should be regularly reviewed and updated as necessary to ensure that it remains effective.

Examples of proactive stakeholder engagement

Proactive stakeholder engagement involves engaging stakeholders early in the project to identify potential issues and prevent them from becoming bigger problems later in the project. Proactive engagement can also help build trust and credibility with stakeholders, which can improve the chances of project success. Examples of proactive stakeholder engagement include:

- Conducting stakeholder workshops or meetings to gather feedback on project goals and objectives.
- Providing stakeholders with regular project updates and progress reports.
- Soliciting feedback from stakeholders on project deliverables and milestones.
- Holding focus groups or surveys to gather feedback on stakeholder satisfaction.

Role of the project manager in stakeholder engagement

The project manager plays a crucial role in stakeholder engagement and should be responsible for ensuring that the project team is gathering feedback, measuring satisfaction levels, and taking corrective action as necessary. The project manager should also be prepared to adjust the stakeholder engagement plan based on feedback and changing circumstances.

The project manager should develop a stakeholder management plan that outlines the goals, objectives, and strategies for managing stakeholders. The plan should be communicated to the project team, and all team members should be aware of their roles and responsibilities regarding stakeholder engagement. The project manager should also ensure that stakeholders are regularly updated on project progress and that their feedback is considered in decision-making.

AGILE AND HYBRID APPROACHES

Agile and Hybrid Approaches are project management methodologies that have gained popularity in recent years.

Agile Manifesto and Principles

This section introduces the Agile Manifesto and its underlying principles, which emphasize collaboration, flexibility, and customer satisfaction.

Agile methodologies have become increasingly popular in project management due to their ability to adapt to changing requirements and provide faster delivery of products or services. The Agile Manifesto, developed by a group of software developers in 2001, outlines the core values and principles of agile methodologies.

The Agile Manifesto consists of four values:

- Individuals and interactions over processes and tools
- Working software over comprehensive documentation
- Customer collaboration over contract negotiation
- Responding to change by following a plan

These values prioritize people and interactions, as well as the ability to respond to change, over rigid processes and plans.

Additionally, the Agile Manifesto is supported by 12 underlying principles, which provide guidance on how to apply the values in practice. Some of these principles include:

- Deliver working software frequently, with a preference for shorter timescales
- Welcome changing requirements, even if they occur late in the project
- Build projects around motivated individuals and give them the support they need
- The most efficient and effective method of conveying information to and within a team is face-to-face conversation
- Working software is the primary measure of progress

Agile methodologies have become increasingly popular in recent years as a way to manage projects in a more flexible and responsive manner. At its core, Agile is a set of values and principles that prioritize individuals and interactions, working software, customer collaboration, and responding to change over following a strict plan.

Agile methodologies are often contrasted with the traditional Waterfall approach to project management. Waterfall is a sequential, phased approach that involves following a strict plan and completing each phase before moving on to the next. Waterfall works well for projects with a clear scope and well-defined requirements. Nonetheless, it can be difficult to adapt to changes in scope or requirements mid-project.

Agile methodologies allow for more flexibility and adaptability. Agile teams work in short sprints, allowing them to respond quickly to changes in scope or requirements. This approach works well for projects with evolving requirements or uncertain scope.

Agile frameworks and methodologies

This section provides an overview of popular Agile frameworks and methodologies, including Scrum, Kanban, and Lean.

Agile methodologies are a set of principles and practices that are designed to deliver software development projects in an iterative and incremental manner. These methodologies focus on delivering value to the customer in a timely and efficient manner, while also responding to changing requirements throughout the project lifecycle.

The three most popular Agile frameworks are Scrum, Kanban, and Lean, and each has its unique approach to software development.

Scrum: Scrum is an Agile framework that is used for managing complex projects. It is based on the principles of transparency, inspection, and adaptation. Scrum involves a series of ceremonies, including daily stand-ups, sprint planning, sprint reviews, and sprint retrospectives, which are used to manage the development process. The Scrum framework is typically used for software development projects, but it can also be used for other types of projects.

Kanban: Kanban is an Agile methodology that is used for managing workflow. It is based on the principles of visualizing work, limiting work in progress, and managing flow. Kanban involves the use of a visual board that shows the status of work items in various stages of completion. The goal of Kanban is to optimize workflow and to deliver value to the customer as quickly as possible.

Lean: Lean is an Agile methodology that is based on the principles of minimizing waste, maximizing customer value, and optimizing the entire value stream. Lean involves a series of techniques and tools, including value stream mapping, continuous improvement, and just-in-time delivery. The goal of Lean is to deliver value to the customer in the most efficient and effective manner possible.

Examples of how these Agile frameworks and methodologies are used in practice:

Scrum can be used to manage the development of a new software application. The team would use a series of sprints to deliver small, incremental pieces of functionality, which would be tested and reviewed at the end of each sprint.

Kanban can be used to manage the workflow of a customer service team. The team would use a visual board to track the status of customer requests, and they would limit the number of requests they were working on at any one time to ensure that they could deliver value to customers as quickly as possible.

Lean can be used to optimize the manufacturing process of a car company. The company would use value stream mapping to identify areas of waste in the manufacturing process, and they would implement continuous improvement initiatives to streamline the process and deliver cars to customers more efficiently.

Agile methodologies have become increasingly popular in the project management world due to their ability to deliver projects efficiently and effectively. Agile is an iterative and collaborative approach that focuses on delivering value to the customer through frequent and incremental deliveries. This text will provide an overview of Agile frameworks and methodologies, highlight the benefits of using Agile methodologies, discuss popular Agile project management tools, compare Agile to traditional project management, and touch on the Agile principles and values.

Agile Frameworks and Methodologies

There are several Agile frameworks and methodologies, including Scrum, Kanban, Lean, and XP. Scrum is the most popular Agile framework and is widely used for software development projects. It involves working in sprints, which are time-boxed iterations, to deliver a working product incrementally. Kanban is another Agile methodology that focuses on visualizing work, limiting work in progress, and continuously delivering small batches of work. Lean is an Agile methodology that emphasizes minimizing waste and maximizing value for the customer. XP (Extreme Programming) is an Agile methodology that emphasizes engineering practices such as pair programming, continuous integration, and test-driven development.

Benefits of Agile Methodologies

One of the main benefits of Agile methodologies is improved customer satisfaction. Agile allows for regular customer feedback, which helps ensure that the end product meets the customer's needs. Additionally, Agile methodologies allow for faster time to market since the product is developed and delivered incrementally. Agile methodologies also offer greater flexibility to changing requirements since the product is developed iteratively and can be adapted easily.

Agile Project Management Tools

There are several popular Agile project management tools that can help teams implement Agile methodologies and manage their projects more effectively. Jira is one such tool that allows teams to plan, track, and release software. Trello is another popular tool that uses a Kanban-style board to visualize work and manage tasks. Asana is a project management tool that offers features such as task management, project tracking, and team collaboration.

Differences between Agile and Traditional Project Management

Agile and traditional project management have several key differences. In traditional project management, the emphasis is on following a strict plan and a sequential approach. In contrast, Agile methodologies emphasize collaboration, customer involvement, and iterative development. Agile also allows for greater flexibility to changing requirements, whereas traditional project management can be rigid and inflexible.

Agile Principles and Values

Agile is based on a set of principles and values that prioritize customer satisfaction, collaboration, and continuous improvement. The Agile Manifesto outlines the following four values:

- Individuals and interactions over processes and tools
- Working software over comprehensive documentation
- Customer collaboration over contract negotiation
- Responding to change over following a plan

Additionally, Agile methodologies prioritize the following principles:

- Deliver working software frequently, with a preference for shorter timescales
- Welcome changing requirements, even late in development
- Collaborate closely with the customer and stakeholders throughout the project
- Build projects around motivated individuals and give them the support and trust they need to succeed
- Use face-to-face communication whenever possible
- Measure progress primarily through working software
- Maintain a sustainable pace of work and focus on continuous improvement

Hybrid approaches and their benefits

This section explains the concept of hybrid project management and the benefits of combining Agile and traditional project management approaches.

Hybrid project management is a methodology that combines the best of Agile and traditional project management approaches. It recognizes that different projects have different needs, and that a "one-size-fits-all" approach to project management is not always effective. Instead, a hybrid approach allows project managers to tailor their approach to the specific needs of each project.

There are several benefits to using a hybrid approach:

Flexibility: A hybrid approach provides more flexibility than a purely Agile or traditional approach. Project managers can adapt their methodology as the project progresses, depending on the project's changing needs.

Improved Communication: By using a hybrid approach, project managers can improve communication between team members, stakeholders, and customers. This can help ensure that everyone is on the same page and that the project is moving in the right direction.

Increased Efficiency: A hybrid approach can help increase project efficiency by combining the best practices of Agile and traditional project management. This can lead to faster project delivery and better outcomes.

Better Risk Management: By using a hybrid approach, project managers can better manage risks associated with the project. This is because the approach is tailored to the specific needs of the project, which allows for better risk identification and mitigation.

Here are a few examples of how a hybrid approach might be used:

A software development project may use Agile methodology for the development phase, but a traditional approach for the testing and quality assurance phase.

A construction project may use a traditional approach for planning and design, but an Agile approach for construction and installation.

A marketing project may use a hybrid approach that combines Agile sprints with traditional project management techniques, such as Gantt charts and Critical path analysis.

Hybrid project management is a project management approach that combines elements of traditional project management and Agile project management. This approach has become increasingly popular in recent years as organizations seek to balance the need for structure and control with the need for flexibility and adaptability.

One of the key benefits of hybrid project management is its ability to align project management practices with organizational strategy. By combining elements of traditional project management and Agile project management, project managers can better understand the bigger picture and make better decisions that are in line with the organization's goals. For example, a manufacturing company may have a strategic objective to reduce the time it takes to bring new products to market. A hybrid project management approach could help the company achieve this objective by combining Agile development methods with traditional project management tools like Gantt charts and Critical path analysis.

Nonetheless, implementing a hybrid approach is not without challenges. These challenges may include resistance to change, difficulty in finding the right balance between Agile and traditional approaches, and the need for clear communication and collaboration. For example, a company that has traditionally used a waterfall approach to project management may struggle to adopt Agile practices, which require a high level of collaboration and communication between team members.

To overcome these challenges, organizations must be willing to invest in training and education for project managers and team members. They must also be willing to adapt their organizational culture to support a hybrid project management approach. For example, a company may need to adopt a more collaborative and flexible culture to support Agile practices.

There are many examples of successful implementation of hybrid project management. For example, a large technology company implemented a hybrid approach to manage a complex software development project. The company used Agile development methods to build the software, but also used traditional project management tools like Gantt charts to manage the project schedule. This approach allowed the company to deliver the software on time and within budget, while also providing the flexibility needed to adapt to changing requirements.

In terms of tools and techniques, there are many that can be used in hybrid project management. These could include Agile tools such as sprint planning and retrospective meetings, as well as traditional tools such as work breakdown structures and Critical path analysis. For example, a project manager may use sprint planning to plan the work to be done in a two-week sprint, while also using a work breakdown structure to break down the overall project into smaller, more manageable pieces.

Agile project management tools and techniques

This section covers the various tools and techniques used in agile project management, such as user stories, burndown charts, and retrospectives.

Agile project management is an iterative approach to managing projects that emphasizes flexibility, collaboration, and customer satisfaction. There are various tools and techniques used in agile project management that help teams deliver high-quality products and services. Here are some of the key tools and techniques:

User stories: User stories are brief, narrative descriptions of a specific feature or functionality from the perspective of the end-user. User stories are used to capture user requirements and are a crucial component of agile project management.

Example: A user story for a social media app might be, "As a user, I want to be able to search for friends based on their location."

Burndown charts: A burndown chart is a visual representation of the amount of work remaining in a project. It shows the amount of work completed and the amount of work remaining, as well as the projected completion date. Burndown charts are used to track progress and identify potential issues early on.

Example: A burndown chart for a software development project might show the amount of work remaining in terms of the number of features or functionalities left to implement, as well as the projected completion date.

Retrospectives: Retrospectives are meetings held at the end of each iteration or sprint to review the team's performance and identify areas for improvement. Retrospectives are used to promote continuous improvement and ensure that the team is delivering high-quality products and services.

Example: A retrospective might involve asking team members to share what went well during the sprint, what didn't go well, and what could be improved. The team can then discuss these issues and develop action plans to address them.

Other tools and techniques used in agile project management include sprint planning, daily stand-ups, backlog grooming, and continuous integration and delivery.

Agile project management is a methodology that prioritizes flexibility, collaboration, and responsiveness in project planning and execution. The Agile approach is based on the Agile Manifesto, which was developed in 2001 by a group of software developers who sought to improve upon traditional project management approaches that they found to be overly rigid and focused on documentation rather than delivering value to customers. The Agile Manifesto consists of four values and twelve principles that guide Agile project management.

The four values of the Agile Manifesto are:

Individuals and interactions over processes and tools: Agile project management prioritizes communication and collaboration among team members over following strict processes and relying on tools.

Working software over comprehensive documentation: Agile project management emphasizes delivering working software that meets customer needs over creating extensive documentation that may not be necessary or useful.

Customer collaboration over contract negotiation: Agile project management involves working closely with customers to understand their needs and priorities rather than relying on strict contracts or agreements.

Responding to change over following a plan: Agile project management is adaptable and responsive to changes in customer needs or project requirements, rather than being bound to a predetermined plan.

The twelve principles of the Agile Manifesto provide more specific guidance for implementing Agile project management. These principles include:

Delivering working software frequently, with a preference for shorter timescales.

Welcoming changing requirements, even late in the project, as a way of providing value to the customer.

Working collaboratively with customers and stakeholders throughout the project.

Building projects around motivated individuals and giving them the support and environment, they need to succeed.

Emphasizing face-to-face communication as the most effective way of conveying information.

Measuring progress through working software rather than documentation.

Promoting sustainable development by maintaining a steady pace and prioritizing technical excellence and good design.

Fostering self-organizing teams that are empowered to make decisions and solve problems.

Reflecting regularly on team performance and using feedback to continuously improve.

Simplifying processes and tools as much as possible to minimize waste.

Recognizing and valuing the importance of individuals and interactions within the team.

Focusing on delivering value to the customer as the primary goal of the project.

One of the key differences between Agile project management and traditional project management approaches is the emphasis on flexibility and responsiveness. Traditional project management approaches, such as the Waterfall model, follow a linear sequence of planning, executing, and monitoring, with each phase completed before moving onto the next. This approach can be inflexible and may not accommodate changes in customer needs or project requirements that arise during the course of the project.

In contrast, Agile project management is designed to be adaptable to changing circumstances. Agile teams work in short iterations, called sprints, and deliver working software at the end of each sprint. This allows the team to respond quickly to changes and feedback from customers and stakeholders. Additionally, Agile project management emphasizes collaboration and communication among team members, as well as between the team and customers and stakeholders.

Agile project management also incorporates a number of tools and techniques to support its principles and values. These include:

User stories: User stories are brief, simple descriptions of a feature or requirement that are written from the perspective of the end user. User stories are used to guide the development process and ensure that the team is focused on delivering value to the customer.

Kanban boards: Kanban boards are visual tools that help teams manage their work and prioritize tasks. Kanban boards typically consist of a board with columns for tasks in various stages of completion, such as "to do," "in progress," and "done."

Scrum meetings: Scrum meetings are daily check-ins that help team members stay aligned and focused on their goals.

Agile project roles and responsibilities

This section describes the roles and responsibilities of the agile project team, including the product owner, scrum master, and development team.

In an agile project, there are typically three main roles: the product owner, the scrum master, and the development team. Each of these roles has specific responsibilities, as outlined below:

Product owner: The product owner is responsible for ensuring that the team is working on the right things and that the product being developed meets the needs of the stakeholders. The product owner is the primary point of contact for the stakeholders and is responsible for prioritizing the backlog of work that the team will be working on. The product owner also works closely with the development team to ensure that they have a clear understanding of the requirements and can deliver a high-quality product.

Scrum master: The scrum master is responsible for ensuring that the agile process is being followed and that the team is working together effectively. The scrum master facilitates the daily stand-up meetings, sprint planning meetings, sprint review meetings, and retrospective meetings. The scrum master also helps the team to identify and remove any obstacles that are preventing them from delivering the product.

Development team: The development team is responsible for delivering the product. This team is self-organizing and cross-functional, meaning that it includes all the skills and expertise needed to deliver the product. The development team works closely with the product owner to understand the requirements and with the scrum master to ensure that the agile process is being followed. The development team is responsible for estimating the work, breaking it down into tasks, and delivering the product incrementally during each sprint.

Examples of how these roles and responsibilities might play out in practice:

Suppose the product owner receives feedback from stakeholders that the product needs to include a new feature. The product owner would work with the development team to prioritize this feature and ensure that it is included in the backlog of work for the next sprint.

During a daily stand-up meeting, the scrum master might notice that one team member is struggling with a particular task. The scrum master would work with that team member to identify any obstacles and help them to find a way to overcome them.

The development team might be working on a new feature and encounter a problem with the code. They would work together to identify the issue, fix it, and test it to ensure that it is working correctly.

Overall, the roles and responsibilities of the agile project team are designed to promote collaboration, flexibility, and a focus on delivering value to the stakeholders. By working together effectively, the team can deliver high-quality products that meet the needs of the customer in a timely and efficient manner.

Agile project management is a modern approach to project management that emphasizes flexibility, collaboration, and responsiveness. Unlike traditional project management methodologies, which tend to be more rigid and structured, agile methods prioritize iteration and feedback, allowing teams to adapt to changing requirements and stakeholder needs.

One of the key features of agile project management is the use of sprints, which are short, time-boxed periods (usually 1-4 weeks) during which the team focuses on completing a set of tasks or user stories. The goal of each sprint is to produce a working product increment that can be reviewed and refined in subsequent sprints.

Agile methods also prioritize frequent communication and collaboration between team members and stakeholders. Rather than relying on extensive documentation and planning upfront, agile teams work together to define requirements and prioritize tasks in a flexible and iterative manner. This allows the team to respond to changing needs and stakeholder feedback, and to avoid common challenges like scope creep.

Another key aspect of agile project management is the use of user stories, which are short, simple descriptions of a feature or requirement from the perspective of the end user. User stories help the team to focus on the needs of the customer and to prioritize features based on their value to the user.

In order to effectively implement agile project management, there are several best practices that teams should follow. First and foremost, it is important to establish a clear vision and goal for the project, and to communicate this vision to all stakeholders. This helps to ensure that everyone is aligned on the project objectives and understands how their work contributes to the larger goal.

It is also important to establish a collaborative team culture that values open communication and feedback. This can be achieved through regular team meetings, daily stand-ups, and other communication channels that facilitate collaboration and feedback.

Another best practice is to establish clear roles and responsibilities for team members. This helps to ensure that everyone knows what they are responsible for and can work effectively together to achieve the project goals. Agile teams often use roles like product owner, scrum master, and development team member to delineate responsibilities and facilitate communication.

In addition, it is important to establish clear metrics for measuring project success. These might include measures like customer satisfaction, product quality, or speed of delivery. By regularly tracking these metrics, the team can identify areas for improvement and make adjustments to the project as needed.

Overall, agile project management is a powerful tool for managing complex projects in a flexible and collaborative manner. By prioritizing iteration, feedback, and collaboration, agile teams are able to respond to changing requirements and stakeholder needs, while avoiding common challenges like scope creep and misaligned expectations. With the right approach and best practices in place, agile project management can help teams to deliver high-quality products that meet the needs of their customers and stakeholders.

Hybrid project management frameworks

This section discusses the various hybrid project management frameworks, such as PRINCE2 Agile and AgilePM, and how they can be used to combine agile and traditional project management approaches.

Hybrid project management frameworks are becoming increasingly popular in today's fast-paced business environment. These frameworks combine the best aspects of both traditional and agile project management methodologies to create a hybrid approach that is customized to fit the unique needs of a specific project.

The most widely known hybrid project management frameworks are PRINCE2 Agile and AgilePM. PRINCE2 Agile combines the proven principles of PRINCE2 with agile concepts, such as iterative development and continuous feedback. It provides a structured framework that allows organizations to manage projects in a controlled manner while still being flexible enough to adapt to changing circumstances.

AgilePM, on the other hand, is a complete agile project management framework that is based on the Agile Business Consortium's Agile Project Framework. It offers a practical and repeatable methodology for delivering agile projects in organizations of any size and across different industries.

Other hybrid project management frameworks include Scrum with Kanban, SAF (Scaled Agile Framework), and PMI's Agile Certified Practitioner (PMI-ACP) certification.

For example, let's say a company wants to develop a new mobile application. They could use a hybrid approach that combines traditional project management techniques, such as a detailed project plan with a fixed scope and budget, with agile methodologies like daily stand-up meetings and continuous delivery. This approach allows the project team to have a clear roadmap while still being flexible enough to adjust to customer feedback and changing market conditions.

Hybrid project management frameworks are becoming increasingly popular in today's business world. A hybrid approach combines traditional project management methodologies with agile project management methodologies, allowing organizations to take advantage of the strengths of each.

Traditional project management frameworks, such as the Waterfall approach, are well-suited for projects with well-defined goals and requirements, a predictable budget, and a fixed timeline. Nonetheless, they can be rigid and inflexible, making it difficult to adjust to changing circumstances or stakeholder needs. On the other hand, agile project management frameworks, such as Scrum or Kanban, are better suited for projects with constantly evolving requirements, high levels of uncertainty, and a need for frequent feedback and adaptation.

A hybrid approach allows organizations to tailor their project management methodology to the specific needs of each project. For example, a software development project might require an agile approach for the coding and testing phases but a more traditional approach for project planning and budgeting. A hybrid approach can also be useful for organizations that are transitioning from a traditional to an agile approach or for projects that require a mix of both approaches.

One of the key benefits of a hybrid approach is increased flexibility. By combining traditional and agile methodologies, organizations can adjust their approach as needed to meet changing project requirements or stakeholder needs. Another benefit is the ability to take advantage of the strengths of each methodology. For example, a hybrid approach can provide the predictability and structure of a traditional approach while also allowing for the flexibility and responsiveness of an agile approach.

Nonetheless, a hybrid approach also has some drawbacks. It can be challenging to implement, as it requires a deep understanding of both traditional and agile methodologies. It can also be difficult to determine which methodology to use for each phase of the project, and to ensure that all team members are aligned and working effectively together.

To ensure that a hybrid approach is implemented effectively, it's important to identify the specific needs of each project and to choose the appropriate methodology for each phase. This requires a deep understanding of both traditional and agile methodologies, as well as effective communication and collaboration among team members. It's also important to establish clear roles and responsibilities for each team member and to establish a clear process for decision-making and problem-solving.

A hybrid approach can be used in a wide range of industries and project types. For example, a construction project might use a traditional approach for planning and budgeting but an agile approach for the construction phase, allowing for quick adjustments to unexpected changes in weather or materials. Similarly, a marketing campaign might use a traditional approach for developing a marketing plan but an agile approach for executing the plan, allowing for quick adjustments to changing market conditions or customer feedback.

Benefits and challenges of using hybrid approaches

This section explores the benefits and challenges of using hybrid approaches, including improved flexibility, faster delivery, and increased stakeholder engagement, as well as potential conflicts between different project management methodologies.

In recent years, there has been an increased interest in hybrid approaches to project management, which combine traditional and Agile methods to deliver projects. The benefits and challenges of using hybrid approaches are many, and it is important to understand them to make informed decisions about which approach to use for a given project.

Benefits of using hybrid approaches

Improved flexibility: Hybrid approaches allow project teams to adapt to changing requirements and deliverables by combining the structured planning and control of traditional project management with the agility and responsiveness of Agile methodologies.

Faster delivery: By adopting Agile practices such as iterative development, continuous delivery, and frequent feedback loops, hybrid approaches can speed up project delivery and reduce time to market.

Increased stakeholder engagement: Hybrid approaches emphasize collaboration and communication between the project team and stakeholders, resulting in greater engagement, participation, and buy-in from all parties involved.

Challenges of using hybrid approaches

Conflicts between methodologies: One of the main challenges of using hybrid approaches is the potential for conflicts between different project management methodologies. For example, traditional project management may emphasize detailed planning and control, while Agile methodologies prioritize flexibility and responsiveness. Project teams need to carefully balance these different approaches to avoid conflicts and ensure project success.

Complexity: Hybrid approaches can be more complex and difficult to manage than traditional or Agile approaches alone. Project teams need to carefully plan and coordinate their activities to ensure that all stakeholders are aligned and that project goals are being met.

Cultural change: Hybrid approaches may require significant cultural change within an organization, particularly if there is a strong emphasis on traditional project management practices. Project teams need to ensure that all stakeholders are on board with the new approach and are willing to adapt their roles and responsibilities accordingly.

Examples of hybrid approaches include:

- Scrum with a traditional project management framework such as PMBOK
- Kanban with a traditional project management framework such as PRINCE2
- Waterfall with Agile practices such as continuous delivery and frequent feedback loops.

Hybrid project management approaches have become increasingly popular in recent years as organizations seek to combine the benefits of different methodologies to better address the unique challenges of their projects. A hybrid approach combines elements of traditional and agile project management methodologies to create a tailored approach that best meets the needs of a particular project.

One potential conflict that can arise between different project management methodologies in a hybrid approach is the use of different project artifacts, such as the project charter, scope statement, and project plan. For example, traditional project management typically emphasizes detailed project planning and documentation, while agile project management prioritizes flexibility and adaptability. To resolve this conflict, project managers can work with their project team to identify which artifacts are essential for their project and adapt them accordingly. For instance, they may use a more lightweight project charter and scope statement in an agile project, but still include a detailed project plan to ensure that everyone is clear on the project's goals and timelines.

Another potential conflict in hybrid project management is the use of different project roles and responsibilities. In a traditional project management approach, there are typically clear hierarchies and defined roles, such as project manager, project sponsor, and project team members. In contrast, agile project management emphasizes cross-functional teams and shared responsibilities. To resolve this conflict, project managers can work with their team to establish clear roles and responsibilities that combine the strengths of both approaches. For example, they may assign a project sponsor who is responsible for providing overall project guidance and support, while also having cross-functional team members who share responsibilities for delivering specific project outcomes.

Selecting the appropriate approach for a specific project based on its unique characteristics and requirements is crucial in hybrid project management. One way to do this is to conduct a thorough analysis of the project's scope, timelines, budget, and stakeholders, among other factors. This analysis can help project managers determine which project management methodologies are most appropriate for their project and tailor their approach accordingly. For example, a project with a fixed budget and timeline may benefit from using traditional project management techniques to ensure that the project is completed within budget and on time, while a project with more uncertainty and complexity may require agile project management techniques to allow for more flexibility and adaptability.

Effective implementation and management of hybrid approaches require project managers to possess certain skills and competencies. These include strong leadership skills, the ability to manage teams with diverse backgrounds and expertise, excellent communication and stakeholder management skills, and the ability to adapt and adjust to changing circumstances. Project managers also need to be knowledgeable about different project management methodologies and their strengths and weaknesses to create a tailored approach that meets the specific needs of their project.

Continuous learning and improvement are essential for successful hybrid project management. This includes staying up to date with the latest industry standards and practices, pursuing ongoing professional development opportunities, and continuously pursuing continuous feedback and learning from successes and failures. By doing so, project managers can continue to refine and improve their approach, leading to more successful outcomes for their projects and organizations.

ETHICS AND PROFESSIONAL CONDUCT

Code of Ethics and Professional Conduct

This section covers the ethical principles and guidelines that project managers should follow in their professional conduct. It includes an overview of the PMI Code of Ethics and Professional Conduct, which outlines the expectations for professional conduct and ethical behavior.

The Code of Ethics and Professional Conduct is a crucial component of project management, and it outlines the ethical principles and guidelines that project managers should follow in their professional conduct. The Code is based on four core values: responsibility, respect, fairness, and honesty. Project managers who adhere to these values are more likely to deliver successful projects that benefit all stakeholders.

To illustrate how the Code works in practice, let's consider an example. Suppose that a project manager is leading a team that is responsible for building a new bridge. The project manager has been informed by the construction contractor that they have discovered some issues with the quality of the concrete that has been delivered to the site. The contractor suggests that they can still use the concrete and just hide the defects.

In this scenario, the project manager must adhere to the Code of Ethics and Professional Conduct by prioritizing responsibility, respect, fairness, and honesty. First, the project manager must take responsibility for the project's success and ensure that all work is done to the highest quality. Second, the project manager must show respect to all stakeholders by ensuring that the bridge is safe and meets all relevant standards. Third, the project manager must ensure fairness by not compromising quality in favor of cost or schedule. Finally, the project manager must be honest and transparent about the quality issues, even if it means delaying the project or incurring additional costs.

As a project manager, it is essential to understand the importance of the Code of Ethics and Professional Conduct (CEPC) and the impact it can have on your project's success and your organization's reputation. The CEPC provides a framework of values and principles that guide ethical behavior, integrity, and professional conduct for project managers. It serves as a guide for decision-making and helps project managers ensure they are acting in the best interest of their stakeholders.

The consequences of not adhering to the Code of Ethics and Professional Conduct can be severe. Unethical behavior can lead to project failures, damaged relationships with stakeholders, and reputational harm for the organization. For instance, imagine a project manager who decides to cut corners to meet deadlines, disregarding safety measures and quality standards. This behavior could result in accidents, delays, and rework, jeopardizing the project's success and the safety of the team and stakeholders.

Project managers must be aware of the process for reporting ethical violations. The Project Management Institute (PMI) provides a set of procedures for handling ethical violations. The PMI's Ethics Member Advisory Group (EMAG) is responsible for investigating and resolving ethical complaints. Project managers should report ethical violations promptly, following the established procedures. They can also seek guidance from their peers, mentors, or supervisors if they are unsure how to proceed.

Adhering to the Code of Ethics and Professional Conduct has significant benefits. It can lead to increased trust, better relationships with stakeholders, and sustainable success for the project and the organization. For example, imagine a project manager who demonstrates integrity, transparency, and respect for stakeholders' interests. This behavior can build trust, enhance communication, and foster collaboration among team members, stakeholders, and partners. It can also increase the likelihood of achieving project objectives and creating long-term value for the organization.

Responsibilities of a project manager

This section covers the roles and responsibilities of a project manager, as defined by the PMBOK Guide 2021. It includes an overview of the project manager's duties, such as defining project objectives, managing project scope, and ensuring project quality. It also covers the project manager's responsibilities in terms of stakeholder management, communication, risk management, and project closure.

Essential roles and responsibilities of a project manager in ensuring the success of a project. As per the PMBOK Guide 2021, a project manager is responsible for defining the project objectives, managing project scope, and ensuring project quality.

To define project objectives, a project manager must first understand the project's requirements and goals. Based on this understanding, the project manager should define clear and measurable project objectives that align with the organization's strategic goals. For example, if the project is to develop a new software product, the project manager must define the features and functionality required by the end-users, the timelines for development, and the budget allocated for the project.

Managing project scope involves identifying and documenting project requirements, creating a project scope statement, and monitoring project progress against the defined scope. The project manager must ensure that the project remains within the defined scope, and any changes to the scope are managed through the appropriate change control processes.

Ensuring project quality involves defining and implementing a quality management plan, including quality standards, metrics, and processes. The project manager should ensure that the project team adheres to the defined quality management plan and implements corrective actions to address any quality issues.

The project manager also has several responsibilities related to stakeholder management, communication, risk management, and project closure. These include identifying and managing project stakeholders, communicating project status and updates, identifying and mitigating project risks, and ensuring a smooth project closure.

For example, stakeholder management involves identifying all stakeholders involved in the project, understanding their needs and expectations, and developing a stakeholder engagement plan to manage their involvement throughout the project. Effective communication involves establishing communication channels, defining communication protocols, and regularly updating stakeholders on project progress.

Risk management involves identifying and assessing project risks, developing risk response plans, and monitoring and controlling risks throughout the project. The project manager should also ensure a smooth project closure by verifying that all project deliverables have been completed, conducting project reviews, and documenting lessons learned.

As a project manager, you have a wide range of responsibilities that are crucial to the success of your project. In this section, we will cover the main responsibilities of a project manager as defined by the PMBOK Guide 2021 and other relevant sources. We will also provide examples to further clarify certain points.

Stakeholder Management One of the most important responsibilities of a project manager is stakeholder management. A stakeholder is anyone who has an interest in the project or who is impacted by the project. This can include project team members, customers, sponsors, vendors, and other key stakeholders.

Managing stakeholders effectively involves identifying and analyzing the needs, expectations, and potential impact of each stakeholder. For example, a customer may have specific requirements that must be met in order for them to be satisfied with the project outcome. A vendor may have specific technical expertise that is required to complete the project successfully.

In addition, stakeholders may have conflicting interests or priorities that must be managed effectively. For example, a project team member may have a personal interest in completing their work quickly, while a sponsor may have a financial interest in keeping costs low.

To manage stakeholders effectively, you must communicate with them regularly and proactively address any concerns or issues that arise. This may involve holding regular meetings, providing progress reports, and maintaining open lines of communication.

Risk Management Another crucial responsibility of a project manager is risk management. This involves identifying potential risks that could impact the project, assessing the likelihood and potential impact of each risk, and developing strategies to mitigate or avoid those risks.

There are many different types of risks that can arise in a project. For example, technical risks may involve problems with hardware or software that could delay the project. Schedule risks may involve delays caused by unforeseen circumstances, such as weather or supply chain issues. Cost risks may involve unexpected expenses that exceed the budget for the project.

To manage risks effectively, you must prioritize them based on their likelihood and potential impact. This may involve developing a risk matrix or other tool to help you assess and prioritize risks.

Once you have identified and prioritized the risks, you must develop strategies to mitigate or avoid them. This may involve developing contingency plans, establishing risk mitigation teams, or adjusting project schedules or budgets.

Project Planning and Execution Project planning and execution is another key responsibility of a project manager. This involves defining project objectives, creating a project plan, and managing the project team to ensure that the project is completed on time, within budget, and to the desired level of quality.

Project planning involves defining the scope of the project, identifying project requirements, and creating a project schedule and budget. This may involve working with key stakeholders to ensure that their needs and expectations are taken into account.

Once the project plan is in place, the project manager must manage the project team to ensure that the project is executed successfully. This may involve assigning tasks to team members, monitoring progress, and providing support and guidance as needed.

Quality Management Finally, quality management is another key responsibility of a project manager. This involves ensuring that the project meets the desired level of quality and that any issues are identified and resolved in a timely manner.

To manage quality effectively, the project manager must define quality standards and ensure that they are met throughout the project. This may involve establishing quality metrics, conducting regular inspections, and providing training to project team members to ensure that they are able to meet the required quality standards.

PROJECT MANAGEMENT EXAM PREP

This comprehensive exam preparation guide is designed to help you pass the PMP exam with confidence. We have included the latest updates from the PMBOK Guide 2021, ECO 2021, and other relevant resources. Our goal is to provide you with the most superior and comprehensive content available.

With our comprehensive exam preparation guide, you will have everything you need to pass the PMP exam with confidence:

Exam Tips and Tricks

   Time management techniques: This section covers proven time management techniques to help you optimize your study time and manage time effectively during the exam. We will provide you with strategies for creating a study schedule, allocating time during the exam, and managing your time efficiently.

Time management techniques are essential for any project manager, and this is especially true when preparing for the PMP exam. The exam is notoriously challenging, with a four-hour time limit to answer 200 multiple-choice questions. Therefore, effective time management techniques are crucial to ensure that you can complete the exam on time and with a passing score.

Here are some examples of time management techniques that can help you optimize your study time and manage your time effectively during the PMP exam:

Create a study schedule: Creating a study schedule can help you stay organized and manage your time effectively. It can also help you identify areas where you need to focus more attention. For example, you may want to allocate more time to studying the areas where you are weaker.

   Use a timer: Using a timer can help you manage your time during the exam. For example, you may want to allocate a specific amount of time to each question, so you don't spend too much time on any one question.

   Eliminate distractions: Distractions can significantly impact your productivity and concentration. It's essential to eliminate any potential distractions during your study time and during the exam. For example, you may want to turn off your phone or email notifications during your study time or use noise-canceling headphones during the exam.

   Prioritize tasks: Prioritizing tasks can help you manage your time effectively. For example, you may want to prioritize studying the areas where you are weaker, so you have more time to focus on those areas.

   Practice time management techniques: Practicing time management techniques during your study time can help you develop good habits that will carry over to the exam. For example, you may want to set a timer for each study session and take regular breaks to stay focused.

Effective time management is a crucial factor in passing the PMP exam. To prepare for the exam, learners must be able to manage their time efficiently and effectively to maximize their study time and minimize stress. Here are some time management techniques that can help learners prepare for the PMP exam:

Use of mnemonic devices: Mnemonic devices can be helpful in remembering key concepts and formulas required for the PMP exam. For example, to remember the five process groups, learners can use the acronym "I-P-O-C-C" (Initiating, Planning, Executing, Monitoring and Controlling, Closing). Another example is to remember the nine knowledge areas by using the acronym "S-C-Q-R-H-R-S-C-C" (Scope, Cost, Quality, Resource, Human Resource, Risk, Stakeholder, Communication, and Procurement). Encourage learners to create their own memory aids that work for them.

Importance of a good night's sleep: Adequate rest is essential for effective time management. Encourage learners to get a good night's sleep before the exam, so they are refreshed and focused. For example, learners should aim to get at least 7-8 hours of sleep the night before the exam to ensure they are alert and able to concentrate during the exam.

Practice exams: Taking practice exams can help learners get familiar with the exam format and time constraints. It's an effective way to test their knowledge, identify areas where they need more focus and practice time management techniques. For example, learners can take simulated PMP exams using exam simulators, review their answers, and identify areas where they need to improve their time management skills.

Personal time management strategies: Encourage learners to identify their preferred time management strategies that work for them, such as creating to-do lists, using calendars, or breaking down tasks into smaller achievable goals. For example, learners can create a study schedule that allows them to allocate time for each knowledge area and process group. They can also use a timer to measure their study time and avoid getting distracted.

Time management is a crucial aspect of preparing and taking the Project Management Professional (PMP) exam. To effectively manage your time, it is important to understand the exam structure, use mind maps and flowcharts, manage stress and anxiety, and set realistic goals.

Understanding the Exam Structure: To effectively manage your time during the exam, it is crucial to understand its structure. The PMP exam consists of 200 multiple-choice questions that must be completed within four hours. Understanding the exam's scoring system is also essential. The exam is scored on a scale of 0 to 1000, and a passing score is 61%.

An example of how understanding the exam structure can help with time management is to break down the four hours of the exam into four sections of one hour each. This way, you can allocate enough time for each section and ensure that you answer all the questions in the allotted time.

Use of Mind Maps and Flowcharts: Mind maps and flowcharts can be useful tools to organize and connect information, especially for visual learners. They help in breaking down complex information into smaller, more manageable parts.

An example of how mind maps can be used is by creating a mind map of the five process groups and their respective knowledge areas. This way, you can visualize how each process group relates to the knowledge areas and understand the interconnections between them.

Managing Stress and Anxiety: Stress and anxiety can negatively affect your performance during the exam. It is essential to manage your stress levels to stay focused during the exam. Some relaxation techniques that can be helpful include deep breathing, meditation, and progressive muscle relaxation.

An example of how to manage stress and anxiety is by practicing deep breathing exercises before and during the exam. This can help calm your nerves and reduce stress levels, allowing you to perform better.

Setting Realistic Goals: Setting realistic goals for studying and exam preparation can help learners manage their time effectively and reduce the risk of burnout. It is important to create a study plan that considers your daily schedule and other commitments.

An example of how to set realistic goals is by breaking down the knowledge areas into smaller chunks and allocating a specific amount of time to study each chunk. This way, you can track your progress and adjust your study plan accordingly.

Exam-taking strategies

This section will give you tips on how to approach and tackle the exam questions. We will provide you with strategies for analyzing questions, eliminating wrong answers, and identifying the correct answer. These strategies are designed to help you maximize your score and minimize the chances of missing any crucial questions.

When it comes to taking any exam, it's important to have a solid strategy in place. The PMP exam is no exception. In this section of the book, we'll cover various strategies that can help you approach the exam questions in a more effective manner. These strategies are designed to help you save time, avoid common mistakes, and increase your chances of answering questions correctly.

Here are some exam-taking strategies that we'll cover in the book:

Read the question carefully: This may seem obvious, but it's important to read each question carefully and thoroughly before attempting to answer it. Pay attention to details such as keywords, phrases, and instructions. Sometimes, a single word can completely change the meaning of the question.

Eliminate wrong answers: If you're not sure about the correct answer, try to eliminate any options that you know are incorrect. This will increase your chances of guessing the correct answer. Look for options that are completely irrelevant or contradict the information provided in the question.

Use your scratch paper: During the exam, you'll be provided with scratch paper. Use it to jot down notes, formulas, or any other information that might be helpful while answering questions. This will help you stay organized and save time.

Pace yourself: The PMP exam is a four-hour test, which means you'll have an average of 1.2 minutes to answer each question. It's important to pace yourself and not spend too much time on any single question. If you're not sure about a question, skip it and come back to it later.

Focus on high-value areas: Certain areas of the exam are weighted more heavily than others. For example, the Initiating and Planning domains account for a larger percentage of the exam than the other domains. Make sure to focus your study efforts on these high-value areas.

Use process of elimination: If you're not sure about the correct answer, try to eliminate any options that you know are incorrect. This will increase your chances of guessing the correct answer. Look for options that are completely irrelevant or contradict the information provided in the question.

Take breaks: The PMP exam is a long and mentally taxing test. It's important to take breaks to recharge your brain and stay focused. You'll have the option to take two 10-minute breaks during the exam.

Here are a few examples of how these strategies might be applied:

Example 1: You come across a question that asks you to identify the best tool for stakeholder analysis. You're not sure about the answer, but you do know that brainstorming is not a tool used for stakeholder analysis. By eliminating this option, you're left with fewer choices and a better chance of guessing the correct answer.

Example 2: You're running low on time and still have several questions left to answer. Rather than trying to answer every question, focus on the ones that are worth more points or are in the high-value domains. This will help you maximize your score and avoid running out of time before completing the entire exam.

Preparing for the Project Management Professional (PMP) exam can be a challenging and overwhelming task, especially if you're unfamiliar with the exam format and content. However, with the right strategies and study materials, you can increase your chances of passing the exam and earning your PMP certification.

To start, it's important to familiarize yourself with the PMP exam format. The exam consists of 180 multiple-choice questions and is administered as a computer-based test (CBT). It's important to understand how to navigate through the questions, mark questions for review, and manage your time effectively during the exam.

One way to practice time management is by taking several timed practice tests before the actual exam. This can help you get a sense of how much time to allocate for each question and improve your pacing. Additionally, you should develop a study plan that includes a combination of study materials such as books, online courses, and practice exams.

It's also crucial to have a good understanding of the PMBOK Guide, which is the primary reference for the PMP exam. The guide covers a wide range of project management concepts and terminology, and many exam questions are based on it. Therefore, it's important to thoroughly read and understand the guide, and use it as a reference throughout your exam preparation.

When it comes to managing exam anxiety, it's important to develop coping mechanisms that work for you. Some techniques include deep breathing, positive self-talk, and visualization exercises. Practicing these techniques regularly can help you feel more confident and calmer during the exam.

In addition to the strategies mentioned above, there are a few other tips to keep in mind. First, make sure to read and understand the PMP Exam Content Outline (ECO), which outlines the topics and knowledge areas that will be covered on the exam. This can help you prioritize your study materials and ensure that you're focusing on the most important topics.

Second, be familiar with the PMI Code of Ethics and Professional Conduct, which outlines the ethical standards that project managers are expected to uphold. Understanding these standards can help you answer ethical questions on the exam and demonstrate your commitment to ethical behavior as a project manager.

Finally, make sure to practice answering sample exam questions to get a sense of the types of questions that will be on the actual exam. There are many resources available for sample questions, including the PMBOK Guide, the PMP Exam Prep Simplified book, and online practice exams.

For example, a sample question might ask: "During which process do you develop a project charter?" The correct answer would be "Initiating," as this is the process where the project charter is developed and approved.

What is the PMP Exam? The Project Management Professional (PMP) exam is a globally recognized certification exam for project managers. It assesses their knowledge, skills, and abilities in project management based on the Project Management Body of Knowledge (PMBOK) Guide. The exam is designed to ensure that certified project managers can handle complex projects in a wide range of industries and domains.

What is the Content and Format of the PMP Exam? The PMP exam consists of 180 multiple-choice questions that cover five project management domains:

Initiating (13%)

Planning (24%)

Executing (31%)

Monitoring and Controlling (25%)

Closing (7%)

The exam has a time limit of four hours, during which you need to answer all the questions. You can mark questions for review and go back to them later. However, once you submit your answers, you cannot change them.

The PMP exam is computer-based, and you will take it at a Pearson VUE test center or online from your home or office. If you take it online, you will need a computer with a webcam, microphone, and reliable internet connection.

What Types of Questions Are on the PMP Exam? The PMP exam includes three types of questions:

Situational questions: These are hypothetical scenarios that require you to apply project management concepts and techniques to solve a problem or make a decision. For example, "Your project sponsor has just informed you that the budget has been reduced by 20%. What actions will you take to ensure that the project stays on track?"

Knowledge-based questions: These are direct questions that test your understanding of project management concepts and terminology. For example, "What is the difference between a milestone and a deliverable?"

Formula-based questions: These questions require you to apply mathematical formulas and calculations to solve a problem. For example, "What is the estimated cost of the project if the budget is $500,000, and the planned value is $400,000?"

How is the PMP Exam Scored? The PMP exam is scored on a scale of 0-200. To pass the exam, you need to score at least 141 out of 180 questions. The passing score is determined by a psychometric analysis process that ensures the fairness and reliability of the exam. The exam result will show whether you passed or failed; it will not show your exact score.

What are the Exam-Taking Strategies for the PMP Exam? Here are some exam-taking strategies that can help you pass the PMP exam:

Study the PMBOK Guide thoroughly: The PMBOK Guide is the primary source of exam content. It is recommended that you read the guide at least twice and understand all the concepts, processes, and techniques.

Use additional study materials: Besides the PMBOK Guide, you can use other study materials such as the PMP Exam Prep Simplified book and the 35-hour PMP e-learning course. These materials will provide you with additional insights, tips, and practice questions.

Practice with sample questions: Practice questions can help you familiarize yourself with the exam format and types of questions. The PMI website provides sample questions that you can use for practice.

Develop a study plan: Create a study plan that suits your learning style and schedule. Allocate enough time for each domain, and make sure you cover all the topics.

Take breaks during the exam: The exam can be stressful, and you may feel

Earned value management (EVM) is a crucial tool for project managers to track the progress of their projects and make data-driven decisions. EVM involves measuring and comparing the actual cost and work performed against the planned cost and work scheduled. By doing so, project managers can determine whether their projects are on track or not and take corrective actions if needed.

There are several types of EVM calculations, including:

Planned value (PV): This is the budgeted cost of the work scheduled to be completed at a certain point in time. PV is often referred to as the "budgeted cost of work scheduled" (BCWS).

For example, if a project has a total budget of $100,000 and the project manager plans to complete 50% of the work by the end of the first month, then the PV for the first month would be $50,000.

Actual cost (AC): This is the actual cost of the work performed to date. AC is often referred to as the "actual cost of work performed" (ACWP).

For example, if a project has a budget of $100,000 and the project manager has spent $40,000 to date, then the AC would be $40,000.

Earned value (EV): This is the budgeted cost of the work actually completed to date. EV is often referred to as the "budgeted cost of work performed" (BCWP).

For example, if a project has a budget of $100,000 and the project manager has completed 30% of the work, then the EV would be $30,000.

By comparing these values, project managers can calculate important performance metrics, such as schedule variance (SV), cost variance (CV), schedule performance index (SPI), and cost performance index (CPI).

SV measures the difference between the earned value and the planned value, while CV measures the difference between the earned value and the actual cost. SPI and CPI measure the project's efficiency in terms of schedule and cost, respectively. An SPI or CPI of 1 indicates that the project is on track, while values less than 1 indicate that the project is behind schedule or over budget.

It is important to note that EVM is just one tool in the project manager's toolkit. Other tools and techniques, such as risk management and issue management, are also important for project success.

Risk management involves identifying, analyzing, and responding to project risks. Risks are events or conditions that could have a negative impact on the project, such as budget overruns, schedule delays, or quality issues. Project managers use risk management techniques to minimize the likelihood or impact of these risks.

Issue management, on the other hand, involves identifying, analyzing, and resolving project issues. Issues are problems or challenges that have already occurred and need to be addressed, such as a team member leaving the project or a supplier failing to deliver on time. Project managers use issue management techniques to minimize the impact of these issues and keep the project on track.

When it comes to the PMP exam, it is important to approach each question with a clear understanding of the knowledge areas and process groups. The knowledge areas represent the different areas of expertise that project managers need to have, such as project integration management, project scope management, project time management, and so on.

The process groups, on the other hand, represent the different stages of a project, such as initiating, planning, executing, monitoring and controlling, and closing. It is important to understand the different processes within each process group and how they relate to the overall project.

As a PMP aspirant, it's important to have a solid understanding of the PMBOK Guide and the concepts and terminology covered in it. The PMBOK Guide is the primary reference for the PMP exam, and having a good grasp of it is crucial for passing the exam.

The PMBOK Guide provides a framework for managing projects and is divided into ten knowledge areas, including integration management, scope management, time management, cost management, quality management, resource management, communication management, risk management, procurement management, and stakeholder management. Each of these knowledge areas is further broken down into processes, inputs, outputs, tools, and techniques.

For example, the integration management knowledge area includes processes such as developing a project charter, developing a project management plan, directing and managing project work, monitoring and controlling project work, performing integrated change control, and closing a project or phase. The inputs for these processes may include project charters, stakeholder registers, and project management plans, while the outputs may include project documents, change requests, and work performance data. The tools and techniques used in these processes may include expert judgment, project management information systems, and change control tools.

It's important to thoroughly read and understand the PMBOK Guide and use it as a reference throughout the exam preparation. The guide should be used in conjunction with other study materials and the PMP Exam Content Outline (ECO). The ECO outlines the topics and knowledge areas that will be covered on the exam and should be reviewed to ensure all areas are adequately covered in the exam preparation.

In addition to understanding the PMBOK Guide and the ECO, exam-taking strategies should also be employed to improve exam performance. Some of these strategies include taking practice exams, managing time effectively during the exam, and reviewing and double-checking answers before submitting the exam.

Exam anxiety management is also important to address. Some strategies to manage exam anxiety include taking breaks during the exam, practicing relaxation techniques, and getting a good night's sleep before the exam.

Finally, it's important to be familiar with the ethical standards that guide the project management profession. The PMI Code of Ethics and Professional Conduct should be reviewed to ensure that ethical standards are upheld throughout the exam preparation and in the professional practice of project management.

Key concepts and formulas to remember

This section covers essential concepts and formulas that are frequently tested on the PMP exam. We will provide you with a concise summary of the 10 knowledge areas, 49 processes, and formulas related to earned value management. By understanding these crucial project management concepts, you will be better prepared to pass the PMP exam.

In this section of the book, you will find a concise summary of the key concepts and formulas related to project management that are frequently tested on the PMP exam. The section is designed to help you better understand these crucial concepts and improve your chances of passing the exam.

The section covers essential concepts and formulas related to the ten knowledge areas, which are as follows:

- Project Integration Management
- Project Scope Management
- Project Schedule Management
- Project Cost Management
- Project Quality Management
- Project Resource Management
- Project Communication Management

- Project Risk Management
- Project Procurement Management
- Project Stakeholder Management

For each of these knowledge areas, the section provides an overview of the key concepts and formulas that are important to understand. Additionally, the section covers formulas related to earned value management, which is an important topic on the PMP exam.

Some of the key concepts and formulas covered in this section include:

- Critical path method (CPM) calculations
- Cost variance (CV)
- Schedule variance (SV)
- Cost performance index (CPI)
- Schedule performance index (SPI)
- Estimate at completion (EAC)
- Estimate to complete (ETC)

Here are a few examples to help illustrate some of the concepts and formulas covered in this section:

Example 1: Let's say you are managing a project and your current project cost is $100,000. The project was supposed to be completed in 10 weeks, but it is now the end of week 8 and only 50% of the work has been completed. What is the cost variance (CV) and schedule variance (SV) for the project?

CV = Earned Value (EV) - Actual Cost (AC) = 50% of $100,000 - $100,000 = -$50,000 (negative value means over budget)

SV = Earned Value (EV) - Planned Value (PV) = 50% of $100,000 - 80% of $100,000 = -$10,000 (negative value means behind schedule)

Example 2: Let's say your project has a budget of $500,000 and you are currently halfway through the project timeline. The project has spent $300,000 so far and the work completed is estimated to be worth $250,000. What is the cost performance index (CPI) and schedule performance index (SPI) for the project?

CPI = Earned Value (EV) / Actual Cost (AC) = $250,000 / $300,000 = 0.83 (a value less than 1 means the project is over budget)

SPI = Earned Value (EV) / Planned Value (PV) = $250,000 / $250,000 = 1 (a value less than 1 means the project is behind schedule)

Project management is a vital process for ensuring the success of any project. The PMP (Project Management Professional) exam tests your knowledge of project management concepts, including the ability to apply various formulas. In this comprehensive guide, we will cover essential concepts and formulas related to project management, including practical tips and strategies for memorizing and applying them. Our goal is to provide you with a clear understanding of the exam material, so you can pass the PMP exam with flying colors.

One of the essential concepts in project management is the project life cycle. A project life cycle refers to the phases a project goes through from initiation to closure. There are typically five phases of a project life cycle: initiation, planning, execution, monitoring and controlling, and closure. The project life cycle provides a framework for managing a project and helps ensure that all necessary steps are taken to achieve project goals.

Another important concept in project management is the project charter. The project charter is a document that outlines the project's objectives, scope, and stakeholders. It is typically created during the initiation phase of the project life cycle and serves as a reference point throughout the project. The project charter is crucial because it helps ensure that all stakeholders have a clear understanding of the project's goals and objectives.

One formula that is frequently tested on the PMP exam is the Cost Performance Index (CPI). The CPI is a measure of a project's cost efficiency. It is calculated by dividing the earned value (EV) by the actual cost (AC). If the CPI is greater than one, it indicates that the project is under budget. If the CPI is less than one, it indicates that the project is over budget. For example, if a project has an EV of $100,000 and an AC of $120,000, the CPI would be 0.83, indicating that the project is over budget.

Another formula that is frequently tested on the PMP exam is the Schedule Performance Index (SPI). The SPI is a measure of a project's schedule efficiency. It is calculated by dividing the earned value (EV) by the planned value (PV). If the SPI is greater than one, it indicates that the project is ahead of schedule. If the SPI is less than one, it indicates that the project is behind schedule. For example, if a project has an EV of $100,000 and a PV of $120,000, the SPI would be 0.83, indicating that the project is behind schedule.

To memorize these formulas, you can use mnemonic devices or step-by-step methods. For example, to remember the CPI formula, you could use the acronym EV/AC (Earned Value over Actual Cost) and remember that if the result is greater than one, the project is under budget. Similarly, to remember the SPI formula, you could use the acronym EV/PV (Earned Value over Planned Value) and remember that if the result is greater than one, the project is ahead of schedule.

Ethics is another crucial aspect of project management. The PMP exam tests your knowledge of the PMI Code of Ethics and Professional Conduct. The code outlines four key values that project managers should uphold: responsibility, respect, fairness, and honesty. These values provide a framework for ethical behavior in project management and help ensure that all stakeholders are treated fairly and with respect.

Finally, to pass the PMP exam, you must also have a solid understanding of project management processes. The PMBOK (Project Management Body of Knowledge) Guide outlines 49 project management processes that are organized into five process groups: initiating, planning, executing, monitoring and controlling, and closing. Each process group contains a set of processes that are designed to help ensure that the project is completed successfully.

Practice questions and answers

This section includes a comprehensive set of practice questions designed to simulate the PMP exam. We have included detailed explanations and references to the PMBOK Guide, ECO 2021, and other relevant resources. Our practice questions cover all knowledge areas and process groups, allowing you to test your understanding and identify areas where you need further study.

In this section of the book, we will provide readers with a comprehensive set of practice questions designed to simulate the PMP exam. These questions will cover all knowledge areas and process groups, and will be accompanied by detailed explanations and references to the PMBOK Guide, ECO 2021, and other relevant resources.

The purpose of this section is to help readers test their understanding of the material and identify areas where they may need further study. By practicing these questions, readers can gain confidence in their ability to pass the PMP exam and improve their chances of success.

To ensure that our practice questions are as effective as possible, we will strive to make them as similar as possible to the actual PMP exam questions. This means that they will be written in the same format and style as the real exam questions, and will cover the same topics and knowledge areas.

Before we begin, to start familiarizing yourself with the exam, please answer these next 5 questions based on everything we have learned from the guide, once answered please look at the answer, once you have finished the 5 questions the 200+ practice questions will begin with the answer to prepare you with the exam, good luck:

1. What is the primary purpose of a project charter?

    a. To define the scope and objectives of the project

    b. To identify project risks and develop risk management strategies

    c. To create a detailed project plan and schedule

    d. To monitor and control project performance

Answer: a. To define the scope and objectives of the project

Explanation: The project charter is a document that formally authorizes the existence of a project and provides the project manager with the authority to apply organizational resources to project activities. The primary purpose of a project charter is to define the scope and objectives of the project, and to establish the project's high-level requirements, assumptions, and constraints.

2. Which of the following is NOT a tool or technique used in the Develop Project Charter process?

      a. Expert judgment

      b. Project selection methods

      c. Project management information system (PMIS)

      d. Project management plan

Answer: b. Project selection methods

Explanation: The Develop Project Charter process is the process of developing a document that formally authorizes the existence of a project and provides the project manager with the authority to apply organizational resources to project activities. Tools and techniques used in this process include expert judgment, PMIS, and project management plan. Project selection methods are not used in this process.

3. What is the purpose of a stakeholder register?

      a. To identify all project stakeholders and their roles

      b. To track stakeholder engagement levels throughout the project

      c. To document stakeholder requirements and expectations

      d. To analyze stakeholder influence and interest

Answer: a. To identify all project stakeholders and their roles

Explanation: A stakeholder register is a document that identifies all project stakeholders and provides details on their roles, responsibilities, and communication requirements. The purpose of the stakeholder register is to ensure that all stakeholders are identified and that their needs and expectations are understood and managed throughout the project. While stakeholder engagement levels, requirements, and influence are important considerations, the primary purpose of the stakeholder register is to identify stakeholders and their roles.

4. During which process group is the project schedule developed?

      a. Planning

      b. Execution

      c. Monitoring and controlling

      d. Closing

Answer: a. Planning

Explanation: The project schedule is developed during the Planning process group, specifically in the Develop Schedule process. This process involves analyzing activity sequences, durations, resource requirements, and schedule constraints to create a project schedule that meets the project objectives. The project schedule is an essential component of the project management plan and is used to guide project execution and monitoring and controlling activities.

5. Which of the following is NOT a responsibility of the project manager during the Close Project or Phase process?

 a. Reviewing project deliverables for completeness

 b. Documenting lessons learned

 c. Obtaining acceptance of project deliverables from the customer

 d. Developing the project charter

Answer: d. Developing the project charter

Explanation: The Close Project or Phase process is the final process group in the project management life cycle, and it involves closing out the project or project phase in a systematic way. The project manager's responsibilities during this process include reviewing project deliverables for completeness, obtaining acceptance of project deliverables from the customer, documenting lessons learned, and archiving project records. Developing the project charter is not a responsibility of the project manager during the Close Project or Phase process, as the project charter is developed during the Initiating process group.

TEST PMP EXAM

CATEGORY OF QUESTIONS	CONTENT	NUMBER OF QUESTIONS
SITUATIONAL	Scenarios and case studies that test the ability to apply the knowledge acquired in real situations.	40
KNOWLEDGE-BASED QUESTIONS	Questions that assess theoretical knowledge and understanding of project management concepts, processes and techniques.	26
FORMULA-BASED QUESTIONS	Questions that require the application of mathematical and statistical formulas used in project management.	18
INTERPERSONAL AND LEADERSHIP SKILLS	Questions that evaluate the candidate's leadership, communication and teamwork skills.	20

ETHICS AND PROFESSIONAL RESPONSIBILITY	Questions about the PMI Code of Ethics and Professional Conduct and its application in everyday project management situations.	**18**
Proficiency in Project Management		
Initiating		**24**
Planning		**25**
Executing		**25**
Monitoring and Controlling		**25**
Closing		**25**

SITUATIONAL

1. **Your project team is experiencing conflict over how to approach a crucial project issue. What conflict resolution technique should you use to help them reach a resolution?**

    a. Forcing

    b. Smoothing

    c. Compromising

    d. Collaborating

Answer: d. Collaborating

Explanation: Collaborating is a conflict resolution technique that involves working together to find a mutually acceptable solution. In this scenario, the project manager should encourage the team members to work together to identify the underlying issues causing the conflict and brainstorm solutions that meet the needs of all parties involved. This approach can lead to a more creative and effective solution that everyone can support.

2. **During the execution phase of your project, a key stakeholder expresses concern about the project timeline. They believe that the project is behind schedule and that the team needs to take immediate action to get back on track. What should you do as the project manager?**

    a. Ignore the stakeholder's concerns and focus on executing the project plan as planned.

    b. Schedule a meeting with the stakeholder to discuss their concerns and review the project schedule together.

    c. Immediately add additional resources to the project to speed up the timeline.

    d. Reassure the stakeholder that the project is on track and that any delays will be addressed during the monitoring and controlling phase.

Answer: b. Schedule a meeting with the stakeholder to discuss their concerns and review the project schedule together.

Explanation: As a project manager, it's important to listen to the concerns of stakeholders and take appropriate action to address them. In this scenario, the project manager should schedule a meeting with the stakeholder to discuss their concerns and review the project schedule together. This will allow the project manager to gain a better understanding of the stakeholder's concerns and identify any potential issues that need to be addressed to keep the project on track. It also demonstrates the project manager's commitment to communication and stakeholder engagement.

3. **How do you identify project risks?**

    a. By conducting a stakeholder analysis

b. By creating a work breakdown structure

c. By performing a SWOT analysis

d. By using a risk management plan

Answer: d. By using a risk management plan

Explanation: A risk management plan is a document that outlines the approach to identify, assess, and manage risks throughout the project. To identify project risks, the project team should use the risk management plan as a guide and perform risk identification techniques such as brainstorming, expert judgment, and historical information review. By using these techniques, the project team can identify potential events or situations that could have a positive or negative impact on the project objectives.

4.   **Your project team is experiencing conflict due to differences in communication styles. What actions will you take to resolve the conflict?**

a. Provide conflict resolution training to the team

b. Encourage team members to work separately

c. Assign a mediator to facilitate communication between team members

d. Change the project plan to accommodate communication preferences

Answer: c. Assign a mediator to facilitate communication between team members

Explanation: Conflict is a natural part of project teams, and it can arise due to various factors, such as differences in communication styles, cultural backgrounds, and personalities. To resolve the conflict, the project manager should first identify the root cause of the conflict and then select an appropriate conflict resolution technique. In this case, assigning a mediator to facilitate communication between team members can help to promote understanding and collaboration among team members with different communication styles.

5.   **What is the purpose of earned value management (EVM)?**

a. To measure project performance against the project plan

b. To identify project risks and develop risk management strategies

c. To allocate resources to project activities

d. To track project expenses

Answer: a. To measure project performance against the project plan

Explanation: Earned value management (EVM) is a project management technique that integrates scope, schedule, and cost measures to assess project performance and progress. The purpose of EVM is to provide project managers with a comprehensive view of project performance, and to enable them to make informed decisions based on accurate and timely data. EVM compares the actual project performance to the planned performance, and provides early warning signals if the project is behind schedule or over budget.

6. **Your project team is tasked with developing a new software application. During the planning phase, one of the team members suggests using an Agile approach instead of the traditional Waterfall approach. What should you do as the project manager?**

   a. Ignore the team member's suggestion and proceed with the Waterfall approach as planned.

   b. Conduct research on Agile and Waterfall methodologies and make an informed decision on which approach to use.

   c. Immediately switch to the Agile approach without conducting any further analysis or discussion.

   d. Acknowledge the team member's suggestion and explore the benefits and drawbacks of both approaches with the team.

Answer: d. Acknowledge the team member's suggestion and explore the benefits and drawbacks of both approaches with the team.

Explanation: As a project manager, it's important to encourage and consider suggestions from the project team. In this scenario, the project manager should acknowledge the team member's suggestion and facilitate a discussion to explore the benefits and drawbacks of both the Agile and Waterfall approaches with the team. This will allow the team to make an informed decision on which approach to use based on the unique characteristics of the project. It also demonstrates the project manager's commitment to collaboration and inclusiveness.

7. **Your project is running behind schedule, and you need to take action to get it back on track. One of your options is to fast-track the project by overlapping some of the activities. What should you consider before deciding to fast-track the project?**

   a. The impact on project quality and risk.

   b. The availability of resources to support fast-tracking.

   c. The impact on project costs and stakeholder expectations.

   d. All of the above.

Answer: d. All of the above.

Explanation: Fast-tracking a project can help to expedite the schedule, but it also has potential drawbacks that should be considered before making a decision. The project manager should consider the impact on project quality and risk, as fast-tracking may increase the likelihood of errors or issues. The availability of resources should also be considered, as fast-tracking may require additional resources to support the accelerated schedule. Finally, the impact on project costs and stakeholder expectations should also be evaluated, as fast-tracking may lead to increased costs or changes in stakeholder expectations.

8.   **Your project team is experiencing a high level of turnover, with several key team members leaving the project. What should you do as the project manager to mitigate the impact of this turnover?**

a. Work with human resources to recruit new team members as quickly as possible.

b. Re-evaluate the project plan and schedule to determine if adjustments need to be made.

c. Conduct a lessons learned session to identify the reasons for the turnover and address any issues that may have contributed to it.

d. All of the above.

Answer: d. All of the above.

Explanation: High turnover can have a significant impact on project performance, so it's important for the project manager to take appropriate action to mitigate its effects. This may include working with human resources to recruit new team members as quickly as possible, re-evaluating the project plan and schedule to determine if adjustments need to be made to account for the loss of key team members, and conducting a lessons learned session to identify the reasons for the turnover and address any issues that may have contributed to it. By taking these actions, the project manager can help to minimize the impact of turnover on the project and keep it on track.

9.   **Your project team is responsible for implementing a new software system that will be used by multiple departments within your organization. How will you ensure that the system is adopted and used effectively by all stakeholders?**

a. Develop a comprehensive training plan that covers all aspects of the system and provide ongoing support to users.

b. Force all stakeholders to use the system by implementing consequences for non-compliance.

c. Assume that stakeholders will naturally adopt the system and only provide minimal training.

d. Create a rewards program for stakeholders who successfully use the system.

Answer: a. Develop a comprehensive training plan that covers all aspects of the system and provide ongoing support to users.

Explanation: Change management is an important aspect of project management, and it's important to ensure that stakeholders are adequately prepared for changes in their work processes. In this scenario, the project manager should develop a comprehensive training plan that covers all aspects of the new software system and provide ongoing support to users. This will help stakeholders understand how to use the system effectively and minimize resistance to the change. It also demonstrates the project manager's commitment to supporting stakeholders through the transition.

10. **Your project team has been working on a crucial deliverable for several weeks, but the quality of the work is not up to the expected standard. What actions should you take as the project manager?**

   a. Review the work with the team and identify areas for improvement.

   b. Accept the work as is and move on to the next task.

   c. Assign blame to individual team members for the poor-quality work.

   d. Ignore the issue and hope that it doesn't impact the overall project outcome.

Answer: a. Review the work with the team and identify areas for improvement.

Explanation: Quality management is an important aspect of project management, and it's important to ensure that project deliverables meet the expected quality standards. In this scenario, the project manager should review the work with the team and identify areas for improvement. This will help the team understand what went wrong and how they can improve their work in the future. It also demonstrates the project manager's commitment to quality and continuous improvement.

11. **Your project team is responsible for implementing a new marketing campaign for a product launch. How will you measure the success of the campaign?**

   a. Use key performance indicators (KPIs) to track campaign performance against established goals.

   b. Ask stakeholders for their subjective opinions on the success of the campaign.

   c. Use social media metrics to gauge the popularity of the campaign.

   d. Use financial metrics to track the revenue generated by the campaign.

Answer: a. Use key performance indicators (KPIs) to track campaign performance against established goals.

Explanation: Project success should be measured against established goals and objectives. In this scenario, the project manager should use key performance indicators (KPIs) to track campaign performance against established goals. This will provide an objective measure of the campaign's success and allow the project manager to make data-driven decisions about future campaigns. It also demonstrates the project manager's commitment to performance measurement and accountability.

12. **Your project team is working on a crucial deliverable that is due in two weeks. One team member informs you that they will be taking a planned vacation during that time period. What should you do as the project manager?**

a. Tell the team member they cannot take their vacation and must work on the deliverable instead.

b. Allow the team member to take their vacation and assign another team member to complete their tasks.

c. Ask the team member to delay their vacation until after the deliverable is complete.

d. Re-evaluate the project schedule to see if the deadline can be extended to accommodate the team member's vacation.

Answer: d. Re-evaluate the project schedule to see if the deadline can be extended to accommodate the team member's vacation.

Explanation: As a project manager, it's important to balance the needs of the project with the needs of the team members. In this scenario, the project manager should evaluate the project schedule to see if the deadline can be extended to accommodate the team member's vacation. If the deadline cannot be extended, the project manager should consider assigning another team member to complete the tasks or finding other ways to mitigate the impact of the team member's absence. It's important to communicate the revised schedule and any changes to the team members and stakeholders to ensure that everyone is aware of the impact on the project.

13.   **Your project team is working on a complex software development project. During the testing phase, the team discovers a major defect that will require significant rework. What should you do as the project manager?**

a. Ask the team to ignore the defect and move forward with the project as planned.

b. Assign blame to the team member responsible for the defect and reprimand them.

c. Work with the team to identify the root cause of the defect and develop a plan to address it.

d. Terminate the project immediately to avoid any further defects.

Answer: c. Work with the team to identify the root cause of the defect and develop a plan to address it.

Explanation: When a major defect is discovered in a project, it's important to take immediate action to address it. As a project manager, you should work with the team to identify the root cause of the defect and develop a plan to address it. This may involve additional testing, rework, or other corrective actions. It's important to communicate the impact of the defect and any changes to the project schedule or budget to stakeholders. Assigning blame or ignoring the defect will not solve the problem and may have negative consequences for the project.

14.   **Your project team is working on a construction project in a remote location with limited access to resources. During the execution phase, one of the key pieces of equipment breaks down and cannot be repaired on site. What should you do as the project manager?**

142

a. Delay the project until the equipment can be repaired or replaced.

b. Hire a local contractor to complete the work using their equipment.

c. Change the project scope to exclude the work that requires the broken equipment.

d. Find a way to repair or replace the equipment to continue with the project.

Answer: d. Find a way to repair or replace the equipment to continue with the project.

Explanation: In a remote location with limited access to resources, it may not be feasible to delay the project or hire a local contractor. Changing the project scope may also not be an option if the work is crucial to the project's success. As a project manager, you should work with the team to find a way to repair or replace the equipment to continue with the project. This may involve bringing in replacement equipment from another location, renting equipment, or finding alternative ways to complete the work. It's important to consider the impact on the project schedule and budget and communicate any changes to stakeholders.

15.   **Your project is in the closing phase and you need to obtain final acceptance from the customer. What is the best way to obtain final acceptance?**

a. Schedule a meeting with the customer to review the project deliverables and obtain sign-off.

b. Send the customer an email asking for final acceptance.

c. Assume that final acceptance has been obtained because the project has been completed.

d. Ask the project team to obtain final acceptance from the customer.

Answer: a. Schedule a meeting with the customer to review the project deliverables and obtain sign-off.

Explanation: Final acceptance is a crucial component of the project closing phase, as it signifies the customer's acceptance that the project has been completed in accordance with the project scope and requirements. The best way to obtain final acceptance is to schedule a meeting with the customer to review the project deliverables and obtain sign-off. This allows for any final issues or concerns to be addressed and ensures that both the project team and customer are in agreement regarding the completion of the project. It also provides a formal record of the customer's acceptance, which can be used for future reference or in case of any disputes.

16.   **Your project has identified several risks that may impact the project's success. What is the best way to manage these risks?**

a. Avoid the risks by changing the project scope or approach.

b. Transfer the risks to a third party.

c. Mitigate the risks by implementing risk response plans.

d. Accept the risks and hope that they do not occur.

Answer: c. Mitigate the risks by implementing risk response plans.

Explanation: Risk management is a crucial component of project management, as it helps identify potential risks that may impact the project's success and implement strategies to manage or mitigate them. The best way to manage risks is to implement risk response plans, which involve taking proactive measures to minimize the likelihood and impact of identified risks. This may include developing contingency plans, implementing workarounds, or allocating additional resources to mitigate the risks. Avoiding the risks by changing the project scope or approach may not be feasible or practical, and accepting the risks without any mitigation strategies can lead to negative consequences for the project.

17. **Your project team is struggling to complete a crucial task within the designated timeline. The team members have already put in significant effort, but the task remains incomplete. What action should you take as the project manager?**

   a. Reprimand the team members for not completing the task on time.

   b. Adjust the project timeline to accommodate the delay.

   c. Reallocate resources to the task to help the team complete it on time.

   d. Work with the team to identify the root cause of the delay and develop a plan to address it.

Answer: d. Work with the team to identify the root cause of the delay and develop a plan to address it.

Explanation: It's important for project managers to take a proactive approach to addressing project delays. In this scenario, the project manager should work with the team to identify the root cause of the delay and develop a plan to address it. This may involve re-sequencing tasks, re-allocating resources, or adjusting the project schedule. By working collaboratively with the team, the project manager can help ensure that the project stays on track and that team morale remains high.

18. **Your project team is working on a crucial task when a key team member unexpectedly resigns. The team member had unique skills and knowledge that are crucial to the task's completion. What should you do as the project manager?**

   a. Ignore the situation and hope that the team can complete the task without the missing team member.

   b. Reassign the task to another team member without providing any additional support.

   c. Bring in a new team member with the necessary skills and knowledge to complete the task.

   d. Work with the team to identify any potential workarounds or alternative approaches that can be used to complete the task.

Answer: d. Work with the team to identify any potential workarounds or alternative approaches that can be used to complete the task.

Explanation: Losing a key team member can be a significant challenge for any project. In this scenario, the project manager should work with the team to identify any potential workarounds or alternative approaches that can be used to complete the task. This may involve re-sequencing tasks, re-allocating resources, or adjusting the project schedule. By working collaboratively with the team, the project manager can help ensure that the project stays on track and that team morale remains high.

19. **Your project team has identified a potential risk that could have a significant impact on the project's timeline and budget. What should you do as the project manager?**

a. Ignore the risk and hope that it doesn't materialize.

b. Develop a contingency plan to address the risk if it materializes.

c. Immediately terminate the project to avoid any potential negative impacts.

d. Reallocate resources to the task to help mitigate the risk.

Answer: b. Develop a contingency plan to address the risk if it materializes.

Explanation: Risks are an inherent part of any project, and it's important for project managers to be proactive in identifying and addressing them. In this scenario, the project manager should develop a contingency plan to address the risk if it materializes. This may involve adjusting the project schedule, re-allocating resources, or implementing additional controls to mitigate the risk. By taking a proactive approach, the project manager can help ensure that the project stays on track and that any potential negative impacts are minimized.

20. **You are the project manager of a software development project, and your team has just discovered a crucial defect in the software code during the testing phase. What is the first thing you should do?**

a. Notify the project sponsor and stakeholders immediately.

b. Work with the team to develop a plan to fix the defect.

c. Evaluate the impact of the defect on the project schedule and budget.

d. Stop all work on the project until the defect is resolved.

Answer: b. Work with the team to develop a plan to fix the defect.

Explanation: When a crucial defect is discovered, the project manager should work with the team to develop a plan to fix it as soon as possible. This includes identifying the root cause of the defect, developing a plan to address it, and prioritizing the fix based on its impact on the project schedule and budget. While it is important to keep the project sponsor and stakeholders informed, the focus should be on resolving the issue as quickly as possible to minimize its impact on the project.

21. **Your project is running behind schedule, and the project sponsor has asked you to provide a revised project schedule that shows how the project can be completed on time. What tool or technique can you use to develop this revised schedule?**

    a. Critical Path Method (CPM)

    b. Earned Value Management (EVM)

    c. Monte Carlo Simulation

    d. Ishikawa Diagram

Answer: a. Critical Path Method (CPM)

Explanation: The Critical Path Method (CPM) is a project management tool used to identify the activities that are critical to the project's success and determine the shortest possible duration for completing the project. This tool can be used to develop a revised project schedule that shows how the project can be completed on time. By identifying the critical path and determining which activities can be accelerated, delayed, or eliminated, the project manager can create a realistic schedule that meets the project sponsor's requirements.

22. **You are the project manager of a construction project, and you have just received a change request from the project sponsor to add an additional floor to the building. What is the first thing you should do?**

    a. Evaluate the impact of the change on the project scope, schedule, and budget.

    b. Immediately reject the change request as it was not included in the original project scope.

    c. Work with the team to develop a plan to incorporate the change into the project.

    d. Consult the project charter to determine if the change is within the project's scope.

Answer: a. Evaluate the impact of the change on the project scope, schedule, and budget.

Explanation: When a change request is received, the project manager should evaluate its impact on the project scope, schedule, and budget before making any decisions. This includes assessing the feasibility of the change, identifying any additional resources that may be required, and determining how the change will affect the overall project timeline. Based on this evaluation, the project manager can determine whether the change is feasible and what steps need to be taken to incorporate it into the project.

23. **You are the project manager for a software development project. During the planning phase, one of your team members suggests that you use an agile approach to manage the project. What is an advantage of using an agile approach for software development projects?**

    a. Agile approaches prioritize comprehensive documentation over working software.

    b. Agile approaches require a detailed project plan before work can begin.

c. Agile approaches allow for more flexibility and adaptability to changing requirements.

d. Agile approaches are only suitable for small projects with limited scope.

Answer: c. Agile approaches allow for more flexibility and adaptability to changing requirements.

Explanation: Agile approaches are designed to be flexible and adaptive to changing requirements throughout the project. This is particularly useful in software development projects where requirements can change frequently. Agile approaches prioritize working software over comprehensive documentation, allowing the team to focus on delivering functionality that meets the customer's needs. While a project plan is still important in agile projects, it is less detailed and more adaptable to change than in traditional project management approaches. Agile approaches can be used on projects of any size and scope, as long as they are well-suited to an iterative and incremental approach to development.

24. **During the closing phase of your project, you realize that one of your team members did not complete their assigned tasks on time, causing delays to the project schedule. What should you do as the project manager?**

a. Ignore the issue and focus on closing out the project.

b. Document the team member's performance issues and address them during their next performance review.

c. Hold a meeting with the team member to discuss the issue and identify any underlying causes.

d. Terminate the team member's employment immediately.

Answer: c. Hold a meeting with the team member to discuss the issue and identify any underlying causes.

Explanation: As a project manager, it's important to address performance issues as they arise to minimize the impact on the project. In this scenario, the project manager should hold a meeting with the team member to discuss the issue and identify any underlying causes. This will allow the project manager to understand why the team member was not able to complete their tasks on time and identify any potential solutions to prevent similar issues in the future. Terminating the team member's employment should only be considered as a last resort, and after other options such as reassignment or additional training have been explored.

25. **Your project has encountered a significant issue that requires a change to the project scope. What should you do as the project manager?**

a. Ignore the issue and hope that it resolves itself.

b. Implement the scope change without consulting the project sponsor or other stakeholders.

147

c. Assess the impact of the scope change on the project schedule, budget, and other constraints.

d. Delay the project until the issue can be resolved without changing the project scope.

Answer: c. Assess the impact of the scope change on the project schedule, budget, and other constraints.

Explanation: When a significant issue arises that requires a change to the project scope, it's important to assess the impact of the change on the project schedule, budget, and other constraints. This will allow the project manager to determine the feasibility of the change and identify any potential risks or issues that need to be addressed. Implementing the scope change without consulting the project sponsor or other stakeholders can lead to misunderstandings and conflict, while ignoring the issue or delaying the project can lead to missed deadlines and budget overruns. As such, assessing the impact of the scope change and communicating with stakeholders is the best course of action.

26. **Your project sponsor has just informed you that the budget has been reduced by 20%. What actions will you take to ensure that the project stays on track?**

a. Reduce the scope of the project

b. Increase the project schedule

c. Request additional funding from the sponsor

d. Revisit the project requirements to identify potential cost savings

Answer: d. Revisit the project requirements to identify potential cost savings

Explanation: When faced with a budget reduction, the project manager should first assess the impact of the change on the project's objectives and scope. If the budget reduction requires a change in scope, the project manager should work with the stakeholders to identify the most crucial project requirements and prioritize them based on their business value. If the budget reduction can be addressed without a change in scope, the project manager should review the project requirements to identify areas where cost savings can be achieved without compromising quality or functionality.

27. **Your project team is experiencing conflict over how to approach a crucial project issue. What conflict resolution technique should you use to help them reach a resolution?**

a. Forcing

b. Smoothing

c. Compromising

d. Collaborating

Answer: d. Collaborating

Explanation: Collaborating is a conflict resolution technique that involves working together to find a mutually acceptable solution. In this scenario, the project manager should encourage the team members to work together to identify the underlying issues causing the conflict and brainstorm solutions that meet the needs of all parties involved. This approach can lead to a more creative and effective solution that everyone can support.

28. **You are managing a project that involves developing a new product. During the project planning phase, you realize that the product design requires a new manufacturing process that is not currently available in your organization. What should you do?**

   a. Hire external consultants to develop the manufacturing process

   b. Revisit the product design to eliminate the need for the new manufacturing process

   c. Delay the project until the new manufacturing process can be developed

   d. Work with the stakeholders to identify alternative manufacturing processes that are available in the organization

Answer: d. Work with the stakeholders to identify alternative manufacturing processes that are available in the organization

Explanation: When faced with a resource constraint, the project manager should first assess the impact of the change on the project's objectives and scope. If the resource constraint requires a change in scope, the project manager should work with the stakeholders to identify the most crucial project requirements and prioritize them based on their business value. If the resource constraint can be addressed without a change in scope, the project manager should review the available resources to identify alternatives that can be used to achieve the project objectives.

29. **Your team is behind schedule on a crucial task. What actions can you take to get the project back on track?**

   a. Increase the number of resources assigned to the task

   b. Reduce the scope of the task

   c. Increase the duration of the task

   d. All of the above

Answer: It depends on the specific situation, but option d. All of the above could be possible solutions.

Explanation: If the team is behind schedule on a crucial task, the project manager needs to analyze the situation and determine the best course of action. Increasing the number of resources assigned to the task could help get it done faster, but this may not always be feasible due to resource availability or budget constraints. Reducing the scope of the task could also be an option, but this may impact the quality of the project deliverables. Finally, increasing the duration of the task could provide more time to complete it, but this could impact the overall project schedule. The project manager should weigh the pros and cons of each option and choose the one that will have the least negative impact on the project.

30. **Your project sponsor has just informed you that the project's budget has been reduced by 20%. What actions will you take to ensure that the project stays on track?**

    a. Reduce the project scope

    b. Negotiate with the sponsor for additional funding

    c. Re-estimate the remaining work to see if it can be completed within the new budget

    d. All of the above

Answer: c. Re-estimate the remaining work to see if it can be completed within the new budget

Explanation: If the project's budget has been reduced, the project manager needs to re-evaluate the project plan and determine if it can still be completed within the new budget. This involves re-estimating the remaining work and adjusting the project plan accordingly. If the remaining work cannot be completed within the new budget, then the project scope may need to be reduced. Negotiating with the sponsor for additional funding could also be an option, but this may not always be possible due to budget constraints. The project manager should prioritize the crucial project tasks and ensure that they are completed within the new budget.

31. **Your project team is experiencing communication issues. What actions can you take to improve communication within the team?**

    a. Schedule regular team meetings to discuss project progress and issues

    b. Encourage open and honest communication

    c. Use a communication plan to define roles and responsibilities for communication

    d. All of the above

Answer: d. All of the above

Explanation: To improve communication within the project team, the project manager should schedule regular team meetings to discuss project progress and issues. Encouraging open and honest communication is also important, as it can help team members feel comfortable sharing their thoughts and concerns. Using a communication plan to define roles and responsibilities for communication can also help ensure that everyone is on the same page and knows what is expected of them. The project manager should also use effective communication techniques, such as active listening and clarifying questions, to ensure that everyone understands the project goals and requirements.

32. **Your project team is working remotely due to the COVID-19 pandemic. What actions can you take to ensure that the project stays on track?**

a. Use collaboration tools to facilitate communication and collaboration

b. Set clear expectations for project deliverables and deadlines

c. Monitor team progress and provide regular feedback

d. All of the above

Answer: d. All of the above

Explanation: Working remotely can present unique challenges for project teams, but there are several actions that the project manager can take to ensure that the project stays on track. Using collaboration tools, such as video conferencing and online project management software, can help facilitate communication and collaboration among team members. Setting clear expectations

33. One of your team members has consistently been underperforming and failing to meet project deadlines. What actions should you take as the project manager?

a. Ignore the team member's performance issues and hope that they will improve on their own.

b. Provide the team member with additional training and resources to help improve their performance.

c. Address the team member's performance issues through coaching and feedback, and if necessary, take disciplinary action.

d. Reassign the team member to a different role within the project to minimize the impact of their performance issues.

Answer: c. Address the team member's performance issues through coaching and feedback, and if necessary, take disciplinary action.

Explanation: As a project manager, it's important to address performance issues as they arise to minimize the impact on the project. In this scenario, the project manager should address the team member's performance issues through coaching and feedback, providing support and resources to help improve their performance. If the team member's performance continues to be a problem, the project manager may need to take disciplinary action in accordance with the organization's policies and procedures. Reassigning the team member may not be the best solution if their performance issues are not addressed and resolved, as they may continue to underperform in their new role.

34. A change request has been submitted by a stakeholder that would significantly impact the project scope and budget. What steps should you take as the project manager?

a. Reject the change request and inform the stakeholder that it is outside of the project scope.

b. Approve the change request without conducting an analysis of its impact on the project.

c. Analyze the impact of the change request on the project scope, schedule, and budget, and consult with stakeholders before making a decision.

d. Approve the change request without consulting with stakeholders or analyzing its impact on the project.

Answer: c. Analyze the impact of the change request on the project scope, schedule, and budget, and consult with stakeholders before making a decision.

Explanation: As a project manager, it's important to carefully consider the impact of any change request on the project before making a decision. In this scenario, the project manager should analyze the impact of the change request on the project scope, schedule, and budget, and consult with stakeholders before making a decision. This will allow the project manager to understand the potential consequences of the change request and make an informed decision that balances the needs of the stakeholder with the project objectives. Approving the change request without analysis or consultation can lead to scope creep, budget overruns, and delays. Rejecting the change request outright may not be appropriate if it aligns with the project objectives and can be accommodated within the project constraints.

35.   **Your project team is experiencing high turnover rates, with several team members leaving the project within the past few weeks. What actions should you take as the project manager to address this issue?**

   a. Ignore the turnover and continue with the project as planned, assuming that new team members will be able to catch up quickly.

   b. Conduct an investigation into the reasons for the turnover and take steps to address any underlying issues, such as low morale or poor team dynamics.

   c. Immediately hire new team members to replace those who have left, without conducting any analysis into the causes of the turnover.

   d. Ask the remaining team members to take on additional responsibilities to compensate for the loss of team members.

Answer: b. Conduct an investigation into the reasons for the turnover and take steps to address any underlying issues, such as low morale or poor team dynamics.

Explanation: High turnover rates can be a sign of underlying issues within the project team or organization. As a project manager, it's important to investigate the reasons for the turnover and take appropriate steps to address any issues that may be contributing to it. This could involve conducting surveys or interviews with team members to get feedback on their experiences, or working with HR to address any broader organizational issues that may be affecting team morale. Ignoring the turnover or simply hiring new team members without addressing the underlying issues is unlikely to be an effective solution and may ultimately lead to additional turnover.

36.   **Your project team is comprised of individuals from diverse backgrounds and cultures. During a team meeting, you notice that some team members appear uncomfortable and**

are not participating in the discussion. **What actions will you take to encourage team participation and collaboration?**

a. Ignore the situation and continue with the meeting as planned.

b. Address the situation directly with the unengaged team members and ask for their input.

c. Modify the meeting agenda to accommodate the cultural differences of the team members.

d. Assign additional tasks to the unengaged team members to motivate them to participate.

Answer: b. Address the situation directly with the unengaged team members and ask for their input.

Explanation: As a project manager, it is important to recognize and address communication and collaboration issues within the project team. In this scenario, the project manager should directly address the unengaged team members to understand the root cause of their discomfort and encourage their participation. This can help to foster a collaborative environment where all team members feel valued and can contribute to the project's success. Option C is a possible solution but it may not necessarily address the root cause of the problem, and Option D can lead to increased workload and potential resentment from the team members.

37. **Your team has just completed a major deliverable on the project, but you've noticed that there are some errors in the work. What should you do as the project manager?**

a. Ignore the errors and move forward with the project as planned.

b. Correct the errors yourself to ensure that the project stays on track.

c. Assign someone else on the team to correct the errors.

d. Work with the team to identify the root cause of the errors and develop a plan to correct them.

Answer: d. Work with the team to identify the root cause of the errors and develop a plan to correct them.

Explanation: As a project manager, it's important to ensure that the project deliverables are of high quality and meet the project requirements. In this scenario, the project manager should work with the team to identify the root cause of the errors and develop a plan to correct them. This will help to prevent similar errors from occurring in the future and ensure that the project remains on track. Ignoring the errors or correcting them yourself may result in further issues down the line, and assigning someone else to correct them without identifying the root cause may not address the underlying issue.

38. **During the planning phase of your project, you realize that one of your key deliverables requires a specialized skill set that your team doesn't currently possess. What should you do as the project manager?**

a. Reduce the scope of the deliverable to eliminate the need for the specialized skill set.

b. Assign the task to a team member who has some experience in the area and hope for the best.

c. Hire a contractor with the required skill set to complete the deliverable.

d. Provide training or professional development opportunities to team members to acquire the required skill set.

Answer: c. Hire a contractor with the required skill set to complete the deliverable.

Explanation: When faced with a skills gap in the team, the project manager should consider hiring a contractor with the required skill set to complete the deliverable. This ensures that the project remains on track and that the quality of the deliverable is not compromised. It is important to carefully evaluate and select the contractor to ensure that they have the necessary qualifications and experience. The other options, such as reducing the scope of the deliverable or assigning the task to a team member with little experience, may lead to suboptimal results and negatively impact the project's success. Providing training or professional development opportunities can be a good long-term solution, but it may not be feasible in the short term when the project is time-sensitive.

39. **Your project team is in the planning phase and is working on identifying all of the project risks. One team member suggests that the project team should also identify opportunities in addition to risks. What should you do as the project manager?**

a. Thank the team member for their suggestion, but explain that the project team does not have the time to identify opportunities at this stage.

b. Dismiss the team member's suggestion and focus solely on identifying risks.

c. Encourage the team member's suggestion and ask them to lead a discussion on identifying project opportunities.

d. Ignore the team member's suggestion and focus solely on the project risks identified by the team.

Answer: c. Encourage the team member's suggestion and ask them to lead a discussion on identifying project opportunities.

Explanation: Identifying project opportunities in addition to risks can help the project team to maximize the potential benefits of the project. As a project manager, it's important to encourage team members to share their ideas and perspectives. By asking the team member to lead a discussion on identifying opportunities, the project manager is not only demonstrating their support for the team member's suggestion but also providing an opportunity for the team member to develop their leadership skills. It also shows a commitment to fostering a collaborative team environment where all ideas are valued.

40. **Your team is working on a project to develop a new software application. During the testing phase, several bugs are discovered that will require additional work to fix.**

However, fixing the bugs will delay the project schedule and potentially impact the budget. What should you do as the project manager?

a. Ignore the bugs and continue with the project schedule as planned.

b. Delay the project schedule to fix the bugs immediately.

c. Conduct a cost-benefit analysis to determine the impact of fixing the bugs on the project schedule and budget.

d. Ask the team to work overtime to fix the bugs and meet the original project schedule.

Answer: c. Conduct a cost-benefit analysis to determine the impact of fixing the bugs on the project schedule and budget.

Explanation: In this scenario, the project manager should conduct a cost-benefit analysis to determine the impact of fixing the bugs on the project schedule and budget. This will help the project manager make an informed decision on whether to fix the bugs immediately or delay the project schedule. By conducting the analysis, the project manager can weigh the potential costs of fixing the bugs, such as increased labor and materials, against the potential benefits, such as improved quality and customer satisfaction. This will enable the project manager to make a well-informed decision that balances the needs of the project and the stakeholders.

KNOWLEDGE-BASED QUESTIONS

41. **What is the difference between a milestone and a deliverable?**

a. A milestone is a significant point in the project schedule that represents the completion of a major task or phase, while a deliverable is a tangible outcome or result that is produced as part of the project.

b. A milestone is a tangible outcome or result that is produced as part of the project, while a deliverable is a significant point in the project schedule that represents the completion of a major task or phase.

c. A milestone and a deliverable are the same thing and can be used interchangeably in project management.

d. A milestone is a point in the project schedule that represents the completion of a minor task, while a deliverable is a point in the project schedule that represents the completion of a major task or phase.

Answer: a. A milestone is a significant point in the project schedule that represents the completion of a major task or phase, while a deliverable is a tangible outcome or result that is produced as part of the project.

Explanation: A milestone is a specific point in time during a project where a major achievement or stage has been completed, while a deliverable is a specific output or result that is produced as part of the project. Milestones are used to track progress and measure the success of the project, while deliverables are the tangible outcomes that are expected from the project. Knowing the difference between milestones and deliverables is important for project managers to effectively plan and track the progress of their projects.

42.   What is the difference between a project and a program?

a. A project is a temporary endeavor undertaken to create a unique product, service, or result, while a program is a group of related projects managed in a coordinated way to obtain benefits and control not available from managing them individually.

b. A project is a group of related initiatives undertaken to achieve a specific objective, while a program is a large-scale effort to achieve a strategic goal.

c. A project is a long-term endeavor aimed at creating a sustainable outcome, while a program is a short-term initiative focused on achieving immediate results.

d. A project is a series of sequential tasks designed to deliver a specific output, while a program is a set of activities designed to improve organizational performance.

Answer: a. A project is a temporary endeavor undertaken to create a unique product, service, or result, while a program is a group of related projects managed in a coordinated way to obtain benefits and control not available from managing them individually.

Explanation: Understanding the difference between a project and a program is important in project management. A project is a temporary endeavor that has a defined beginning and end and is undertaken to create a unique product, service, or result. On the other hand, a program is a group of related projects that are managed in a coordinated way to obtain benefits and control not available from managing them individually. Programs are often used to achieve strategic goals and objectives, and they may involve multiple projects, as well as ongoing operations and maintenance activities. Therefore, option a is the correct answer as it accurately defines both project and program, and shows the difference between them.

43.   What is the primary benefit of a project charter?

a. It outlines the detailed project plan

b. It provides a high-level overview of the project goals and objectives

c. It lists all the project stakeholders

d. It defines the roles and responsibilities of the project team

Answer: b. It provides a high-level overview of the project goals and objectives

Explanation: A project charter is a document that provides a high-level overview of the project goals and objectives, including the project scope, budget, timeline, and major deliverables. It also defines the project stakeholders and their roles and responsibilities. The primary benefit of a project charter is that it helps to ensure that all stakeholders have a clear understanding of the project goals and objectives.

44.   Which of the following is NOT a project constraint?

   a. Scope

   b. Quality

   c. Resources

   d. Creativity

Answer: d. Creativity

Explanation: Project constraints are factors that limit the ability to achieve the project goals and objectives. The three primary project constraints are scope, time, and resources. Quality is sometimes considered a fourth constraint, as it is often impacted by the other constraints. Creativity is not a project constraint.

45.   Which of the following is a tool used for risk identification?

   a. Ishikawa diagram

   b. Pareto chart

   c. SWOT analysis

   d. Brainstorming

Answer: d. Brainstorming

Explanation: Brainstorming is a tool used for risk identification. It is a technique in which a group of people come together to generate ideas and potential solutions to a problem. In the context of project management, it can be used to identify potential risks and develop risk response plans.

46.   What is the difference between a milestone and a deliverable?

   a. Milestones are completed activities, while deliverables are measurable results

   b. Deliverables are completed activities, while milestones are measurable results

   c. Milestones are project goals, while deliverables are project objectives

   d. Deliverables are project goals, while milestones are project objectives

Answer: a. Milestones are completed activities, while deliverables are measurable results

Explanation: Milestones are significant events or achievements in a project that mark progress towards the project goals. They are often used to track and communicate project status. Deliverables are tangible results that are produced by the project, such as a report, software, or hardware. They are often used to measure project success.

47. **During the planning phase of your project, you identify a potential risk and develop a plan to mitigate it. However, during the execution phase, the risk actually occurs. What should you do?**

   a. Implement the risk response plan that was developed during the planning phase

   b. Develop a new risk response plan to address the risk

   c. Ignore the risk and continue with the project plan as planned

   d. Stop the project and re-evaluate the project plan

Answer: a. Implement the risk response plan that was developed during the planning phase

Explanation: When a risk occurs, it's important to implement the risk response plan that was developed during the planning phase. This plan should outline the actions that need to be taken to minimize the impact of the risk. If the risk response plan is not effective, a new plan may need to be developed to address the risk.

48. **Which of the following is NOT a type of dependency in project management?**

   a. Mandatory dependency

   b. Discretionary dependency

   c. External dependency

   d. Internal dependency

Answer: d. Internal dependency

Explanation: All other options are valid types of dependencies in project management. A mandatory dependency is one that must be completed before the successor activity can begin, a discretionary dependency is one that is preferred but not mandatory, and an external dependency is one that is outside of the project team's control.

49. **What is the difference between a risk and an issue in project management?**

   a. A risk is a potential future event, while an issue is a current problem.

   b. A risk is a positive event, while an issue is a negative event.

   c. A risk is a certain event, while an issue is a potential future event.

   d. A risk and an issue are the same thing.

Answer: a. A risk is a potential future event, while an issue is a current problem.

Explanation: Risks are uncertain events that may happen in the future and can have positive or negative impacts on the project. Issues, on the other hand, are current problems that need to be resolved to keep the project on track.

50. **Which of the following is NOT a type of power in project management?**

a. Coercive power

b. Reward power

c. Expert power

d. Emotional power

Answer: d. Emotional power

Explanation: Emotional power is not a recognized type of power in project management. Coercive power is based on the ability to punish, reward power is based on the ability to reward, and expert power is based on knowledge and expertise.

51.   What is the formula for calculating the expected monetary value (EMV) of a project?

a. EMV = P x V

b. EMV = P / V

c. EMV = P + V

d. EMV = P – V

Answer: a. EMV = P x V

Explanation: The expected monetary value (EMV) of a project is calculated by multiplying the probability (P) of a particular outcome by the value (V) of that outcome.

52.   What is the difference between a change request and a change order in project management?

a. A change request is a formal written document, while a change order is a verbal agreement.

b. A change request is a formal written document submitted to the project sponsor, while a change order is a formal written document submitted to the project team.

c. A change request is a request for a change to the project scope, while a change order is a request for a change to the project schedule.

d. A change request and a change order are the same thing.

Answer: b. A change request is a formal written document submitted to the project sponsor, while a change order is a formal written document submitted to the project team.

Explanation: A change request is a formal written document submitted to the project sponsor requesting a change to the project scope, schedule, or budget. A change order is a formal written document submitted to the project team authorizing the change requested in the change request.

53.   What is the primary objective of the Plan Quality Management process?

a. To define how quality will be measured

b. To define the quality standards for the project

c. To implement the quality control activities

d. To develop the quality management plan

Answer: d. To develop the quality management plan

Explanation: Although defining quality standards and measuring quality are important, the primary objective of Plan Quality Management is to develop a quality management plan that will guide the quality assurance and control activities for the project.

54. **Which of the following is NOT a characteristic of a project?**

a. Temporary

b. Unique

c. Ongoing

d. Cross-functional

Answer: c. Ongoing

Explanation: A project is defined as a temporary endeavor to create a unique product, service, or result. Projects have a defined start and end date, and are not ongoing.

55. **Which of the following is NOT a tool or technique of the Identify Stakeholders process?**

a. Stakeholder analysis

b. Expert judgment

c. Brainstorming

d. Project charter

Answer: d. Project charter

Explanation: The Identify Stakeholders process uses tools and techniques such as stakeholder analysis, expert judgment, and brainstorming to identify stakeholders. The project charter is a document that authorizes the project and is created during the Develop Project Charter process.

56. **Which of the following is NOT an output of the Plan Procurement Management process?**

a. Procurement management plan

b. Procurement documents

c. Source selection criteria

d. Project schedule

Answer: d. Project schedule

Explanation: The Plan Procurement Management process produces outputs such as the procurement management plan, procurement documents, and source selection criteria. The project schedule is not an output of this process.

57.   Which of the following is NOT a type of power in the context of stakeholder management?

a. Legitimate power

b. Expert power

c. Reward power

d. Conformity power

Answer: d. Conformity power

Explanation: The four types of power in stakeholder management are legitimate power, expert power, reward power, and coercive power. Conformity power is not a recognized type of power in this context.

58.   Which of the following is NOT a component of the Cost of Quality?

a. Prevention costs

b. Appraisal costs

c. Failure costs

d. Maintenance costs

Answer: d. Maintenance costs

Explanation: The three components of the Cost of Quality are prevention costs, appraisal costs, and failure costs. Maintenance costs are not considered a part of the Cost of Quality.

59.   Which of the following is NOT an input to the Plan Risk Responses process?

a. Risk management plan

b. Risk register

c. Stakeholder register

d. Enterprise environmental factors

Answer: c. Stakeholder register

Explanation: Inputs to the Plan Risk Responses process include the risk management plan, risk register, and enterprise environmental factors. The stakeholder register is not an input to this process.

60.   Which of the following is NOT a project constraint?

a. Scope

b. Quality

c. Cost

d. Time

e. Risk

Answer: b. (Quality) Explanation: Scope, cost, time, and risk are all considered project constraints because they can impact the project's overall success. Quality is not a constraint but is considered a project objective.

61. **Which type of contract places the most risk on the seller?**

a. Fixed Price

b. Cost Plus Fixed Fee

c. Time and Material

d. Cost Plus Incentive Fee

e. None of the above

Answer: c. (Time and Material) Explanation: A time and material contract places the most risk on the seller because the final cost is unknown, and the seller is responsible for any cost overruns.

62. **Which of the following is an example of a project assumption?**

a. The project team will consist of five members.

b. The project will be completed within six months.

c. The project will require a budget of $100,000.

d. The project will be executed using the agile methodology.

e. None of the above.

Answer: D (The project will be executed using the agile methodology.)

Explanation: A project assumption is a factor that is considered to be true but has not yet been proven or validated. The assumption that the project will be executed using the agile methodology is an example of a project assumption.

63. **Which of the following tools is used to identify potential risks?**

a. Ishikawa diagram

b. Gantt chart

c. SWOT analysis

d. Risk probability and impact matrix

e. None of the above

Answer: c (SWOT analysis)

Explanation: SWOT analysis is a tool used to identify potential risks by analyzing an organization's strengths, weaknesses, opportunities, and threats.

64.   Which of the following is a type of project life cycle?

a. Predictive

b. Incremental

c. Agile

d. Hybrid

e. All of the above

Answer: e. (All of the above)

Explanation: There are several types of project life cycles, including predictive, incremental, agile, and hybrid.

65.   Which of the following is NOT a component of a project charter?

a. Project purpose or justification

b. Stakeholder identification

c. Project budget

d. Project scope statement

e. Project objectives

Answer: c. (Project budget)

Explanation: A project charter typically includes the project purpose or justification, stakeholder identification, project scope statement, project objectives, and high-level risks and assumptions. A project budget is typically included in the project plan.

66.   Which of the following is NOT a risk response strategy?

a. Avoidance

b. Mitigation

c. Transference

d. Enhancement

e. Acceptance

Answer: d. (Enhancement)

Explanation: The risk response strategies are avoidance, mitigation, transference, and acceptance. Enhancement is not a recognized risk response strategy.

67. **Which of the following is NOT an output of the Monitor and Control Project Work process?**

    a. Change requests

    b. Work performance reports

    c. Project management plan updates

    d. Deliverables

    e. None of the above

Answer: d. (Deliverables)

Explanation: The Monitor and Control Project Work process is focused on tracking, reviewing, and regulating the progress and performance of the project. Deliverables are not an output of this process.

FORMULA-BASED QUESTIONS

68. **What is the earned value (EV) of a project if the actual cost (AC) is $50,000, the planned value (PV) is $60,000, and the schedule performance index (SPI) is 0.8?**

    a. $40,000

    b. $48,000

    c. $50,000

    d. $60,000

Answer: b. $48,000

Explanation: $EV = PV * SPI = \$60,000 * 0.8 = \$48,000$.

69. **If a project has a CPI (cost performance index) of 0.9 and a budget at completion (BAC) of $100,000, what is the estimated total cost of the project?**

    a. $90,000

    b. $100,000

    c. $110,000

    d. $120,000

Answer: d. $120,000

Explanation: Estimated total cost = $BAC / CPI = \$100,000 / 0.9 = \$111,111$ (rounded to the nearest dollar).

70. **What is the schedule variance (SV) of a project if the earned value (EV) is $80,000, and the planned value (PV) is $100,000?**

    a. -$20,000

b. $0

c. $20,000

d. $80,000

Answer: a. -$20,000

Explanation: SV = EV - PV = $80,000 - $100,000 = -$20,000.

71.   **If a project has a schedule performance index (SPI) of 1.2 and a planned value (PV) of $120,000, what is the earned value (EV)?**

   a. $100,000

   b. $120,000

   c. $140,000

   d. $160,000

Answer: c. $140,000

Explanation: EV = PV * SPI = $120,000 * 1.2 = $140,000.

72.   **What is the estimate at completion (EAC) of a project if the budget at completion (BAC) is $500,000, the actual cost (AC) is $250,000, and the earned value (EV) is $300,000?**

   a. $400,000

   b. $450,000

   c. $500,000

   d. $550,000

Answer: d. $550,000

Explanation: EAC = BAC / CPI = $500,000 / (EV/AC) = $500,000 / (300,000/250,000) = $550,000.

73.   **What is the cost performance index (CPI) of a project if the earned value (EV) is $75,000, and the actual cost (AC) is $100,000?**

   a. 0.25

   b. 0.75

   c. 0.9

   d. 1.25

   Answer: b. 0.75

Explanation: CPI = EV / AC = $75,000 / $100,000 = 0.75.

74.   **What is the formula for calculating Earned Value (EV) in project management?**

a. EV = AC - PV

b. EV = PV - AC

c. EV = AC + PV

d. EV = PV x AC

Answer: b. EV = PV - AC

Explanation: Earned Value (EV) is calculated by subtracting Actual Cost (AC) from Planned Value (PV).

75. **What is the formula for calculating Schedule Variance (SV) in project management?**

a. SV = EV - AC

b. SV = AC - EV

c. SV = EV / AC

d. SV = AC / EV

Answer: b. SV = AC - EV

Explanation: Schedule Variance (SV) is calculated by subtracting Earned Value (EV) from Actual Cost (AC).

76. **What is the formula for calculating Cost Performance Index (CPI) in project management?**

a. CPI = EV / AC

b. CPI = AC / EV

c. CPI = EV - AC

d. CPI = AC - EV

Answer: a. CPI = EV / AC

Explanation: Cost Performance Index (CPI) is calculated by dividing Earned Value (EV) by Actual Cost (AC).

77. **What is the formula for calculating Schedule Performance Index (SPI) in project management?**

a. SPI = EV / PV

b. SPI = PV / EV

c. SPI = EV - PV

d. SPI = PV - EV

Answer: a. SPI = EV / PV

Explanation: Schedule Performance Index (SPI) is calculated by dividing Earned Value (EV) by Planned Value (PV).

78. **If the budget for a project is $1,000,000, and the Actual Cost (AC) is $750,000, what is the Cost Variance (CV) for the project?**

    a. $500,000

    b. $250,000

    c. -$250,000

    d. -$500,000

Answer: b. $250,000

Explanation: Cost Variance (CV) is calculated by subtracting Actual Cost (AC) from Earned Value (EV). Since EV = Budget = $1,000,000, CV = $1,000,000 - $750,000 = $250,000.

79. **If the Planned Value (PV) for a project is $500,000, and the Earned Value (EV) is $450,000, what is the Schedule Variance (SV) for the project?**

    a. $50,000

    b. $100,000

    c. -$50,000

    d. -$100,000

Answer: c. -$50,000

Explanation: Schedule Variance (SV) is calculated by subtracting Earned Value (EV) from Planned Value (PV). Since PV > EV in this case, SV = $500,000 - $450,000 = -$50,000.

80. **If the Cost Performance Index (CPI) for a project is 0.8, what does it mean?**

    a. The project is under budget.

    b. The project is over budget.

    c. The project is on budget.

    d. None of the above.

Answer: b. The project is over budget.

Explanation: Cost Performance Index (CPI) less than 1 indicates that the project is over budget. A CPI greater than 1 indicates that the project is under budget.

81. **What is the cost variance (CV) if the earned value (EV) of a project is $50,000 and the actual cost (AC) is $60,000?**

    a. $10,000 over budget

b. $10,000 under budget

c. $50,000 over budget

d. $50,000 under budget

Answer: a. $10,000 over budget.

Explanation: CV = EV - AC, which in this case is $50,000 - $60,000 = -$10,000. A negative CV indicates that the project is over budget.

82. **What is the schedule variance (SV) if the earned value (EV) of a project is $80,000 and the planned value (PV) is $100,000?**

   a. $20,000 behind schedule

   b. $20,000 ahead of schedule

   c. $80,000 behind schedule

   d. $80,000 ahead of schedule

Answer: a. $20,000 behind schedule.

Explanation: SV = EV - PV, which in this case is $80,000 - $100,000 = -$20,000. A negative SV indicates that the project is behind schedule.

83. **What is the cost performance index (CPI) if the earned value (EV) of a project is $40,000, and the actual cost (AC) is $30,000?**

   a. 1.33

   b. 0.75

   c. 0.67

   d. 1.25

Answer: d. 1.25.

Explanation: CPI – EV / AC, which in this case is $40,000 / $30,000 – 1.33. A CPI greater than 1 indicates that the project is under budget.

84. **What is the schedule performance index (SPI) if the earned value (EV) of a project is $60,000, and the planned value (PV) is $50,000?**

   a. 0.83

   b. 1.2

   c. 1.5

   d. 0.8

Answer: b. 1.2.

Explanation: SPI = EV / PV, which in this case is $60,000 / $50,000 = 1.2. An SPI greater than 1 indicates that the project is ahead of schedule.

85. **What is the estimate at completion (EAC) if the budget at completion (BAC) of a project is $500,000, the actual cost (AC) is $300,000, and the earned value (EV) is $250,000?**

    a. $400,000

    b. $625,000

    c. $575,000

    d. $525,000

Answer: c. $575,000.

Explanation: EAC = BAC / CPI, which in this case is $500,000 / (250,000 / 300,000) = $575,000. EAC is an estimate of the total cost of the project based on its current performance.

INTERPERSONAL AND LEADERSHIP SKILLS

86. **Which of the following leadership styles is characterized by high concern for people and low concern for results?**

    a. Autocratic

    b. Democratic

    c. Laissez-faire

    d. Transformational

Answer: b. Democratic

Explanation: The democratic leadership style is characterized by a high concern for people and a high concern for results, whereas the autocratic leadership style is characterized by a low concern for people and a high concern for results. The laissez-faire style is characterized by a low concern for both people and results, and the transformational style is characterized by a high concern for both.

87. **Which of the following is an example of a soft skill?**

    a. Project management

    b. Technical writing

    c. Time management

    d. Emotional intelligence

Answer: d. Emotional intelligence

Explanation: Emotional intelligence is a soft skill that refers to the ability to understand and manage one's own emotions and those of others.

88. **Which of the following is not a component of emotional intelligence?**

    a. Self-awareness

    b. Self-regulation

    c. Social awareness

    d. Technical knowledge

Answer: d. Technical knowledge

Explanation: Technical knowledge is not a component of emotional intelligence. The other three options are all components of emotional intelligence.

89. **Which of the following conflict resolution techniques involves a neutral third party helping the parties involved reach a mutually agreeable solution?**

    a. Avoidance

    b. Accommodation

    c. Collaboration

    d. Mediation

Answer: d. Mediation

Explanation: Mediation involves a neutral third party helping the parties involved in a conflict reach a mutually agreeable solution.

90. **Which of the following conflict resolution techniques involves one party giving in to the demands of the other party?**

    a. Avoidance

    b. Accommodation

    c. Collaboration

    d. Compromise

Answer: b. Accommodation

Explanation: Accommodation involves one party giving in to the demands of the other party.

91. **Which of the following communication methods is best for conveying complex technical information?**

    a. Email

b. Phone

c. In-person meeting

d. Video conference

Answer: c. In-person meeting Explanation: In-person meetings are the best option for conveying complex technical information, as they allow for visual aids and more detailed explanations.

92. **Which of the following communication methods is best for quick updates or requests?**

a. Email

b. Phone

c. In-person meeting

d. Video conference

Answer: a. Email Explanation: Email is the best option for quick updates or requests, as it allows for a quick exchange of information without requiring an immediate response.

93. **Which of the following is an example of a stakeholder who has high power and high interest?**

a. A team member with low technical skills

b. A project sponsor with limited budget

c. A customer with a limited need for the product

d. A government agency with strict regulations

Answer: d. A government agency with strict regulations

Explanation: Stakeholders with high power and high interest are those who have a significant impact on the project and are highly invested in its success. A government agency with strict regulations fits this description.

94. **Which of the following is the most important characteristic of a project manager in terms of their interpersonal and leadership skills?**

a. Technical expertise

b. Task-oriented mindset

c. Emotional intelligence

d. Strong decision-making skills

Answer: c. Emotional intelligence

Explanation: Emotional intelligence is the most important characteristic of a project manager in terms of their interpersonal and leadership skills because it helps them to understand their own emotions and the emotions of others, which is essential for effective communication and collaboration. A project manager who has high emotional intelligence can build trust and rapport with team members, resolve conflicts, and inspire and motivate others. While technical expertise and strong decision-making skills are also important, they are not sufficient on their own to make a project manager an effective leader.

95. **Which of the following leadership styles is most effective for a project manager who is leading a team of highly skilled and experienced professionals?**

   a. Autocratic leadership

   b. Democratic leadership

   c. Transformational leadership

   d. Laissez-faire leadership

Answer: b. Democratic leadership

Explanation: Democratic leadership is the most effective style for a project manager who is leading a team of highly skilled and experienced professionals because it allows team members to have input into the decision-making process and to take ownership of their work. This style of leadership fosters creativity, innovation, and collaboration, and it helps to build a sense of shared responsibility for the success of the project. Autocratic leadership can be effective in certain situations, but it can also lead to resentment and demotivation among team members, while laissez-faire leadership is generally ineffective in a project management context.

96. **Which of the following is an example of a communication barrier in a multicultural project team?**

   a. Language differences

   b. Technical jargon

   c. Lack of trust

   d. Time zone differences

Answer: a. Language differences

Explanation: Language differences can be a significant communication barrier in a multicultural project team because they can lead to misunderstandings, confusion, and misinterpretation of messages. Project managers need to be aware of the language capabilities of their team members and provide appropriate language support, such as translation services or language training, to ensure effective communication. Technical jargon, lack of trust, and time zone differences can also be communication barriers, but they are not specific to multicultural teams.

97. **Which of the following conflict resolution techniques is most effective when there is a high degree of interdependence among team members?**

a. Compromising

b. Collaborating

c. Forcing

d. Avoiding

Answer: b. Collaborating

Explanation: Collaborating is the most effective conflict resolution technique when there is a high degree of interdependence among team members because it involves finding a solution that meets the needs and interests of all parties involved. This technique requires active listening, open communication, and a willingness to explore different perspectives, which can help to build trust and respect among team members. Compromising can be effective when there is some degree of interdependence, but it may not fully address the underlying issues. Forcing and avoiding are generally ineffective in a project management context.

98. **What is the best approach for a project manager to take when dealing with a team member who consistently misses deadlines?**

a. Provide additional training

b. Reassign tasks to other team members

c. Hold the team member accountable and document performance

d. Give the team member a break

Answer: c. Hold the team member accountable and document performance.

Explanation: While additional training and task reassignment may be helpful in some situations, holding the team member accountable and documenting their performance is the most effective way to address consistent missed deadlines. This helps to maintain clear expectations and consequences for team members and ensures that project timelines and goals are not compromised.

99. **What is the best approach for a project manager to take when dealing with a team member who is not receptive to feedback?**

a. Provide additional incentives for improvement

b. Avoid addressing the issue to avoid conflict

c. Modify communication approach to better align with team member's style

d. Provide negative feedback and consequences

Answer: c. Modify communication approach to better align with team member's style.

Explanation: Providing additional incentives or negative feedback may not be effective if the team member is not receptive to feedback. The best approach is to adjust the communication approach to better align with the team member's style, which can help to build trust and increase receptiveness to feedback over time.

100. **What is the best approach for a project manager to take when dealing with a team member who frequently disagrees with the rest of the team?**

a. Ignore the team member's opinions to maintain team cohesion

b. Encourage the team member to be more cooperative

c. Facilitate open and respectful communication among team members

d. Remove the team member from the project team

Answer: c. Facilitate open and respectful communication among team members.

Explanation: Ignoring the team member's opinions or removing them from the project team may not be effective solutions, and may even harm team cohesion and morale. Encouraging the team member to be more cooperative may also not be effective if there are underlying issues causing the disagreements. The best approach is to facilitate open and respectful communication among team members, encouraging all team members to express their opinions and work towards finding common ground.

101. **What is the best approach for a project manager to take when dealing with a team member who is consistently negative and crucial of the project?**

a. Ignore the team member's negative comments

b. Address the team member's behavior in private and provide constructive feedback

c. Encourage the team member to share their concerns with the team in a constructive manner

d. Remove the team member from the project team

Answer: b. Address the team member's behavior in private and provide constructive feedback.

Explanation: Ignoring the team member's negative comments may lead to further negativity and conflict, while removing the team member from the project team should be a last resort. Encouraging the team member to share their concerns constructively may not be effective if there are underlying issues causing the negativity. The best approach is to address the team member's behavior in private and provide constructive feedback, focusing on the impact of their behavior on the team and the project.

102. **Which of the following is not a characteristic of a transformational leader?**

a. Inspiration

b. Intellectual Stimulation

c. Individualized Consideration

d. Control

Answer: d. Control

Explanation: Transformational leaders inspire and motivate their followers to achieve their goals and realize their full potential. They do this by providing intellectual stimulation, challenging the status quo, and offering individualized consideration to each team member. They do not rely on control as their primary means of leadership. Transformational leaders believe in empowerment, delegation, and trust, which leads to higher levels of engagement and productivity.

103.   Which of the following leadership styles is best suited for a high-performing team?

   a. Autocratic

   b. Laissez-faire

   c. Participative

   d. Democratic

Answer: d. Democratic

Explanation: The democratic leadership style is best suited for high-performing teams because it involves collaboration, teamwork, and shared decision-making. This style allows team members to have a voice in the decision-making process, which leads to higher levels of engagement, commitment, and ownership. The democratic leadership style fosters a sense of empowerment and trust, which is essential for a high-performing team.

104.   Which of the following is not a common communication barrier?

   a. Noise

   b. Language

   c. Time zone differences

   d. Active listening

Answer: d. Active listening

Explanation: Communication barriers are obstacles that prevent effective communication. Common communication barriers include noise, language, cultural differences, time zone differences, and technology. Active listening, on the other hand, is a technique that helps to overcome communication barriers. Active listening involves fully concentrating on what is being said, understanding the message, and responding appropriately.

105.   Which of the following is not a conflict resolution technique?

   a. Collaboration

   b. Competing

   c. Avoiding

d. Confronting

Answer: b. Competing

Explanation: Conflict resolution techniques are methods used to resolve conflicts in a constructive and positive manner. The most common conflict resolution techniques include collaboration, compromising, avoiding, and confronting. Competing is not a conflict resolution technique; it is a win-lose approach that focuses on achieving one's goals at the expense of the other party's goals. This approach can lead to resentment and mistrust, which is not conducive to effective conflict resolution.

ETHICS AND PROFESSIONAL RESPONSIBILITY

106. **Which of the following is the most important reason why a project manager should ensure that all stakeholders are fully informed of the ethical standards to be followed on a project?**

    a. To avoid negative publicity

    b. To meet legal requirements

    c. To maintain stakeholder trust and confidence

    d. To increase profits

Answer: c. To maintain stakeholder trust and confidence

Explanation: Project managers have a professional responsibility to ensure that ethical standards are followed on their projects. When all stakeholders are fully informed of these standards, it helps to build and maintain trust and confidence in the project team and its outcomes. This can lead to a more positive project environment, improved communication, and better overall project performance. While avoiding negative publicity and meeting legal requirements are also important considerations, they are not as crucial as maintaining stakeholder trust and confidence.

107. **A project manager has identified a potential conflict of interest between the project and a stakeholder. What is the most appropriate course of action for the project manager to take?**

    a. Ignore the conflict and continue with the project

    b. Disclose the conflict to the stakeholder and continue with the project

    c. Disclose the conflict to the stakeholder and modify the project plan

    d. Withdraw from the project to avoid the conflict

Answer: c. Disclose the conflict to the stakeholder and modify the project plan

Explanation: Project managers have a responsibility to identify and manage conflicts of interest on their projects. When a conflict arises between the project and a stakeholder, the most appropriate course of action is to disclose the conflict to the stakeholder and work together to modify the project plan to minimize the impact of the conflict. Ignoring the conflict or withdrawing from the project are not appropriate options, as they can lead to negative consequences for both the project and the stakeholder.

108. **Which of the following is the best way for a project manager to ensure that all project team members are aware of the ethical standards to be followed on a project?**

    a. Provide a copy of the code of ethics to each team member

    b. Conduct a training session on ethical standards for the team

    c. Include ethical standards in the project charter

    d. Request each team member to sign a document confirming their awareness of the ethical standards

Answer: b. Conduct a training session on ethical standards for the team

Explanation: While providing a copy of the code of ethics, including ethical standards in the project charter, or requesting team members to sign a document confirming their awareness of the ethical standards can be helpful, the most effective way to ensure that all team members are aware of the ethical standards to be followed on a project is to conduct a training session. This allows for interactive discussion, clarification of any questions, and a deeper understanding of the ethical principles and standards that should be followed on the project.

109. **A project manager is approached by a stakeholder who offers a bribe in exchange for a change in the project scope. What is the most appropriate course of action for the project manager to take?**

    a. Report the offer to the appropriate authority

    b. Accept the offer to keep the stakeholder satisfied

    c. Discuss the offer with the project team and modify the project plan accordingly

    d. Ignore the offer and continue with the original project scope

Answer: a. Report the offer to the appropriate authority

Explanation: Bribery is a serious violation of ethical standards and is illegal in most jurisdictions. Project managers have a professional responsibility to report any attempts at bribery to the appropriate authorities. Accepting the offer, discussing it with the project team, or ignoring it are not appropriate options and can lead to negative consequences.

110. **Which of the following scenarios represents a violation of the PMP Code of Ethics and Professional Conduct?**

a. A project manager allows a team member to take credit for work that was not completed by them

b. A project manager takes credit for a team member's work without their knowledge or consent

c. A project manager promotes a team member based on their qualifications and experience rather than personal relationships

d. A project manager provides constructive feedback to a team member about their performance

Answer: b. A project manager taking credit for a team member's work without their knowledge or consent.

Explanation: Is a violation of the PMP Code of Ethics and Professional Conduct, specifically the section on integrity. Project managers are expected to act honestly and transparently in all their dealings and to give credit where it is due. Taking credit for someone else's work is dishonest and unethical.

111. **A project manager discovers that a supplier has offered them a kickback in return for awarding them a contract. What is the appropriate course of action for the project manager?**

a. Accept the kickback and award the contract to the supplier

b. Report the offer to their manager and the appropriate authorities

c. Decline the offer and award the contract to the supplier based on merit

d. Request a larger kickback from the supplier before awarding the contract

Answer: b. The appropriate course of action for the project manager is to report the offer to their manager and the appropriate authorities.

Explanation: This situation violates the PMP Code of Ethics and Professional Conduct, specifically the sections on honesty and transparency, and conflicts of interest. Project managers are expected to act with integrity and impartiality in all their dealings and to avoid any conflicts of interest that could compromise their professional judgment.

112. **A project manager is asked to provide inaccurate information about the progress of a project to a senior executive. What is the appropriate course of action for the project manager?**

a. Provide the inaccurate information to avoid conflict with the senior executive

b. Refuse to provide the inaccurate information and explain the actual progress of the project

c. Provide the inaccurate information and document the actual progress of the project separately

d. Provide the inaccurate information and blame the team for any issues or delays

Answer: b. The appropriate course of action for the project manager is to refuse to provide the inaccurate information and explain the actual progress of the project.

Explanation: This situation violates the PMP Code of Ethics and Professional Conduct, specifically the section on honesty. Project managers are expected to be truthful and transparent in all their dealings and to provide accurate information to stakeholders.

113. **Which of the following is not a component of the PMI Code of Ethics and Professional Conduct?**

a. Responsibility

b. Respect

c. Fairness

d. Loyalty

Answer: d. Loyalty.

Explanation: The PMI Code of Ethics and Professional Conduct consists of four components: responsibility, respect, fairness, and honesty. Loyalty is not one of the components.

114. **A project manager is faced with a dilemma in which one of their team members has been falsifying their hours to get paid for more time than they actually worked. What is the best course of action for the project manager?**

a. Ignore the situation since it is the team member's responsibility to be honest about their hours.

b. Confront the team member and threaten to report them if they do not stop.

c. Report the situation to the appropriate authority within the organization.

d. Tell the team member to stop and keep it a secret from everyone else.

Answer: c. Report the situation to the appropriate authority within the organization.

Explanation: As a project manager, it is important to uphold the standards of ethics and professional responsibility set forth in the PMI Code of Ethics and Professional Conduct. This includes being honest and transparent in all business dealings. Falsifying hours is a serious offense and should be reported to the appropriate authority within the organization.

115. **A project manager has been offered a bribe by a vendor in exchange for selecting their company for a project. What should the project manager do?**

a. Accept the bribe and select the vendor's company for the project.

b. Refuse the bribe and report the vendor to the appropriate authority within the organization.

c. Negotiate a higher bribe before making a decision.

d. Consult with their supervisor before making a decision.

Answer: b. Refuse the bribe and report the vendor to the appropriate authority within the organization.

Explanation: Accepting a bribe is a violation of the PMI Code of Ethics and Professional Conduct, which requires project managers to maintain high standards of honesty and integrity in all business dealings. The project manager should refuse the bribe and report the vendor to the appropriate authority within the organization.

116. **A project manager has discovered that a team member is engaging in behavior that violates the PMI Code of Ethics and Professional Conduct. What should the project manager do?**

a. Ignore the behavior since it is the team member's responsibility to uphold ethical standards.

b. Confront the team member and give them a warning.

c. Report the behavior to the appropriate authority within the organization.

d. Do nothing and wait for the behavior to stop on its own.

Answer: c. Report the behavior to the appropriate authority within the organization.

Explanation: It is the responsibility of the project manager to maintain high standards of ethics and professional responsibility on the project team. If a team member is engaging in behavior that violates these standards, it should be reported to the appropriate authority within the organization.

117. **Which of the following is not a principle of the PMI Code of Ethics and Professional Conduct?**

a. Responsibility

b. Honesty

c. Respect

d. Competence

Answer: d. Competence.

Explanation: The PMI Code of Ethics and Professional Conduct consists of four principles: responsibility, honesty, respect, and fairness. Competence is not one of the principles. However, project managers are expected to possess the necessary skills and knowledge to effectively manage their projects.

118. **Which of the following best describes the ethical responsibilities of a project manager in relation to stakeholders?**

a. Prioritize the needs of the project team over those of stakeholders

b. Prioritize the needs of stakeholders over those of the project team

c. Strike a balance between the needs of the project team and stakeholders

d. Avoid considering the needs of stakeholders to prevent conflicts

Answer: c. Strike a balance between the needs of the project team and stakeholders.

Explanation: Project managers have a responsibility to balance the interests of all stakeholders, including the project team, sponsor, customer, and other stakeholders. It is essential to prioritize the needs of stakeholders while considering the interests of the project team to ensure project success. Therefore, striking a balance between the two is crucial for effective project management.

119. **Which of the following best describes a project manager's responsibility when presented with a conflict of interest?**

a. Disclose the conflict and avoid making a decision that would favor one party over the other

b. Favor the party that has the most significant impact on the project's success

c. Prioritize the needs of the stakeholders who have a direct impact on the project's success

d. Ignore the conflict and proceed with making decisions as usual

Answer: a. Disclose the conflict and avoid making a decision that would favor one party over the other.

Explanation: A conflict of interest arises when a project manager's personal interests interfere with their professional judgment. In such situations, project managers should disclose the conflict and avoid making decisions that could favor one party over the other. This approach ensures that the project is executed objectively, and stakeholders' interests are not compromised.

120. **What should a project manager do if they observe unethical behavior in their team?**

a. Ignore the behavior and continue with the project as planned

b. Report the behavior to the project sponsor

c. Address the behavior with the team member privately

d. Report the behavior to the appropriate authority or governance body

Answer: d. Report the behavior to the appropriate authority or governance body.

Explanation: Ethical behavior is crucial in project management. A project manager must report any unethical behavior to the appropriate authority or governance body, regardless of who committed the behavior. This approach ensures that the behavior is investigated and that corrective measures are taken.

121. **What is the primary reason for a project manager to establish a code of conduct for their team?**

    a. To provide guidance on the expected behavior of team members

    b. To ensure the project's success

    c. To avoid conflicts with stakeholders

    d. To establish project timelines and deliverables

Answer: a. To provide guidance on the expected behavior of team members.

Explanation: A code of conduct provides guidance on the expected behavior of team members, outlining the ethical principles and standards that they must adhere to. This helps establish a culture of ethical behavior, ensuring that team members work together effectively and efficiently.

122. **Which of the following is an example of a conflict of interest in project management?**

    a. A project manager hiring a close friend or family member to work on the project team

    b. A project manager disclosing confidential information to a competitor

    c. A project manager favoring a particular vendor without evaluating other options

    d. A project manager ignoring safety regulations to complete the project on time

Answer: a. A project manager hiring a close friend or family member to work on the project team.

Explanation: A conflict of interest arises when a project manager's personal interests interfere with their professional judgment.

123. **You are a project manager on a construction project. You have been offered a substantial bribe by a subcontractor to use their materials on the project. What should you do?**

    a. Accept the bribe and use the subcontractor's materials

    b. Report the incident to the project sponsor or other senior management

    c. Consider the offer but only if it benefits the project

    d. Consult with the project team to see if they agree with the use of the subcontractor's materials

Answer: b. Report the incident to the project sponsor or other senior management

Explanation: Bribery is a clear violation of professional conduct and ethics. As a project manager, you should immediately report any attempt at bribery to senior management. Accepting the bribe would compromise your professional integrity and could result in serious consequences for you and your organization.

INITIATING

124. **Which of the following is not an input to the Initiating process group?**

    a. Business documents

    b. Project charter

    c. Stakeholder register

    d. Scope baseline

Answer: d. Scope baseline

Explanation: The four inputs to the Initiating process group are business documents, the project charter, the stakeholder register, and agreements. The scope baseline is an output of the Define Scope process within the Planning process group, not an input to the Initiating process group.

125. **Which of the following is a characteristic of a project charter?**

    a. It is created by the project manager

    b. It is a formal document that authorizes the project

    c. It includes detailed project requirements

    d. It is created during the Planning process group

Answer: b. It is a formal document that authorizes the project

Explanation: The project charter is a high-level document that formally authorizes the project and gives the project manager the authority to use organizational resources for the project. It is usually created by a sponsor or senior management, not the project manager. The project charter does not include detailed project requirements, and it is created during the Initiating process group, not the Planning process group.

126. **Which of the following is not a tool or technique used in the Identify Stakeholders process?**

    a. Stakeholder analysis

    b. Expert judgment

    c. Change requests

    d. Meetings

Answer: c. Change requests

Explanation: The tools and techniques used in the Identify Stakeholders process include stakeholder analysis, expert judgment, meetings, and document analysis. Change requests are not used in the Identify Stakeholders process, but they are used in the Monitoring and Controlling process group.

127. **Which of the following is an output of the Develop Project Charter process?**

   a. Stakeholder register

   b. Project management plan

   c. Business case

   d. Project statement of work

Answer: c. Business case

Explanation: The Develop Project Charter process is responsible for creating the project charter, which is a high-level document that formally authorizes the project and gives the project manager the authority to use organizational resources for the project. The business case, which describes the business need for the project and how it aligns with organizational objectives, is one of the outputs of the Develop Project Charter process. The stakeholder register is an output of the Identify Stakeholders process, the project management plan is an output of the Develop Project Management Plan process, and the project statement of work is an input to the Develop Project Charter process.

128. **Which of the following is an example of a project constraint?**

   a. The project team's skill levels

   b. The project scope

   c. The project budget

   d. The project risks

Answer: c. The project budget

Explanation: A project constraint is any factor that limits the project team's ability to complete the project. Common project constraints include time, cost, and scope. The project budget is a constraint because it limits the amount of money available to complete the project. The project team's skill levels, project scope, and project risks are not constraints, but they can impact the project's success.

129. **Which of the following is NOT an output of the Develop Project Charter process?**

   a. Stakeholder register

   b. Assumption log

   c. Project charter

   d. Business case

Answer: a. Stakeholder register is NOT an output of the Develop Project Charter process.

Explanation: The Stakeholder register is an output of the Identify Stakeholders process, which comes before the Develop Project Charter process. The Project charter, Business case, and Assumption log are all outputs of the Develop Project Charter process.

130. During the Identify Stakeholders process, a stakeholder has been identified who has a high level of interest in the project but low level of power. Which of the following actions should be taken?

a. Monitor the stakeholder closely

b. Keep the stakeholder informed

c. Manage the stakeholder actively

d. Engage the stakeholder regularly

Answer: b. Keep the stakeholder informed.

Explanation: Stakeholders with high interest but low power should be kept informed about the project. Although they may not have the ability to affect project outcomes directly, they can still exert some influence and may become advocates for the project.

131. Which of the following is NOT a component of the project management plan?

a. Scope baseline

b. Risk management plan

c. Quality management plan

d. Work breakdown structure

Answer: d. Work breakdown structure is NOT a component of the project management plan.

Explanation: The work breakdown structure is an output of the Create WBS process, which comes after the Develop Project Management Plan process. The Scope baseline, Risk management plan, and Quality management plan are all components of the Project Management Plan.

132. Which of the following is NOT a tool or technique used in the Identify Stakeholders process?

a. Expert judgment

b. Data analysis

c. Project management information system

d. Pareto chart

Answer: d. Pareto chart is NOT a tool or technique used in the Identify Stakeholders process.

Explanation: Pareto chart is a tool used in Quality Control, which is a part of the Monitoring and Controlling process group. Expert judgment, Data analysis, and Project management information system are all tools and techniques used in the Identify Stakeholders process.

133. During the Develop Project Charter process, a business case has been developed. Which of the following is NOT included in the business case?

a. Cost-benefit analysis

b. Feasibility study

c. Stakeholder analysis

d. Project timeline

Answer: d. Project timeline is NOT included in the business case.

Explanation: The project timeline is a part of the Project Management Plan, not the business case. The business case includes the cost-benefit analysis, feasibility study, stakeholder analysis, and other relevant information to justify the project.

134. What is the primary objective of the project charter in the initiating process group?

a. To identify the project scope

b. To define the project objectives

c. To authorize the project

d. To establish the project team

Answer: c. To authorize the project Explanation

Explanation: The project charter is a document that authorizes the project and gives the project manager the authority to apply organizational resources to project activities. It outlines the project's purpose, objectives, stakeholders, and key performance indicators (KPIs) to ensure that everyone involved in the project has a clear understanding of what needs to be done. Therefore, option C is the correct answer.

135. Which of the following is NOT a typical element of the project statement of work (SOW)?

a. Project scope description

b. Business need

c. Project objectives

d. Project team roles and responsibilities

Answer: d. Project team roles and responsibilities

Explanation: The project statement of work (SOW) is a document that describes the project's business need, objectives, and scope, including high-level requirements, constraints, and assumptions. It is typically provided by the customer or sponsor and is used as input to the project charter. While it may include a high-level description of the project team, it does not typically include specific roles and responsibilities, making option D the correct answer.

136. **What is the main output of the Identify Stakeholders process in the initiating process group?**

   a. Stakeholder register

   b. Stakeholder management plan

   c. Project charter

   d. Project management plan

Answer: a. Stakeholder register

Explanation: The Identify Stakeholders process involves identifying all individuals, groups, and organizations that may be affected by or have an impact on the project, and documenting their interests, involvement, and potential impact on the project's success. The main output of this process is the stakeholder register, which is a document that provides an overview of the stakeholders, their interests, and their level of influence on the project.

137. **Which of the following is a tool or technique used in the Develop Project Charter process?**

   a. Brainstorming

   b. Ishikawa diagram

   c. SWOT analysis

   d. Monte Carlo analysis

Answer: a. Brainstorming

Explanation: The Develop Project Charter process is used to develop a document that formally authorizes a project or a phase, and defines the project objectives, requirements, and key stakeholders. Brainstorming is a technique used in this process to generate ideas and facilitate the identification of key project elements such as project objectives, high-level requirements and risks.

138. **Which of the following is NOT a typical component of the project management plan developed in the initiating process group?**

   a. Schedule management plan

   b. Scope management plan

   c. Cost management plan

   d. Resource allocation plan

Answer: d. Resource allocation plan

Explanation: The project management plan is a document that integrates all subsidiary plans and baselines into a comprehensive, coordinated plan that guides project execution and control. It typically includes components such as scope, schedule, cost, quality, risk, communication, and procurement management plans, as well as baselines for these components. However, a specific resource allocation plan is not typically included in the project management plan developed during the initiating process group, making option D the correct answer.

139. Which of the following is a key output of the Initiating process group?

   a. Resource calendar

   b. Risk register

   c. Issue log

   d. Change request

Correct answer: b. Risk register

Explanation: The Risk Register is a key output of the Initiating process group. It is a document that captures all identified risks, their potential impact on the project, and the planned responses to those risks.

140. Who is typically responsible for approving the Project Charter?

   a. The project team

   b. The project sponsor

   c. The project manager

   d. The project stakeholders

Correct answer: b. The project sponsor

Explanation: The Project Sponsor is typically responsible for approving the Project Charter. The Project Charter outlines the project's high-level scope, objectives, assumptions, constraints, and stakeholders, and serves as the official authorization for the project to begin.

141. What is the main purpose of the Stakeholder Register?

   a. To identify project risks

   b. To document stakeholder requirements

   c. To track stakeholder engagement

   d. To capture stakeholder feedback

Correct answer: c. To track stakeholder engagement

Explanation: The Stakeholder Register is a document that tracks key information about project stakeholders, including their interests, needs, and potential impact on the project. Its primary purpose is to help the project team plan, manage, and monitor stakeholder engagement throughout the project lifecycle.

142. **Which of the following is NOT typically included in the Business Case?**

  a. Project scope

  b. Project benefits

  c. Project risks

  d. Project budget

Correct answer: d. Project budget

Explanation: While the Business Case does outline the projected costs of the project, it does not typically include a detailed project budget. Instead, the Business Case focuses on the strategic and financial justifications for the project, including its potential benefits, risks, and alignment with organizational goals.

143. **Which of the following is NOT included in the project charter?**

  a. Project objectives

  b. Stakeholder analysis

  c. Business case

  d. Project budget

Answer: d. Project budget

Explanation: The project charter outlines the high-level project information, including project objectives, business case, project scope, major stakeholders, and high-level risks. It does not include the project budget, which is typically developed later in the planning process.

144. **Which of the following is a characteristic of a well-defined project scope?**

  a. It is flexible and can be easily changed

  b. It is vague and open to interpretation

  c. It is documented and agreed upon by stakeholders

  d. It is not necessary for the success of the project

Answer: c. It is documented and agreed upon by stakeholders

Explanation: A well-defined project scope is documented and agreed upon by all stakeholders. It provides clarity and direction to the project team, reduces the risk of scope creep, and helps to ensure that project deliverables meet stakeholder expectations.

145. **Which of the following documents is used to formally authorize a project?**

  a. Project plan

  b. Project charter

c. Business case

d. Project proposal

Answer: b. Project charter

Explanation: The project charter is used to formally authorize a project. It outlines the project objectives, high-level project information, and provides the project manager with the authority to apply organizational resources to project activities.

146.   Which of the following is a component of the stakeholder register?

   a. Change requests

   b. Risk management plan

   c. Stakeholder analysis

   d. Project schedule

Answer: c. Stakeholder analysis

Explanation: The stakeholder register is a document that contains information about all project stakeholders, including their roles, interests, and level of influence. Stakeholder analysis is a component of the stakeholder register, and it involves identifying, assessing, and prioritizing stakeholders.

147.   Which of the following is NOT a tool or technique used in the Develop Project Charter process?

   a. Expert judgment

   b. Project selection methods

   c. Data analysis techniques

   d. Decomposition

Answer: d. Decomposition

Explanation: Decomposition is a tool used in the Develop Project Management Plan process. The Develop Project Charter process involves tools and techniques such as expert judgment, project selection methods, and data analysis techniques to develop the project charter.

PLANNING

148.   Which of the following is not a tool or technique used in the Define Scope process?

   a. Expert judgment

   b. Product analysis

   c. Workshops

d. Inspection

Answer: d. Inspection is not a tool or technique used in the Define Scope process.

Explanation: The correct answer is based on the PMBOK Guide 2021, which identifies expert judgment, product analysis, and workshops as tools and techniques used in the Define Scope process.

149.   During which process group is the project charter developed?

   a. Planning

   b. Execution

   c. Monitoring and Controlling

   d. Closing

Answer: a. Planning

Explanation: The project charter is developed during the Planning process group. This is because the project charter is an input to the planning processes and is created during the project initiation phase.

150.   Which of the following is not a component of the project management plan?

   a. Resource plan

   b. Change control plan

   c. Procurement management plan

   d. Issue resolution plan

Answer: d. Issue resolution plan

Explanation: Issue resolution plan is not a component of the project management plan. While issue resolution is an important aspect of project management, it is typically addressed in the context of the project's issue log, which is a separate document from the project management plan.

151.   Which of the following is a benefit of using a Monte Carlo analysis in project risk management?

   a. It provides a deterministic estimate of project outcomes

   b. It allows for the identification of Critical path activities

   c. It helps to identify low-probability, high-impact risks

   d. It enables team members to perform quantitative risk analysis

Answer: c. One benefit of using a Monte Carlo analysis in project risk management is that it helps to identify low-probability, high-impact risks.

Explanation: Monte Carlo analysis is a probabilistic technique that uses simulations to model the likelihood of different outcomes, which can be particularly useful in identifying risks that have a low probability of occurring but would have a high impact if they did.

152. In which process group is the risk management plan developed?

   a. Planning

   b. Execution

   c. Monitoring and Controlling

   d. Closing

Answer: a. The risk management plan is developed during the Planning process group.

Explanation: The risk management plan is a key output of the Plan Risk Management process, which is the first process in the Risk Management knowledge area.

153. Which of the following is NOT an input to the Plan Scope Management process?

   a. Project Charter

   b. Project Management Plan

   c. Enterprise Environmental Factors

   d. Organizational Process Assets

Answer: a. Project Charter

Explanation: The Project Charter is an input to the Develop Project Charter process, not to the Plan Scope Management process. The inputs to the Plan Scope Management process are the Project Management Plan, Enterprise Environmental Factors, and Organizational Process Assets.

154. What is the purpose of the Define Scope process?

   a. To create a detailed project schedule

   b. To determine the requirements for the project deliverables

   c. To establish the project budget

   d. To identify project risks

Answer: b. To determine the requirements for the project deliverables

Explanation: The Define Scope process is used to develop a detailed description of the project and its deliverables. This includes determining the requirements for the project deliverables and defining the scope of the project.

155. Which of the following is an output of the Plan Schedule Management process?

   a. Schedule Baseline

b. Activity Resource Requirements

c. Risk Register

d. Cost Management Plan

Answer: d. Cost Management Plan

Explanation: The Plan Schedule Management process is used to develop a plan for how the project schedule will be created, monitored, and controlled. The output of this process is the Schedule Management Plan, which includes information on how the schedule will be developed, monitored, and controlled. The Cost Management Plan is an output of the Plan Cost Management process.

156. What is the purpose of the Identify Stakeholders process?

a. To document the roles and responsibilities of project team members

b. To develop a communication plan

c. To identify all stakeholders who may be impacted by the project

d. To define the project scope

Answer: c. To identify all stakeholders who may be impacted by the project

Explanation: The purpose of the Identify Stakeholders process is to identify all stakeholders who may be impacted by the project and to document their interests, involvement, and impact on the project. This information is used to develop a Stakeholder Management Plan.

157. Which of the following is a tool and technique used in the Define Activities process

a. Decomposition

b. Expert Judgment

c. Variance Analysis

d. Cost-Benefit Analysis

Answer: a. Decomposition

Explanation: The Define Activities process is used to break down the project deliverables into smaller, more manageable components. Decomposition is a tool and technique used in this process, which involves breaking down the project deliverables into smaller, more manageable components. Expert Judgment is a tool and technique used in many project management processes, while Variance Analysis and Cost-Benefit Analysis are typically used in the Monitor and Control Project Work process.

158. Which of the following is NOT a component of a Project Management Plan (PMP)?

a. Scope Management Plan

b. Quality Management Plan

c. Communication Management Plan

d. Requirements Management Plan

Answer: d. Requirements Management Plan

Explanation: The PMP is a comprehensive document that outlines how the project will be executed, monitored, and controlled. It includes several components, such as the Scope Management Plan, Quality Management Plan, Communication Management Plan, Risk Management Plan, etc. However, the Requirements Management Plan is not a component of the PMP, as it is a part of the Requirements Documentation.

159. **Which of the following is the MOST important tool for identifying stakeholders in a project?**

a. Project Management Information System (PMIS)

b. Stakeholder Analysis

c. Communication Management Plan

d. Risk Management Plan

Answer: b. Stakeholder Analysis

Explanation: Stakeholder Analysis is the process of identifying, analyzing, and managing stakeholders in a project. It is an essential tool for identifying the stakeholders' needs, interests, expectations, and potential impact on the project. Stakeholder Analysis helps in developing a Stakeholder Management Plan, which outlines the strategy for engaging with the stakeholders throughout the project.

160. **Which of the following is NOT a component of a Work Breakdown Structure (WBS)?**

a. Control Accounts

b. Work Packages

c. Cost Baselines

d. Planning Packages

Answer: c. Cost Baselines

Explanation: A WBS is a hierarchical decomposition of the project scope into smaller, manageable components. It includes several components, such as Work Packages, Control Accounts, Planning Packages, etc. However, Cost Baselines are not a component of the WBS, as they are a part of the Cost Management Plan.

161. **Which of the following is the MOST effective technique for managing changes in a project?**

a. Change Control Board (CCb.

b. Change Request Form

c. Change Management Plan

d. Configuration Management System (CMS)

Answer: a. Change Control Board (CCb.

Explanation: A Change Control Board (CCb. is a group of stakeholders responsible for reviewing, approving, and managing changes in a project. It is an effective technique for managing changes, as it ensures that all changes are documented, analyzed, and approved before implementation. The CCB also helps in minimizing the impact of changes on the project scope, schedule, and budget.

162. **Which of the following is NOT a characteristic of a well-defined project objective?**

a. Specific

b. Measurable

c. Achievable

d. Relevant

Answer: d. Relevant

Explanation: A well-defined project objective should be Specific, Measurable, Achievable, Realistic, and Time-bound (SMART). The objective should be clear, concise, and focused on the desired outcome of the project. Relevant is not a characteristic of a well-defined project objective, as it is more related to the project scope and requirements.

163. **Which of the following is NOT an input to the Develop Project Charter process?**

a. Business case

b. Stakeholder register

c. Project selection criteria

 d. Project management plan

Answer: d. Project management plan is not an input to the Develop Project Charter process.

Explanation: The inputs to this process are business case, agreements, enterprise environmental factors, organizational process assets, and project selection criteria.

164. **In which of the following planning processes is a resource calendar typically developed?**

a. Estimate Activity Resources

b. Estimate Activity Durations

c. Plan Resource Management

d. Plan Schedule Management

Answer: c. Plan Resource Management

Explanation: Plan Resource Management is the planning process in which a resource calendar is typically developed. The purpose of this process is to identify, document, and assign project roles, responsibilities, and reporting relationships, as well as to create a staffing management plan.

165. Which of the following is a tool and technique used in the Control Quality process?

a. Statistical sampling

b. Inspection

c. Benchmarking

d. Cost of quality

Answer: b. Inspection

Explanation: Inspection is a tool and technique used in the Control Quality process. It involves examining work results to ensure that they comply with the requirements and standards specified for the project.

166. Which of the following is a valid reason for using a matrix organizational structure

a. To minimize communication overhead

b. To promote team-building and collaboration

c. To increase the flexibility of resource utilization

d. To reduce conflicts between functional managers and project managers

Answer: c. To increase the flexibility of resource utilization

Explanation: A matrix organizational structure is used to increase the flexibility of resource utilization. In this structure, team members have two or more reporting lines, allowing them to be assigned to multiple projects or functional areas simultaneously.

167. Which of the following is NOT an output of the Plan Procurement Management process?

a. Procurement management plan

b. Procurement statement of work

c. Source selection criteria

d. Approved change requests

Answer: d. Approved change requests is not an output of the Plan Procurement Management process.

Explanation: The outputs of this process are procurement management plan, procurement statement of work, source selection criteria, make-or-buy decisions, and procurement documents.

168. Which of the following is NOT a tool or technique used in the Define Scope process

> a. Decomposition
>
> b. Expert judgment
>
> c. Document analysis
>
> d. Pareto chart

Answer: d. Pareto chart

Explanation: A Pareto chart is not a tool or technique used in the Define Scope process, but it is a useful tool for other project management activities. Decomposition, expert judgment, and document analysis are all valid tools and techniques used in Define Scope.

169. What is the primary output of the Plan Procurement Management process?

> a. Procurement management plan
>
> b. Source selection criteria
>
> c. Procurement statement of work
>
> d. Procurement documents

Answer: a. Procurement management plan

Explanation: The primary output of the Plan Procurement Management process is the procurement management plan, which provides guidance on how procurement activities will be managed throughout the project. Source selection criteria, procurement statement of work, and procurement documents are all secondary outputs of this process.

170. During which process does the project manager determine the order in which activities will be performed?

> a. Define Activities
>
> b. Sequence Activities
>
> c. Develop Schedule
>
> d. Control Schedule

Answer: b. Sequence Activities

Explanation: The Sequence Activities process is where the project manager determines the order in which activities will be performed. The Define Activities process is where the activities themselves are identified and described. The Develop Schedule process is where the project schedule is created, and the Control Schedule process is where progress is monitored and adjustments are made.

171. **What is the purpose of the Identify Risks process?**

   a. To develop a plan to respond to identified risks

   b. To prioritize risks based on their impact and likelihood

   c. To identify potential risks that may impact the project

   d. To monitor risks throughout the project lifecycle

Answer: c. To identify potential risks that may impact the project

Explanation: The purpose of the Identify Risks process is to identify potential risks that may impact the project. This process does not involve developing a plan to respond to identified risks, prioritizing risks, or monitoring risks throughout the project lifecycle.

172. **Which of the following is an output of the Estimate Costs process?**

   a. Cost baseline

   b. Activity cost estimates

   c. Cost management plan

   d. Project budget

Answer: b. Activity cost estimates

Explanation: The Estimate Costs process produces the activity cost estimates, which are an estimate of the costs associated with each individual project activity. The cost management plan and cost baseline are developed later in the project, and the project budget is developed based on the cost estimates and other project inputs.

EXECUTING

173. **What is the primary objective of the executing process in project management?**

   a. Develop project schedule

   b. Monitor project risks

   c. Implement project plan

   d. Define project scope

Answer: c. Implement project plan.

Explanation: The executing process is all about carrying out the project plan as per the defined scope, schedule, and budget. This process involves coordinating people and resources to complete the tasks required to achieve project objectives.

174. **What is the primary output of the executing process?**

   a. Project charter

b. Stakeholder register

c. Change request

d. Deliverables

Answer: d. Deliverables.

Explanation: The executing process involves creating and delivering the project deliverables as per the defined specifications, timeline, and budget. Deliverables are the tangible results of a project that are accepted by the project sponsor or customer.

175. **During the executing process, the project manager notices that one of the project team members is consistently missing deadlines. What should the project manager do first**

    a. Update the project schedule

    b. Inform the project sponsor

    c. Meet with the team member to understand the issue

    d. Assign the task to a different team member

Answer: c. Meet with the team member to understand the issue.

Explanation: It's important for the project manager to understand the root cause of the problem before taking any action. Meeting with the team member can help the project manager to identify the underlying issues and work on solutions to address them.

176. **Which of the following is NOT a tool or technique used in the executing process?**

    a. Expert judgment

    b. Change control tools

    c. Project management information system

    d. Risk management plan

Answer: d. Risk management plan.

Explanation: The risk management plan is part of the planning process and is used to identify, assess, and prioritize risks that may impact the project. While it's important to monitor and control risks during the executing process, the risk management plan is not a tool or technique used during this process.

177. **During the executing process, the project team identifies a defect in one of the project deliverables. What should the project team do first?**

    a. Issue a change request

    b. Inform the project sponsor

    c. Take corrective action to fix the defect

d. Verify the defect with the customer

Answer: c. Take corrective action to fix the defect.

Explanation: Corrective action is the first step to address any defects or issues that arise during the executing process. It's important to address the defect as soon as possible to minimize any negative impacts on the project. Once the issue has been resolved, the project team can then determine if a change request is necessary to update the project plan.

178. **Which of the following is a tool or technique used in the Control Procurements process?**

    a. Bidder conferences

    b. Contract change control system

    c. Contract negotiation

    d. Expert judgment

Answer: b. Contract change control system

Explanation: The Control Procurements process involves monitoring the performance of the contracted party and managing any changes to the contract. One of the tools and techniques used in this process is the Contract Change Control System, which helps to ensure that any changes to the contract are properly documented, reviewed, and approved before they are implemented.

179. **During which stage of the project life cycle is procurement risk typically the highest**

    a. Initiating

    b. Planning

    c. Executing

    d. Monitoring and Controlling

Answer: c. Executing

Explanation: Procurement risk typically increases during the Executing stage of the project life cycle, when the contracted party is actually performing the work. This is when issues such as delays, quality problems, and scope creep are most likely to occur, and the project team must be vigilant in managing these risks.

180. **Which of the following is a key output of the Control Quality process?**

    a. Project document updates

    b. Work performance data

    c. Quality metrics

    d. Approved change requests

Answer: a. Project document updates

Explanation: The Control Quality process involves monitoring and controlling the quality of the project deliverables. One of the key outputs of this process is updates to the project documents, such as the quality management plan, quality checklists, and test reports.

181. **Which of the following is NOT a valid reason to reject a change request?**

　　a. The change would require additional resources that are not available

　　b. The change would violate regulatory requirements

　　c. The change would result in a lower quality deliverable

　　d. The change would save time and money

Answer: d. The change would save time and money

Explanation: A change request should be evaluated based on its impact on the project's scope, schedule, cost, quality, and other constraints. While some changes may result in time and cost savings, this alone is not a sufficient reason to approve a change request if it would adversely affect other aspects of the project.

182. **Which of the following is an example of a cost-plus-fixed-fee (CPFF) contract?**

　　a. A contract in which the buyer pays the seller a fixed price for each unit of work completed

　　b. A contract in which the buyer pays the seller a fee for completing the work plus a percentage of the total cost

　　c. A contract in which the buyer reimburses the seller for all allowable costs plus a fixed fee

　　d. A contract in which the buyer pays the seller a percentage of the total cost of the project

Answer: c. A contract in which the buyer reimburses the seller for all allowable costs plus a fixed fee

Explanation: In a cost-plus-fixed-fee (CPFF) contract, the buyer reimburses the seller for all allowable costs incurred in performing the work, plus a fixed fee that is intended to cover the seller's overhead and profit. This type of contract is often used when the scope of work is difficult to define or when the risks associated with the project are high.

183. **Which of the following is a key component of the Direct and Manage Project Work process?**

　　a. Developing the project charter

　　b. Developing the project management plan

　　c. Implementing the project management plan

　　d. Controlling the project work

Answer: c. Implementing the project management plan

Explanation: The Direct and Manage Project Work process is responsible for carrying out the project management plan by performing the activities included in the plan, creating the deliverables, and implementing the project management processes. This process group is focused on executing the work defined in the project management plan.

184. **During the execution of a project, a project manager identifies a risk that was not previously identified in the risk management plan. What should the project manager do?**

    a. Add the risk to the risk management plan

    b. Ignore the risk

    c. Address the risk immediately

    d. Revisit the risk management plan during monitoring and controlling

Answer: c. Address the risk immediately

Explanation: When a new risk is identified during the project execution, it should be addressed immediately to minimize its impact. The risk management plan should be updated to include the new risk, but this should not be the first priority. It is important to address the risk immediately to ensure that the project stays on track.

185. **Which of the following is not a tool or technique used in the Control Quality process**

    a. Inspection

    b. Statistical sampling

    c. Pareto chart

    d. Control charts

Answer: c. Pareto chart

Explanation: The Control Quality process involves monitoring and verifying that the project deliverables and work meet the quality standards defined in the quality management plan. Inspection, statistical sampling, and control charts are all tools and techniques used in this process. A Pareto chart is not used in the Control Quality process, but it is a tool used in the Control Chart process.

186. **During project execution, the project team is working on developing a new software application. One of the project team members proposes a change to the software that will increase the functionality but will also increase the cost of the project. What should the project manager do?**

    a. Reject the change request

    b. Implement the change request

    c. Assess the impact of the change request

d. Request additional funding to implement the change request

Answer: c. Assess the impact of the change request

Explanation: During the project execution, change requests may arise that can impact the project scope, schedule, or budget. It is important for the project manager to assess the impact of the change request before making a decision. The project manager should consider the impact of the change on the project objectives and determine whether it is feasible to implement the change within the constraints of the project.

187. **During project execution, the project team is working on constructing a new building. The project manager receives a change request from the customer to change the color of the exterior paint. What should the project manager do?**

   a. Reject the change request

   b. Implement the change request

   c. Assess the impact of the change request

   d. Request additional time to implement the change request

Answer: c. Assess the impact of the change request

Explanation: Change requests can come from various stakeholders during the project execution. The project manager should assess the impact of the change request and determine whether it aligns with the project objectives. In this case, the change request is related to the building's aesthetics and does not impact the project scope or schedule. Therefore, the project manager should assess the impact of the change on the project budget and determine whether it is feasible to implement the change within the constraints of the project.

188. **Which of the following is NOT an input to the Direct and Manage Project Work process?**

   a. Project management plan

   b. Approved change requests

   c. Work performance data

   d. Resource calendars

Answer: c. Work performance data is not an input to the Direct and Manage Project Work process.

Explanation: The project management plan is an input to this process, as it provides guidance on how the work should be executed and controlled.

189. **Which of the following is a tool or technique used in the Manage Project Knowledge process?**

   a. Data analysis

b. Change control tools

c. Expert judgment

d. Performance reporting

Answer: c. Expert judgment is a tool or technique used in the Manage Project Knowledge process.

Explanation: This involves bringing in individuals with specialized knowledge or experience to help with decision-making and problem-solving.

190. Which of the following is a key output of the Control Quality process?

a. Approved change requests

b. Verified deliverables

c. Project documents updates

d. Resource utilization reports

Answer: b. Verified deliverables is a key output of the Control Quality process.

Explanation: This involves reviewing the deliverables to ensure that they meet the specified quality standards and requirements.

191. During which process is the project charter developed?

a. Develop Project Charter

b. Develop Project Management Plan

c. Direct and Manage Project Work

d. Monitor and Control Project Work

Answer: a. The project charter is developed during the Develop Project Charter process.

Explanation: This process involves defining the project and obtaining authorization to begin the project.

192. Which of the following is a tool or technique used in the Control Procurements process?

a. Contract change control system

b. Performance reporting

c. Inspection

d. Bidder conferences

Answer: a. The contract change control system is a tool or technique used in the Control Procurements process.

Explanation: This involves managing changes to the procurement contract, including changes to the scope, schedule, or cost.

193. During the execution of a project, the project manager notices that the project is deviating from the original plan. What should the project manager do first?

a. Review the project plan and adjust it as necessary

b. Identify the cause of the deviation and develop a corrective action plan

c. Communicate the deviation to the project stakeholders

d. Document the deviation for future reference

Answer: b. Identify the cause of the deviation and develop a corrective action plan.

Explanation: During project execution, it is common to experience deviations from the original plan. The project manager should first identify the root cause of the deviation and develop a corrective action plan to address the issue. Reviewing and adjusting the project plan may come later, but it is important to address the deviation as soon as possible to avoid further complications.

194. Which of the following is NOT an input to the Executing process group?

a. Project charter

b. Approved change requests

c. Project management plan

d. Performance reports

Answer: a. Project charter.

Explanation: The project charter is an input to the Initiating process group and provides high-level information about the project. Approved change requests, project management plan, and performance reports are all inputs to the Executing process group.

195. The project manager has identified a risk during the execution of the project. What is the next step in the risk management process?

a. Develop a risk response plan

b. Monitor the risk

c. Identify the risk

d. Evaluate the risk

Answer: a. Develop a risk response plan.

Explanation: Once a risk has been identified during project execution, the next step is to develop a risk response plan to address the risk. Monitoring the risk comes after the risk response plan has been developed.

196. During the execution of a project, the project manager identifies a change that will impact the project scope. What should the project manager do first?

a. Submit a change request

b. Analyze the impact of the change

c. Communicate the change to the project stakeholders

d. Update the project plan

Answer: b. Analyze the impact of the change.

Explanation: Before submitting a change request, it is important to first analyze the impact of the change on the project scope, schedule, and budget. Communicating the change to stakeholders and updating the project plan can come later, but it is important to fully understand the impact of the change before taking any further action.

197. **During the execution of a project, the project manager realizes that one of the team members does not have the necessary skills to complete their assigned tasks. What should the project manager do?**

a. Assign the team member to a different task

b. Provide the team member with additional training

c. Remove the team member from the project

d. Ignore the issue and hope it resolves itself

Answer: b. Provide the team member with additional training.

Explanation: It is the project manager's responsibility to ensure that all team members have the necessary skills to complete their assigned tasks. If a team member is lacking in skills, providing them with additional training is the best option. Assigning them to a different task may not solve the issue, removing them from the project can cause delays, and ignoring the issue is not a viable solution.

MONITORING AND CONTROLLING

198. **What is the primary objective of the Control Quality process?**

a. To ensure that the project deliverables are completed on time.

b. To ensure that the project team adheres to the project schedule.

c. To ensure that the project deliverables meet the established quality standards.

d. To ensure that the project team is meeting its performance objectives.

Answer: c. To ensure that the project deliverables meet the established quality standards.

Explanation: The Control Quality process is focused on ensuring that the project deliverables meet the established quality standards. This involves inspecting the project deliverables to identify any defects or non-conformances, and taking corrective action as needed to address any issues.

199. **Which of the following is a tool or technique used in the Control Scope process?**

a. Variance analysis

b. Control charts

c. Inspection

d. Configuration management

Answer: D Explanation: Configuration management is a tool or technique used in the Control Scope process.

Explanation: This involves identifying, documenting, and controlling changes to the project scope throughout the project lifecycle.

200. **What is the primary output of the Control Procurements process?**

a. Procurement documents

b. Change requests

c. Work performance data

d. Procurement audits

Answer: d. Procurement audits

Explanation: The primary output of the Control Procurements process is procurement audits. These audits are conducted to verify that the procurement processes were followed correctly and to identify any issues or areas for improvement.

201. **Which of the following is a tool or technique used in the Control Communications process?**

a. Issue logs

b. Trend analysis

c. Variance analysis

d. Performance reporting

Answer: a. Issue logs

Explanation: Issue logs are a tool or technique used in the Control Communications process. These logs are used to track and manage any issues or problems related to project communications.

202. **Which of the following is an input to the Control Schedule process?**

a. Resource calendars

b. Schedule baseline

c. Work performance reports

d. Project charter

Answer: b. Schedule baseline

Explanation: The schedule baseline is an input to the Control Schedule process. This baseline represents the approved version of the project schedule, against which actual progress is compared and variances are measured.

203. What is the main objective of the Control Quality process?

a. To ensure that the project produces the desired outcome

b. To ensure that the project meets the defined quality standards

c. To ensure that the project is completed within budget

d. To ensure that the project is completed on time

Answer: b. To ensure that the project meets the defined quality standards.

Explanation: The Control Quality process is focused on monitoring and controlling specific project results to determine if they comply with the relevant quality standards. The process involves inspecting, testing, and verifying that the project deliverables meet the required quality criteria. While it is important to ensure that the project is completed within budget and on time, those are not the primary objectives of this process.

204. Which of the following is an example of a tool or technique used in the Control Schedule process?

a. Gantt charts

b. Pareto charts

c. Flowcharts

d. Ishikawa diagrams

Answer: a. Gantt charts.

Explanation: The Control Schedule process involves monitoring the status of the project to update project progress and managing changes to the schedule baseline. One of the tools and techniques used in this process is the Gantt chart, which is a visual representation of the project schedule that shows the start and finish dates of project activities.

205. What is the primary output of the Control Cost process?

a. Cost baseline

b. Cost management plan

c. Project charter

d. Work performance data

Answer: a. Cost baseline.

Explanation: The Control Cost process involves monitoring the status of project costs and managing changes to the cost baseline. The primary output of this process is an updated cost baseline, which is a time-phased budget that is used as a basis for comparison against actual project costs.

206. What is the main purpose of the Control Risks process?

a. To identify potential risks to the project

b. To assess the likelihood and impact of identified risks

c. To develop strategies to respond to identified risks

d. To monitor and control identified risks throughout the project

Answer: d. To monitor and control identified risks throughout the project.

Explanation: The Control Risks process involves monitoring and controlling identified risks throughout the project life cycle. The process includes implementing risk response plans, tracking identified risks, and evaluating the effectiveness of risk response strategies. While identifying and assessing risks are important steps, the primary purpose of this process is to manage risks throughout the project.

207. What is the primary output of the Control Procurements process?

a. Procurement documents

b. Procurement management plan

c. Change requests

d. Contract documentation

Answer: d. Contract documentation.

Explanation: The Control Procurements process involves monitoring and controlling procurement activities to ensure that they are conducted in accordance with the procurement management plan. The primary output of this process is contract documentation, which includes all of the legally binding agreements between the buyer and seller. While procurement documents and change requests may be outputs of this process, they are not the primary output.

208. Which of the following is not a tool or technique used in the Control Quality process

a. Inspection

b. Statistical sampling

c. Control charts

d. Pareto chart

Correct answer: d. Pareto chart

Explanation: The Control Quality process involves tools and techniques such as inspection, statistical sampling, control charts, and flowcharting. However, the Pareto chart is a tool used in the Control Resources process, not in Control Quality. The Pareto chart is used to identify and prioritize the most significant causes of problems or defects.

209. **During which process is the project scope statement updated to reflect changes?**

a. Control Scope

b. Monitor and Control Project Work

c. Control Schedule

d. Control Cost

Answer: a. Control Scope

Explanation: The Control Scope process involves monitoring the status of the project and product scope and managing changes to the scope baseline. During this process, the project scope statement is updated to reflect changes to the project scope. The other processes listed do not involve updating the project scope statement.

210. **What is the primary purpose of the Monitor and Control Project Work process?**

a. To track, review, and regulate progress and performance of the project

b. To verify that the project work is being done according to the project management plan

c. To monitor the quality of the project deliverables

d. To ensure that the project is meeting stakeholder expectations

Answer: a. To track, review, and regulate progress and performance of the project

Explanation: The Monitor and Control Project Work process is concerned with tracking, reviewing, and regulating the progress and performance of the project. This process involves collecting and analyzing project data to identify variances from the project plan and taking corrective actions as needed. The other options listed are not the primary purpose of this process.

211. **What is the main difference between the Control Quality and Validate Scope processes?**

a. Control Quality is concerned with monitoring and controlling the quality of the project deliverables, while Validate Scope is concerned with acceptance of the deliverables

b. Control Quality is focused on the product quality, while Validate Scope is focused on the scope of the project

c. Control Quality is performed by the quality assurance team, while Validate Scope is performed by the project manager

d. Control Quality is done during project execution, while Validate Scope is done during project planning

Answer: a. Control Quality is concerned with monitoring and controlling the quality of the project deliverables, while Validate Scope is concerned with acceptance of the deliverables

Explanation: The Control Quality process is concerned with monitoring and controlling the quality of the project deliverables, while the Validate Scope process is concerned with acceptance of the deliverables. In other words, Control Quality is focused on inspecting, testing, and verifying that the deliverables meet the required quality standards, while Validate Scope is focused on obtaining formal acceptance from the customer or sponsor that the deliverables meet the requirements specified in the project scope statement.

212.　Which of the following is a tool or technique used in the Control Procurements process?

　　　a. Bidder conferences

　　　b. Bidder proposals

　　　c. Claims administration

　　　d. Make-or-buy analysis

Answer: c. Claims administration

Explanation: The Control Procurements process involves monitoring and controlling the procurement-related activities of the project. Tools and techniques used in this process include contract change control system, procurement performance reviews, inspections and audits, and claims administration. Claims administration involves addressing claims made by the seller, contractor, or supplier related to the contract terms or other issues.

213.　Which of the following is a tool used in the Control Quality process?

　　　a. Ishikawa diagram

　　　b. Scatter diagram

　　　c. Flowchart

　　　d. Control chart

Answer: d. Control chart

Explanation: Control charts are used to monitor the process performance over time and identify any variations that may occur. The other options are tools used in other quality management processes, such as the Ishikawa diagram in the Identify Causes process and the scatter diagram in the Collect Requirements process.

214.　In the Control Procurements process, which of the following is a tool used to ensure that the procurement is completed according to the contract terms?

　　　a. Inspection and audits

　　　b. Procurement performance reviews

c. Contract change control system

d. Claims administration

Answer: c. Contract change control system

Explanation: The contract change control system is used to ensure that any changes to the procurement contract are documented, approved, and implemented. This helps to ensure that the procurement is completed according to the agreed-upon terms. The other options are tools used in other procurement management processes, such as inspection and audits in the Control Quality process.

215. **Which of the following is a key output of the Monitor Risks process?**

a. Risk register updates

b. Project charter

c. Change requests

d. Stakeholder register updates

Answer: a. Risk register updates

Explanation: The Monitor Risks process involves tracking identified risks, monitoring residual risks, identifying new risks, and evaluating risk process effectiveness. The key output of this process is updates to the risk register, which includes information about the identified risks, their status, and any changes to their priority or response plans. The other options are outputs of other project management processes.

216. **Which of the following is NOT an input to the Control Schedule process?**

a. Schedule baseline

b. Work performance data

c. Project management plan

d. Resource calendars

Answer: d. Resource calendars

Explanation: The Control Schedule process involves monitoring the project schedule performance, making changes as necessary, and updating the project schedule. The inputs to this process include the schedule baseline, work performance data, project management plan, and project calendars. Resource calendars are not an input to this process, as they are used to identify when resources are available to work on the project.

217. **Which of the following is a tool used in the Control Communications process?**

a. Issue log

b. Change log

c. Stakeholder engagement assessment matrix

d. Performance reporting

Answer: d. Performance reporting

Explanation: The Control Communications process involves monitoring and controlling communications throughout the project. Performance reporting is a tool used in this process to collect and distribute performance information, such as status reports, progress measurements, and forecasts. The other options are tools used in other project management processes, such as the issue log in the Control Risks process.

218. **Which of the following is a tool or technique used in the Control Quality process?**

a. Root Cause Analysis

b. Ishikawa Diagram

c. Design of Experiments

d. Benchmarking

Answer: c. Design of Experiments

Explanation: The Design of Experiments is a tool or technique used in the Control Quality process. This technique involves systematically changing variables to determine their impact on the outcome of the process. The goal is to identify the best combination of variables that will produce the desired outcome. Root Cause Analysis and Ishikawa Diagram are tools used in the Perform Quality Control process, while Benchmarking is a tool used in the Control Procurements process.

219. **Which of the following is a technique used in the Control Costs process?**

a. Analogous Estimating

b. Three-Point Estimating

c. Reserve Analysis

d. Cost-Benefit Analysis

Answer: a. Analogous Estimating

Explanation: Analogous Estimating is a technique used in the Control Costs process. This technique involves using historical data from similar projects to estimate the cost of the current project. Three-Point Estimating is a technique used in the Estimate Costs process, while Reserve Analysis is a tool used in the Plan Cost Management process. Cost-Benefit Analysis is a technique used in the Control Benefits process.

220. **Which of the following is an output of the Control Schedule process?**

a. Schedule Baseline

b. Change Log

c. Resource Breakdown Structure

d. Activity Resource Requirements

Answer: b. Change Log

Explanation: The Change Log is an output of the Control Schedule process. This document contains a list of all changes that have been made to the project schedule, including the reasons for the changes and the impact on the project. The Schedule Baseline is an output of the Develop Schedule process, while the Resource Breakdown Structure and Activity Resource Requirements are outputs of the Estimate Activity Resources process.

221. **Which of the following is a tool or technique used in the Control Risks process?**

a. Risk Register

b. Risk Audits

c. Reserve Analysis

d. Risk Response Planning

Answer: b. Risk Audits

Explanation: Risk Audits is a tool or technique used in the Control Risks process. This technique involves reviewing the effectiveness of the risk management plan and the risk response strategies to determine if they are working as intended. The Risk Register is an input to the Control Risks process. Reserve Analysis is a tool used in the Plan Risk Responses process, while Risk Response Planning is a process in the Risk Management knowledge area.

222. **Which of the following is an output of the Control Communications process?**

a. Communications Management Plan

b. Stakeholder Engagement Plan

c. Project Management Plan Updates

d. Work Performance Information

Answer: c. Project Management Plan Updates

Explanation: Project Management Plan Updates are an output of the Control Communications process. This document contains updates to the project management plan, including changes to the communications management plan and other plans affected by changes to project communications. The Communications Management Plan and Stakeholder Engagement Plan are outputs of the Plan Communications Management process, while Work Performance Information is an output of the Monitor and Control Project Work process.

CLOSING

223. **Which of the following is NOT an output of the Closing process group?**

a. Final product, service, or result transition

b. Final project report

c. Organizational process assets updates

d. Project charter

Answer: d. Project charter.

Explanation: The project charter is an output of the Initiating process group, not the Closing process group. The other options are all valid outputs of the Closing process group according to the PMBOK Guide.

224. **During the Closing process group, which of the following should be performed first**

a. Verify completion of all project deliverables

b. Obtain final acceptance of project deliverables

c. Obtain sign-off from the customer

d. Archive project records

Answer: a. Verify completion of all project deliverables.

Explanation: Before obtaining final acceptance or sign-off from the customer, it's important to ensure that all project deliverables have been completed and meet the required quality standards. Archiving project records typically occurs after all other Closing activities have been completed.

225. **Which of the following is the purpose of the Close Procurements process?**

a. To verify that all project deliverables have been completed

b. To transfer ownership of project deliverables to the customer

c. To settle all contractual and financial obligations with suppliers

d. To finalize all project activities and formally close the project

Answer: c. To settle all contractual and financial obligations with suppliers.

Explanation: The Close Procurements process is specifically focused on closing out all procurement-related activities, including settling all financial and contractual obligations with suppliers. The other options are more closely associated with the overall Closing process group.

226. **Which of the following is an example of a stakeholder that should be engaged during the Closing process group?**

a. Project manager

b. Sponsor

c. Project team members

d. Vendors

Answer: b. Sponsor.

Explanation: The sponsor is a key stakeholder who should be engaged during the Closing process group to ensure that all project objectives have been met and that the sponsor is satisfied with the final deliverables. The other options may also be involved in Closing activities, but the sponsor is typically the most crucial stakeholder to engage.

227. **Which of the following is an example of a lesson learned that should be documented during the Closing process group?**

a. A change request that was approved during the project

b. A risk that was identified but never materialized

c. A stakeholder who was difficult to engage throughout the project

d. A best practice that was used successfully on the project

Answer: d. A best practice that was used successfully on the project.

Explanation: Documenting best practices is an important part of the lesson learned process, as it allows organizations to leverage successful strategies in future projects. The other options may also be documented during the Closing process group, but best practices are typically the most valuable lesson learned to capture.

228. **Which of the following is NOT a component of the closing process group?**

a. Administrative closure

b. Contract closure

c. Scope verification

d. Close project or phase

Answer: c. Scope verification

Explanation: Scope verification is a component of the monitoring and controlling process group, not the closing process group. The closing process group includes administrative closure, contract closure, and close project or phase.

229. **Which of the following is true of the final product, service, or result transition during the closing process group?**

a. It occurs during administrative closure.

b. It involves transferring ownership from the project team to the customer or sponsor.

c. It involves archiving project documents and other artifacts.

d. It is the responsibility of the project manager.

Answer: b. It involves transferring ownership from the project team to the customer or sponsor.

Explanation: The final product, service, or result transition is a key part of the closing process group. It involves transferring ownership from the project team to the customer or sponsor, as well as any necessary training or support. Administrative closure involves verifying that all project work has been completed and that all project documentation has been archived. The project manager is responsible for overseeing the closing process group as a whole.

230.   Which of the following is a key output of the closing process group?

a. Approved change requests

b. Lessons learned documentation

c. Project schedule

d. Risk register updates

Answer: b. Lessons learned documentation

Explanation: Lessons learned documentation is a key output of the closing process group. It captures the successes and challenges of the project, as well as recommendations for future projects. Approved change requests are an output of the monitoring and controlling process group, while the project schedule and risk register updates are outputs of the planning process group.

231.   Which of the following is an input to the contract closure process?

a. Procurement management plan

b. Requirements documentation

c. Stakeholder register

d. Resource management plan

Answer: a. Procurement management plan

Explanation: The procurement management plan is an input to the contract closure process, which involves completing and settling the terms of the contract. Requirements documentation is an input to the requirements gathering process, while the stakeholder register and resource management plan are inputs to the planning process group.

232.   Which of the following is a benefit of conducting a stakeholder analysis during the closing process group?

a. It helps identify potential risks and opportunities.

b. It helps determine the scope of the project.

c. It helps ensure that project deliverables meet customer requirements.

d. It helps manage stakeholder expectations.

Answer: d. It helps manage stakeholder expectations.

Explanation: Conducting a stakeholder analysis during the closing process group can help manage stakeholder expectations and ensure that their needs have been met. It can also help identify potential risks and opportunities, but this is more closely associated with the risk management process. Determining the scope of the project is typically done during the planning process group, while ensuring that project deliverables meet customer requirements is a key objective throughout the project lifecycle.

233. What is the primary objective of the Closing process?

a. To close the project contract

b. To identify and document lessons learned

c. To release project resources

d. To update the project schedule

Answer: b. To identify and document lessons learned.

Explanation: The primary objective of the Closing process is to formally close the project or project phase. This involves completing all activities across all project management process groups, including monitoring and controlling, executing, planning, and initiating. The final output of this process is the final project or phase report, which includes a summary of project results, lessons learned, and recommendations for future projects.

234. What is the purpose of the lessons learned document in the Closing process?

a. To identify the scope of the project

b. To provide a summary of project results

c. To document stakeholder feedback

d. To provide recommendations for future projects

Answer: d. To provide recommendations for future projects.

Explanation: The lessons learned document is an output of the Closing process that provides a summary of the knowledge gained during the project. It is used to document both the positive and negative experiences, outcomes, and recommendations from the project team and stakeholders. The purpose of this document is to share the lessons learned with future project teams to improve their performance and ensure successful outcomes.

235. Who is responsible for the formal acceptance of project deliverables during the Closing process?

a. Project sponsor

b. Project manager

c. Project team

d. Customer or sponsor representative

Answer: d. Customer or sponsor representative.

Explanation: Formal acceptance of project deliverables is a crucial aspect of the Closing process. The customer or sponsor representative is responsible for accepting the project deliverables, as they are the final recipient of the project output. The project manager should ensure that all deliverables are completed to the customer's satisfaction before requesting formal acceptance.

236.   What is the main purpose of the project closure report?

a. To provide an overview of the project status

b. To identify and document lessons learned

c. To summarize project risks

d. To outline the project schedule

Answer: b. To identify and document lessons learned.

Explanation: The project closure report is an output of the Closing process and provides a summary of the project results, lessons learned, and recommendations for future projects. It includes details of the project scope, objectives, milestones, schedule, budget, risks, and issues. The primary purpose of the project closure report is to capture lessons learned to improve future project performance.

237.   What is the difference between the Closing process and the Contract Closeout process?

a. The Closing process is focused on the formal acceptance of project deliverables, while the Contract Closeout process is focused on closing out the project contract.

b. The Closing process is focused on finalizing all project activities, while the Contract Closeout process is focused on releasing project resources.

c. The Closing process is focused on documenting lessons learned, while the Contract Closeout process is focused on completing all administrative activities related to the project contract.

d. The Closing process is focused on releasing project resources, while the Contract Closeout process is focused on finalizing all project activities.

Answer: a. The Closing process is focused on the formal acceptance of project deliverables, while the Contract Closeout process is focused on closing out the project contract.

Explanation: The Closing process is the last process group in the project management life cycle and focuses on completing all activities related to the project, including the formal acceptance

238. **Which of the following is NOT a component of the project closure document?**

    a. Lessons learned

    b. Final project budget

    c. Change request log

    d. Stakeholder register

Answer: b. Final project budget

Explanation: The project closure document is a comprehensive report that documents the project's final status and closure. It includes several components such as project performance, project success or failure analysis, recommendations, and lessons learned. The final project budget is part of the financial closure process and is documented in the financial closure report.

239. **During project closure, which of the following should the project manager ensure is done FIRST?**

    a. Archive project documents

    b. Collect feedback from stakeholders

    c. Complete a final performance evaluation

    d. Verify that all project objectives are met

Answer: d. Verify that all project objectives are met

Explanation: Before closing out the project, the project manager should ensure that all project objectives have been achieved. This includes delivering all project outputs, meeting the project's scope, schedule, and cost objectives, and meeting any other requirements specified in the project charter.

240. **Which of the following is the BEST way to ensure effective knowledge transfer during project closure?**

    a. Conducting an exit interview with each team member

    b. Creating a knowledge base of project documents and lessons learned

    c. Providing training sessions for new team members

    d. Sending out a project summary report to stakeholders

Answer: b. Creating a knowledge base of project documents and lessons learned

Explanation: Creating a knowledge base of project documents and lessons learned is the best way to ensure effective knowledge transfer during project closure. This allows future project teams to access information about the project and learn from its successes and failures.

241. **Which of the following is a key output of the project closure process?**

a. Project charter

b. Change management plan

c. Final project report

d. Project schedule

Answer: c. Final project report

Explanation: The final project report is a key output of the project closure process. It summarizes the project's final status and provides details on the project's performance, success or failure analysis, recommendations, and lessons learned.

242.   During project closure, which of the following should the project manager do LAST

a. Archive project documents

b. Collect feedback from stakeholders

c. Complete a final performance evaluation

d. Issue a final project report

Answer: a. Archive project documents

Explanation: Archiving project documents is the last step in the project closure process. Once all project objectives have been met, feedback has been collected, and the final performance evaluation has been completed, project documents should be archived for future reference. This ensures that the project's knowledge and information are retained for future use.

243.   Which of the following is NOT a component of the final product, service, or result transition process in the Closing process group?

a. Delivering the final product, service, or result to the customer

b. Obtaining formal acceptance of the final product, service, or result

c. Archiving project records

d. Conducting lessons learned

Answer: d. Conducting lessons learned.

Explanation: Conducting lessons learned is a component of the Project Closeout process, which is a sub-process within the Closing process group. The final product, service, or result transition process includes delivering the final product, service, or result to the customer, obtaining formal acceptance of the final product, service, or result, and archiving project records.

244.   Which of the following is NOT a task within the Close Procurements process in the Closing process group?

a. Completing procurement audits

b. Negotiating contract disputes

c. Administering contract closure

d. Archiving procurement documentation

Answer: b. Negotiating contract disputes is not a task within the Close Procurements process.

Explanation: The Close Procurements process includes completing procurement audits, administering contract closure, and archiving procurement documentation.

245. **Which of the following is NOT a key output of the Close Project process in the Closing process group?**

a. Final product, service, or result

b. Project documents updates

c. Organizational process assets updates

d. Resource calendars

Answer: d. Resource calendars are not a key output of the Close Project process.

Explanation: The key outputs of this process include final product, service, or result, project documents updates, and organizational process assets updates.

246. **Which of the following is NOT a benefit of conducting a lessons learned session as part of the Closing process group?**

a. Capturing and sharing knowledge

b. Identifying project successes and failures

c. Creating a project archive

d. Improving future project performance

Answer: c. Creating a project archive is not a benefit of conducting a lessons learned session.

Explanation: The purpose of a lessons learned session is to capture and share knowledge, identify project successes and failures, and improve future project performance.

247. **Which of the following is an example of a tool or technique used in the Close Project or Phase process in the Closing process group?**

a. Decomposition

b. Expert judgment

c. Change control tools

d. Regression analysis

Answer: b. Expert judgment is a tool or technique used in the Close Project or Phase process.

Explanation: Other tools and techniques used in this process include analytical techniques, such as root cause analysis, and project management information systems.